AF539308

Essays in the Reconstruction of Political Economy

Essays in the Reconstruction of Political Economy

Amit Bhaduri

Essays in the Reconstruction of Political Economy
Amit Bhaduri

First Published 2010

ISBN 978-93-5002-058-6 (Hb)

Published by
AAKAR BOOKS
28 E Pocket IV, Mayur Vihar Phase I, Delhi 110 091
Phone: 011-2279 5505 Telefax : 011-2279 5641
aakarbooks@gmail.com; www.aakarbooks..com

Composed by
Limited Colors, Delhi 110 092

Printed at
Mudrak, 30 A Patparganj, Delhi 110 091

Contents

In Lieu of an Introduction

When political failures are presented as economic achievements, it may not be easy to separate rhetoric from reality. The smoke screen created by a statistically high economic growth rate, the rhetoric surrounding the intrinsic wisdom of the market in guiding us, backed by big money and sleek media and politicians of unusually short memory who change tone the morning after the election or a crisis, seem to make the obvious invisible. Otherwise how do we explain the fact that the spectacle of farmers committing suicide in thousands, Adivasis being dispossessed of their ancient habitats and land for mining, industrialisation or SEZ, and a growing fury engulfing large chunks of the country hardly reach our middle class consciousness or unsettle the 'business as usual' attitude? The fact that nearly one-fourth of the country is virtually independent of central administration is a concrete expression of popular anger; and the governments offer them nothing but police action without a serious attempt at pro-people development, and we turn our back to it as a law-and-order problem. The disconnect between the majority of our citizens and the democratic government is complete. Election verdicts signify little in this context; except of course for those who make a career in political parties. The majority of the electorate vote increasingly with cynical indifference, because they feel there is little to choose among major political parties. Yet they vote, they vote not with hope, but in despair usually to minimise the damage that the coming of a political party to power could inflict on them, especially in the name of development. They want to escape from being 'developed' forcibly and ruthlessly by the governments, and the corporations. This is more than a disconnect, that is fuelling the fury to consume gradually our countryside.

The problem lies principally in the unthinking extension of the 'market principles' in the society by the central, and state governments of different shapes and colour under the influence of national and international corporate bodies. No doubt, the 'market principles' have many things to commend themselves, but the extent to which the market can work in a country which is poor, and yet maintain democracy, is a question of utmost urgency. It should be faced; indeed we would not even have the choice for long of dodging it in India.

Most people of this country are poor, and it is remarkable that, despite widespread subhuman poverty a democratic system is functioning here for over last 60 years without improving significantly the lot of the poor. The combination of these two—political democracy and extensive poverty—makes the Indian case uniquely paradoxical. In Western Europe universal franchise-based democracy had stabilised at per capita income of not less than US dollars 2000. In contrast the democratic system was introduced in our poor country at about one-sixth that level (in purchasing power parity). It survived, but as the country opted increasingly for 'market principles' in the forms of fast track liberalisation, privatisation partly under the compulsions of globalisation, the situation became more volatile. Indeed the political principle of democracy got increasingly traded for the economic principle of success in the market, and our political failure needed to be presented as economic success.

The reason for this state of affairs is not far to seek. Political democracy votes according to the principle of 'one adult, one vote', whereas the market votes according to one's purchasing power. If the task of making the basic necessities of life available to the poor is left to the market, one ends up by not providing such goods and services to them. The deprivations caused to the poor are ventilated through the political channel that democracy permits to some extent but the rest accumulates as fury. The increasing tension that we are witnessing in India in the form of million mutinies and popular resistances over different issues is the result.

The inherent contradiction between the extensive use of market principle and political democracy in a poor country needs a little more elaboration. In market, the decision about 'what to produce' is determined by the pattern of purchasing power. Since the poor do not have the necessary purchasing power–and, accordingly, not enough voting power in the marketplace–they have no role in deciding what should be produced. In this situation, if the state does not come forward to produce what the poor need, the situation seems increasingly unjust to the poor. For instance, on the one side there are state-of-the-art hospitals, and on the other there are no qualified doctors in village health centres, virtually no arrangement for treatment of even common water-borne diseases or malaria afflicting the poor and killing thousands of children. Fancy educational institutions coexist with nearly collapsed building and no teachers for village primary schools.

The second thing that the market does, apart from deciding what to produce, is ruthless 'rationing' through the price mechanism. It simply means if you cannot pay, you are out. Hence if production of even basic necessities of life is left entirely or substantially to the market, the poor find no alternative, but to beg, borrow or steal to access them. For instance, many recent statistics show that especially the very poor spend a bigger percentage of their income on health, and soon get into a debt trap, as health care in public hospitals get increasingly privatised.

In such situations the state could play the role of the mediator between the market principle that does not work for the poor and the democratic principle that works for the poor. The classic example of this model was developed in the post-First World War Scandinavia. Social democratic policies of the governments ensured that citizens are not deprived of basic necessities like education, health, social security, etc. due to insufficient purchasing power. Many European countries emulated this model especially after the Second World War, some more successfully and some less successfully, but all under a systemic challenge from the socialist counties. Our country became politically independent around the same time. It too recognised that the state should amend some of the gross excesses of the market to meet the requirements of political democracy.

However, as fast track pro-market reforms and market friendly policies were pursued especially since 1991, the state began walking away from its role as the mediator between the market principle and democratic principle. One of the major justifications given in favour of this policy stance is that, the state-based delivery system is hopelessly inefficient. The state institutions, it is often said not without justification, are hopelessly inefficient, and fail to deliver. If the state's delivery system fails to provide a service, hand it over to the market that will function more efficiently—thus runs the argument. Such an argument is flawed in its foundation, because it pretends that this political failure due to the nature of state institutions will have an economic solution in the market. It is flawed because a political problem has to be resolved politically. In our case it has to come from deepening rather than giving up the democratic principles of governance as the cornerstone of our politics.

The single most important reason for the failure of the delivery system of the state has been centralised bureaucratisation of the state machinery, and absence of reliance on local democracy. It suits well the centralised political parties, irrespective of their political pronouncements and colours. Consequently, they have been of little help in making the state's delivery system work through decentralisation of power. And yet, alternative institutional arrangement has to replace it, which works far more through local governments, the panchayats and their lower level gram sabhas. If properly empowered, this institution can go a long way in offering a political solution to address the problem of state failure in delivering basic services to the poor. This seems indeed the only way we can begin to resolve the contradiction between the inefficiency of the state and the callousness of the market towards the poor.

Initiating local level democracy in any form in India has at least two major problems. One relates to the reluctance on the part of the higher level elected power-holders (e.g. MLAs and MPs) as well as higher bureaucracy to share powers with the panchayats and the lower local bodies. They are treated as instrumental agents for higher authorities, but not as elected representatives at a lower level with their smaller but own sphere for independent exercise of power. And yet, this is contrary to the spirit of the 73rd Amendment and Article 243 of the Indian Constitution. To enable the state to be an effective pro-poor mediator between the market principle and democratic principle it is necessary for these institutions to share far greater independent power and resources.

The other major problem of panchayats and gram sabhas relates to funding, which is neither adequate nor predictable or free of bureaucratic hurdles. If panchayats are made perpetually dependent on higher level government for adequate, timely and predictable flow of funds, they can never take the initiative to become an agent of change. And yet, it is possible without much difficulty or complication to draw the broad outlines of a feasible scheme. The essence of the scheme is that, without creating a new chain of institutions, the local nationalised bank can be authorised to advance funds to the panchayats or lower level gram sabhas up to a specific credit limit. If a local body succeeds in utilising the fund advanced satisfactorily, it will get more funds at the next round, if not, it will be penalised with less funds. (I had offered the suggestion in some detail of using the nationalised banks in book, *Development with Dignity*, National Book Trust, Delhi, 2006). The essential nature of the fianancial autonomy would rest on accountability of the panchayats to the local banks and, of the banks to the local panchayats in a mutually compatible scheme of incentives in which both can act with less supervision from higher levels. (The analogy with a repeated game resulting in a more cooperative solution is not far to seek for an economist/game theorist.)

The other and probably important question is about the use of natural resources—land, water and forest—over which large parts of the countryside are burning in protest. Deepening of democracy through decentralisation would require wider scope of application of the 1996 PESA (Panchayat Extension to Scheduled Areas) Act. Thus any change in the nature of the existing pattern of land use would require the approval of gram sabha. This means that the holder of landed property would have only the right to use it or to transfer it to somebody else, but diversion of the land to some other use would require the prior approval of gram sabha. This method of deepening of democracy would undoubtedly be embraced by the poor of this country, but not by the corporations, nor by their supporting cast of politicians or even media persons and academics. They are engaged instead in different ways in a deadly game of depriving and dispossessing the poor of natural resources and common property in the name of development. This is increasingly becoming the defining issue of developmental politics of our time, not only in India but in many other parts of the developing world. We have to make informed choices. The essays collected in this volume are intended to help the reader to make that choice which will determine the course of our political future.

Amit Bhaduri

1

The Impact of Globalisation on Indian Economic Development*

A dilemma faces the developing countries today as they find themselves in an awkward corner. The policy space left for the nation state is shrinking gradually in the current phase of globalisation, while that space is being occupied increasingly by the emerging rules of globalisation. And yet, the global rules of the game are flawed, as they are biased strongly in favour of the richer countries, especially the United States. The dilemma arises because the developing countries tend to feel on the one hand that there is no alternative to accepting globalisation in its present form, the so-called TINA syndrome in a uni-polar world dominated by the US. On the other hand, they know that they can rely hardly on the current rules of globalisation to further their developmental objectives. In many cases the dilemma is acute irrespective of how the government decides to present the case to the public. As a result, developmental problems are seldom faced from the standpoint of the developing countries; instead solutions tend to be imposed on them in the name of globalisation.

Let a couple of well-known examples illustrate the point. The issue of a fairer global trade in agricultural commodities, without subsidy to the farmers in richer countries, is required not merely for a freer trade regime; it affects also the poorest

*Dr. John Matthai Lecture, 2006: Calicut University.

one billion people in the world, as most of them are connected directly or indirectly with agricultural activities in the rural areas of developing countries. There is hardly any other trade-related example with greater compatibility between a more efficient international price mechanism operating through freer trade, and greater global equality. And yet, international negotiations governed by immediate and narrow national interests of the richer nations reduced global rule making recently to a 'tit-for-tat' strategy, that led to a breakdown in negotiations, and the tendency to impose solutions by the richer and more powerful nations.

In a parallel vein, one could think of other examples of imposed rather than negotiated solutions. Both the Bretton Woods institutions, namely the IMF (International Monetary Fund) and the World Bank, make policy recommendations to the developing countries in financial difficulties through their standard pro-market 'conditionalities'. The voting systems in these institutions are heavily biased in favour of the richer countries, especially the United States, because of their higher economic contributions to these institutions. The market principle of the-rich-have-more-votes-than-the-poor because of their greater purchasing power holds blatantly in the voting system. As a justification for imposing pro-market conditionalities on developing countries, both these institutions often place a great deal of emphasis on the principle of accountability to the market. However, it is ironical that they themselves remain totally unaccountable for their performances and recommendations, no matter whether an economic collapse occurs in Argentina under their guidance, or an acute financial crisis erupts in east Asia (the only country to escape largely its adverse consequences was Malaysia, which went openly against the IMF prescriptions), or years of stagnation continues despite their recommended large-scale IMF–World Bank sponsored liberalisation in sub-Saharan Africa.

These are mere illustrations of the power the rich nations have over the poor nations. It arises to a large extent from some structural asymmetries inherent in the current process of globalisation. Until we identify them clearly, it would appear that this process of globalisation led by the interests of the rich is a natural phenomenon like an earthquake or a drought. The consequences have to be simply accepted because they cannot be controlled. The analogy is misleading. As we begin to know more about the workings of nature, we start to exert control to varying extents over the fallout of natural phenomena. Similarly, we would be in a position to be able to integrate strategically with the global economy to our advantage, instead of meekly submitting to the process of globalisation, only if we understand better some of these asymmetries that are also the source of asymmetric global power relations.

First, and perhaps the most fundamental asymmetry in the world economy arises today from the freedom of movement of capital, especially financial capital on the one hand, and the restrictions placed on the other, on the movement of labour, especially unskilled labour from developing countries. Despite vast improvements in travel and communications technology, available estimates suggest that labour migration as a proportion of the total world population has been lower in the current phase (approximately 1973 to date) compared to the earlier phase of globalisation (approximately, 1870–1913). On a rough reckoning, about one in six persons crossed national borders for employment or livelihood between 1860 and 1900. They went as indentured labour from China and India, or as colonial settlers from Europe to North, Central and South America and to Australia. Over a comparable period of nearly five decades of the current phase of globalisation, we have estimates suggesting that not more than one in eight persons has migrated despite vast improvements in transport and communication. Contrast this relatively sluggish movement of labour during the current phase of globalisation with the movements of capital, especially financial capital. Rough estimates available from the Bank of International Settlements suggest that the daily volume of private trade in foreign exchange is over 1.2 trillion (10^{12}) US dollars. Of this, less than 2 per cent is accounted for by trade in goods and services, and even if one adds all direct foreign investment it would still be well below 4 per cent. A few days of hostile private trade in the foreign exchange market can wipe out the entire foreign reserve of all the central banks in the world. The defining characteristic of the current phase of globalisation has become this overwhelming supremacy of private financial capital. The world has not seen anything like this before.

The rise to ascendancy of international finance started with successive waves of liberalisation of the major capital markets of the advanced capitalist countries starting from about the mid-1970s. It assumed irresistible momentum by the early 1980s ushering in the current phase of economic globalisation dominated by international finance. Although little explicit note is taken of its implications in public discussions and government pronouncements, its imprint on the pace and pattern on Indian development too has been unmistakable. Economic policies are increasingly formulated by the government as never before with a view to the sentiments of the financial markets. The English language media, especially the electronic media that shape Indian middle class opinion, behave as if the daily fluctuations of the stock market is an accurate barometer of the health of the real economy. However, underlying this is an uncomfortable fact that is overlooked willingly or unwillingly. The Indian stock market is pathetically small in relation to the vast size of global private trade in foreign exchange mentioned earlier. The rupee and Indian stocks can easily be set into an uncontrollable downward spiral by a few large international players speculating against some

Indian stocks or the rupee. This is not at all fanciful. Recall how the Dalal Street nose-dived immediately after the 2004 general elections results, because a few large, mostly foreign institutional investors began to withdraw from the Indian capital market under the fear that a coalition government supported by the Left will be unfriendly towards private businesses. However, as soon as the United Progressive Alliance government named its top economic team, a trio of the prime minister, the finance minister and the deputy chairman of the Planning Commission, all known for their extreme pro-market and corporate-friendly outlook, the stock markets began to stabilise in no time. Nothing had changed about ground realities of the Indian economy in those few weeks, except international finance capital needed assuring political signals. In the process, the future course of economic policies for the country got set.

This story would remain incomplete for India (and for many other developing countries) without mentioning the critical role of the IMF and the World Bank. Since those two institutions are in a pivotal position to influence the perception of private foreign investors like multinational corporations, banks and other financial institutions about a country's investment climate, their role becomes critical. They shape to a significant extent at least in the short run the sentiments of the financial markets. If the economic policies of a government are favourable to the corporations, it generally gets a favourable signal from the pro-market IMF and the World Bank, with the result capital tends to flow in to stabilise or even stimulate the stock market. On the other hand, with an unfavourable signal from the same institutions, the government runs the risk of destabilising capital flights. This is the core game under globalisation in so far as these two institutions are concerned, while academic research on themes like poverty and macro-economic policies are mere sideshows. This has been part of the unwritten script of financial globalisation in so far as developing countries are concerned.

The major players in the financial markets as well as the IMF and the Bank with their pro-market and pro-corporate philosophy, are generally against the expansion of the economic role of the government. So we have in India a Fiscal Responsibility and Budget Management Act (FRBM), which prevents the government from spending additionally in areas like elementary education or expanding employment guarantee or strengthening decentralisation of the panchayat system through adequate fiscal autonomy. Our tribal population and peasants are evicted from lands with little compensation to improve the 'investment climate' for the corporations. If we have the eyes to see, it becomes increasingly apparent that, in the name of development we are typically pursuing policies that might deliver high growth, but it is growth without a democratic content. It does not reach the poorest citizens of India who need to benefit most urgently from the process of growth. However, this sort of pro-market reforms and high growth led by the corporations, might make the IMF, World Bank and some in government happy. It may even be accompanied by a rising trend in the stock market to create the illusion of a healthy state of economic affairs, but all this will remain merely irrelevant statistics for the poor majority in this country. This is why each and every government that has been following this sort of policy gets showered with the approval of the corporate sector, of the IMF and the World Bank, and even of the upper middle class, but loses the general election. The Congress government under the then prime minister Narasimha Rao with Dr. Manmohan Singh as its finance minister spearheading economic reforms lost the general election. Dr. Singh himself personally failed to win a seat. The pattern got repeated. The BJP-led coalition crashed in the elections with its 'shining India' slogan; and, it did especially badly in Andhra which was said to have been shining under the glow of IT industries. There is no reason to believe that things would be any different next time, unless remedial interventions like employment guarantee and fair price and subsidies to farmers despite WTO become sufficiently strong counteracting forces. However, this would require going against the hidden script of globalisation by upsetting the alliance between large multinational corporations and banks including the IMF and the WB, and a pliable domestic government.

Let me turn now to the second important asymmetry in the current phase of globalisation. It arises from the increasingly freer flow of trade in goods and services on the one hand, and the growing restriction on the transfer of knowledge and technology embodied in the production of those goods and services on the other. In the emerging regime of trade-related intellectual property rights (TRIPS), all developing countries including India find it increasingly difficult to learn and adopt the production technology involved in the goods and services they import. The asymmetry of the emerging trade regime has been characterised by freer trade in goods and services coupled with greater restrictions on the flow of productive knowledge. Thus, in the more liberalised trade regime of the World Trade Organisation, India comes under increasing pressure to import goods and services rather than produce them at home, while it is conveniently forgotten that international trade has been the vehicle for learning the technology embodied in the traded goods and new products throughout industrial history. This learning process involved through international trade may well be the most important dynamic gains from freer trade, far outweighing the static gains of existing comparative advantage. By treating knowledge more and more as simply a privately tradeable commodity, the current trade regime shows its bias towards corporations as the generator of knowledge who should be handsomely rewarded, but forgets the importance of other sources of knowledge. It has tended to underplay traditional community-based knowledge to the detriment of many indigenous communities. Submitting blindly to such an asymmetric trade regime in the name of globalisation would serve the interests of the rich and powerful corporations, but would leave the most vulnerable sections of our population especially in agriculture in even greater distress. The suicides of farmers in Maharashtra, Andhra Pradesh, Kerala and Punjab, adding to over 10 thousand in a year, foretell the kind of disaster that the commercialisation of agriculture under WTO regime might bring.

It is in this context that the inevitable consequence of globalisation in terms of the increased relative importance of the external vis-a-vis the internal or domestic market needs to be examined. It has influenced thinking on macro-economic policy in a way, which is seldom highlighted. It emphasises the importance of reducing the costs of production through more efficient supply side policies for increasing the international competitiveness of the national economy; but ignores the problem of creating adequate purchasing power and aggregate demand in the domestic market.

The shift in focus from the demand to the cost or supply side has had serious consequences. The most apparent consequence of this shift concerns labour market 'flexibility', i.e. some form of wage restraint. Lower wages tend to depress the unit cost of production, but also the consumption demand from wage income. Consequently, unless either higher investment or increased export surplus makes up for that reduction in consumption demand in a regime of investment or export-led growth, insufficient aggregate demand at home would be a drag on development.

Similarly, the emphasis on increasing output (value added) per worker or labour productivity to reduce labour cost of business, and use this as a tool for enhancing international competitiveness has a downside. Exclusive attention on productivity separates it from its other consequences on GDP, and the level of employment in the economy. For instance, total output would decrease despite an increase in productivity, if the percentage decrease in the level of employment exceeds the increase in labour productivity. Consequently, the corporate strategy of 'downsizing' the labour force to create a 'lean and efficient corporation' for increasing market share, might turn out to be good for a particular corporation, but macro-economically counter-productive if either total supply, or the size of the domestic market shrinks.

Policies of reducing unit cost in search of greater efficiency, through downsizing the labour force and restraining wages are encouraged under globalisation by the predominance considerations of competitiveness in the external market. However, in many cases, these policies often turn out to be macro-economically flawed. Because while they are efficient on the micro-economic scale of a single corporation or enterprise, such policies can also become counter-productive on the macro-economic scale due to their effect of depressing demand.

The underlying problem is more general. The blurring of the distinction between micro-and macro-efficiency has become a generic problem with many currently pursued economic policies. It stems from the influences of 'methodological individualism' in economics and from 'neo-liberalism' in politics. It gives rise to many 'fallacies of composition' in macro-economic policy by assuming that the individual micro-economic 'parts' have the same properties as the 'whole' macro-economic system. To illustrate the point, an individual corporation restraining wage or shedding labour to raise productivity might raise the efficiency and profit of that corporation. But if many corporations follow this policy at the same time, total demand and employment in the economy will shrink, and even the profit of all corporations might be reduced. Similarly, one country might increase its export more than its imports, but all cannot achieve it; because, one country's export surplus has to be matched by some other country's import surplus. It is a zero sum global game in which all cannot be winners at the same time. And, it would be foolish to rely entirely on the external market if only for this reason.

In the current phase of globalisation a third asymmetry arises from the role assigned to the state in monitoring and regulating economic activities. The market-oriented philosophy intends to curb the role of the state as an economic actor. This often gives rise to an almost schizophrenic view of the capabilities of the state. It is usually claimed that the state cannot be trusted with expansionary monetary and fiscal policies (e.g. FRBM Act mentioned earlier) because the state has an in-built tendency to be financially irresponsible. At the same time however, the same state is relied upon to undertake far more complex financial tasks like extending the scope of the market though privatisation, regulating the stock exchange, etc. This schizophrenic view about the capabilities of the state is rooted in denying the state its developmental and welfare role, but using it to promote the reach of the multinational corporations through measures like privatisation. The result often is greater corruption and lack of transparency in governance.

Finally, in India the most fundamental asymmetry is to be found in the uneasy relation between our political democracy and the market mechanism. The two have come to be treated as mutually reinforcing concepts in neo-liberal philosophy because both the free market and democracy extend the scope of individual choice. And yet, the relationship between the two types of freedom granted by the market economy and by political democracy often tends to be in conflict in developing countries. The democratic principle of 'one-adult-one-vote' coexists rather uneasily with the free market philosophy that the rich, with greater purchasing power, would have more 'votes' than the poor in the marketplace. This asymmetry becomes even more acute, the greater is the inequality in the distribution of income, and the larger is the proportion of the poor with political voting rights, but economically without a 'voice' in the market. In these circumstances, the democratic form of government comes under increasing strain if too much freedom is granted to the market. And yet, the forces unleashed by the process of globalisation tend to drive relentlessly towards a situation in which governments have little control over the free play of the global market forces.

As a matter of fact the history of the relation between economic development and democracy has been far more complex than the currently fashionable 'political correctness' would have us believe. Historically, the per capita income of the Western countries had to reach some minimum of US dollars 2000 per capita per year before the democratic form of government stabilised after the second world war in most of Western Europe. This was a high level compared to India's $200–250 around the time of our first general election in 1952 (measured in 1999 PPP calculation). It is an unparalleled achievement in the recorded political history that political democracy in India could be sustained at that level of poverty despite the tremendous diversity of the country. However, this should not blind us to the fact that democracy historically co-evolved with development without necessarily being either its cause or consequence. The challenge posed to our democratic form of government is different today. It must counter the domination by corporations of the economy through globalisation. Our democracy has to ensure that the process of growth is not corporate driven, but is decentralised and employment driven to allow for the widest participation of our citizens. Only then will the wealth created by growth be fairly shared, and growth itself will assume a democratic content. It will be wealth created by the people, for the people. The nature of globalisation must fit into this objective. This is the compulsion of our time; of our democracy.

References

1. Bank of International Settlement (BIS), 2001, Central Bank Survey of Foreign Exchange and Derivatives Market Activity in April 2001; Global Data, Press Release.
2. Barro, R. and Sala–I–Martin, X. 1995, *Economic Growth*, New York, McGraw Hill.
3. Bhaduri, A. 2002, 'Nationalism and Economic Policy in the Era of Globalisation' in D. Nayyar (ed.), *Governing Globalisation: Issues and Institutions*, Oxford, Oxford University Press.
4. Bhaduri, A. and Marglin, S. 1990, 'Unemployment and the Real Wage: The Economic Basis of Contesting Political Ideologies', *Cambridge Journal of Economics* (14): 375–93.
5. Chang, H–J. 2002, *Kicking Away the Ladder: Development Strategies in Historical Perspective*, London, Anthem Press.
6. Felix, D. 1998, 'Asia and the Crisis of Globalisation' in D. Backer, G. Epstein and R. Pollin (eds.), *Globalisation and Progressive Economic Policies*, Cambridge, Cambridge University Press.
7. Fischer, S. 2003, 'Globalisation and its Challenges', *American Economic Review*, Papers and Proceedings, 93(2).
8. Krugman, P. 1996, *Pop Internationalism*, Cambridge, Massachusetts, MIT Press.
9. Marglin, S. and Bhaduri, A. 1990, 'Profit Squeeze and Keynesian Theory' in S. Marglin and J. Schor (eds.), *The Golden Age of Capitalism*, Oxford, Clarendon Press, pp. 153–187.
10. Nayyar, D. 2002, 'Cross–border Movements of People', D. Nayyar (ed.), *Governing Globalisation*, Oxford, Oxford University Press.
11. OECD. 1998, 'Trends in International Migration', Annual Report, Paris, OECD.
12. Pasinetti, L. 1981, *Structural Change and Economic Growth*, Cambridge, Cambridge University Press.

2
Growing Wasteland*

Economic growth tends to be sustained over a period of time by mutually reinforcing tendencies. This process has appeared in different guises in various fields of enquiry to describe essentially similar phenomena. Biologists have long known it as symbiosis or mutualism between two species; they appear as autocatalysis in chemical reactions, and engineers dealing with electrical circuits call similar mechanisms systems of positive mutual feedbacks. Economists Myrdal and Kaldor tried to capture this phenomenon occurring during the process of economic growth as the mechanism of 'cumulative causation', and 'dynamic increasing returns' respectively. While most processes of economic growth sustained over a period of time might be characterised by this somewhat abstract notion of mutually reinforcing tendencies, each historical process is also different in so far as it generates its own specific tendencies. It is the specificity of these reinforcing tendencies that determine to a large extent the developmental politics underlying this growth process.

The growing despair and anger in a large part of Indian countryside despite India's recent and unprecedented high growth has to be placed in this context. It is not simply that growth coexists with the persistence of widespread poverty and inequality. That has always been the case, and continues

---

* Foundation Day Lecture delivered at The Madras Institute of Development Studies, 2007.

to be so after 60 years of political independence and democratic governance. The current pattern of high growth is different, because it requires rising inequality as its driving force. Growth feeds on increasing inequality, and increasing inequality promotes growth in a mutually reinforcing spiral of positive feedbacks. It is a World Bank–IMF promoted platitude, shared by most economists and all mainstream political parties from the traditional Right to the traditional Left, that this growth and the accompanying pattern of industrialisation would gradually alleviate poverty, as the benefits of growth begin to 'trickle down' to the poor. The actual truth is less comfortable. This high growth based on a certain pattern of industrialisation can continue only so long as inequality and relative poverty in our society is allowed to increase, while growing inequality is justified in the name of liberalisation, globalisation, attracting foreign investment for industrialisation, in short the TINA (there is no alternative) syndrome. It is also absurd to provide ideological justification along the line that the 'socialism' in Vietnam and China follows this route. These countries do not have a functioning democracy. Their extensive pro-poor policies inherited from their revolutions still survive to some extent despite market-oriented reforms. The Indian context is very different. India has a flawed but functioning multi-party democracy. Its most glaring failure has been our inability to remove extensive sub-human poverty to which we continue to subject anywhere around one-third of our citizens. One cannot hope to understand the historical process of growth under Indian democracy, if one ignores this specific historical context.

The mechanism by which growing inequality drives this growth, while growth reinforces further inequality is caused apparently by two different factors. First, while India is experiencing a growth rate of some 7–8 per cent in recent years, the growth in regular employment has hardly exceeded 1 per cent. According to official statistics, between

1991 and 2004 employment fell in the organised public sector, and the private sector did not compensate for it. This means most of the growth, some 5–6 per cent of the GDP, is the result not of employment expansion, but of higher output per worker in contrast to earlier times when less than 4 per cent growth on an average was associated with 2 per cent growth in employment. This high growth in labour productivity comes in turn from two major sources. In the corporate sector, and in some organised industries it comes mostly from mechanisation, longer hours of work and downsising of the labour force. Tata Steel for example, increased in the last decade its output five-fold, but cut down labour force by nearly half, implying an almost ten-fold increase in productivity. Without a corresponding increase in wages and salaries, by cutting down labour cost per unit of output this becomes an enormous source of profit, and also a source of international price competitiveness in a globalising world. One could multiply such examples, but this is broadly the name of the game everywhere in the private corporate sector. Nevertheless, this is not the entire story, perhaps not even the most important part of the story, because the corporate sector belongs to the organised sector, which accounts for at most about one-tenth of the labour force. Simply by the arithmetic of weighted average, a 5–6 per cent growth in labour productivity for the whole economy is possible only if the unorganised sector accounting for the remaining 90 per cent of the labour force also experiences considerable growth in labour productivity. As many field surveys show, this comes mostly from lengthening the hours of work often for the whole family, and not merely for the individual worker in the unorganised sector because has no labour laws worth the name, and no social security to protect workers. Sub-contracting to the unorganised sector along with casualisation of labour becomes a convenient device to force longer hours of work without higher pay as a source of growth in labour productivity as well as corporate profit. In this context self-employment of workers becomes another name for ruthless self–exploitation in a desperate attempt to survive by doing long hours of work with very little hourly earning. It is this category of self-employed workers (about 260 million workers) which has expanded fastest during the high growth regime proving an invisible source of labour productivity growth.

The increase in labour efficiency driving growth is partly the result of economic openness in a globalising world in two respects. The first relevant aspect is trade openness. Given the overall size and rate of expansion of the global market, which is beyond the control of an individual country like India, the thrust of trade-related economic policy becomes capturing a larger share of the global market for exports. In this respect, India like many other countries behaves like a giant corporation, and tries to achieve a greater share of a given and market through higher competitiveness by cutting unit cost of production. This means imposing greater wage restraint on the one hand, and attempts at raising labour productivity through measures like longer hours, mechanisation and downsizing of the labour force on the other, policies needed for greater labour market flexibility. It has turned international trade into an extremely competitive zero sum game, where one country winning through greater export surplus entails some other countries losing through larger export deficit. It should not be forgotten that attempts at enhancing international competitiveness also puts greater pressure on a country to invite direct foreign investments, raising concern at times over dependency to foreigners. For instance, China has been a winner in this zero-sum game, nearly 77 per cent of Chinese Communication Industry is controlled by foreign investors, with foreign capital controlling the top five firms in each and every industry where the Chinese government allows foreign investment. It forced the government to introduce in September 2006 regulations requiring companies to seek official approvals for all mergers and acquisitions involving more than 2000 employees or 25 per cent of market share.

While trade in goods and services is the more visible aspect of openness, the openness to international finance and capital flows, which might well be of greater consequence. Much of India's comfortable foreign reserves position (crossing 230 billion US dollars in 2008), despite the fact that we continue to import more than we export (unlike China) is the result of portfolio investments and short-term capital inflows from foreign financial institutions. To keep the show going in this way constrains government's policy, for it requires the government policies to be compatible with the interests of the financial markets. Successive Indian governments have willingly accepted this, e.g. the Financial Responsibility and Budget Management Act (2003) restricting deficit spending serves this purpose, and so does the complementary idea that the government should raise resources through privatisation but not through raising fiscal deficit, or not imposing a significant turnover tax on transactions of securities. The hidden agenda behind these measures has been to please the large players in the financial markets who mostly take their lead from the IMF and the World Bank. The burden of such policies is borne largely by the poor of this country. It has had a crippling effect on policies for expanding public sector expenditure on health, education, public distribution, as well as on employment generation.

The 'discipline' imposed by the financial markets serves the rich but harms the poor. This is the other reason for growing inequality which expresses itself in the ideological rolling back of public expenditure in social services like health, education, and public distribution. The result is a picture of striking contrasts which is India today. On the front page of its 8 October 2007 edition, the *Times of India* reported that the collective wealth of India's top ten billionaires had increased by over 65 billion US dollars or 27 per cent in the third quarter year of 2007. The number of Indian billionaires rose from 9 in 2004 to 36 in 2006 with a combined wealth of 191 billion US dollars, which works out to about one-fifth of India's current GDP. Estimates based on corporate profits suggest that, since 2000–01 to date, on an average each one additional per cent growth of GDP has led to some 2.5 per cent growth in corporate profits. India's high growth is sheer music to the ears of the corporation. However, for ordinary Indians it is a land devoid of hope. Nearly half of Indian children under 6 years suffer from under-weight and malnutrition, nearly 80 per cent from anaemia, while some 40 per cent of Indian adults suffer from chronic energy deficit. Destitution, chronic hunger and poverty is systematically more acute in rural India, and among more vulnerable groups like females, Dalits and Adivasis and also concentrated in poorer states since recent market-oriented policies have widened regional disparities. After several years of high growth India now has the distinction of being only second to the United States in terms of the combined total wealth of its corporate billionaires coexisting with the largest number of homeless, ill-fed, illiterates. It is this mechanism of the high growth process that we need to analyse. This is a process of high growth which traps roughly one in three citizens of India in extreme poverty with no possibility of escape. The high growth scene of India appears to them like a wasteland leading to the Hell once described by the great Italian poet Dante. On the gate of this imagined Hell is written, "This is the land you enter after abandoning all hopes".

Extremely slow growth in employment and feeble public action exacerbates inequality, as a disproportionately large share of the increasing output and income from growth goes to the rich, not more than say the top 20 per cent of the income groups. With their income rapidly growing, this group of privileged Indians demand a set of goods which lie mostly outside the reach of the rest in the society. The market expands rapidly, but only for a selected set of high income goods; typically they also have high service content. For instance, we are told that more than 3 in 4 Indians do not have a daily income of Rupees 20, roughly equivalent in purchasing power to 2 US dollars. They can hardly be a part of this growing market. Since the market votes with purchasing power, its logic is to produce those goods for which there is enough demand backed by money so that high prices can be charged and handsome profit can be made. As the income of the privileged grows rapidly in the process of this growth, the goods they demand expand even faster through the operation of the 'income elasticities of demand' which roughly measures the percentage growth in the demand for a particular commodity due to one per cent growth in income. Typically, goods consumed by the rich have income elasticities greater than unity. Consequently, the demand for the goods consumed by the rich expands even faster than the growth in their income. As a result, a lopsided composition of goods emerges in our otherwise poor country. Examples abound. We have state-of-the-art corporate-run expensive hospitals and nursing homes for the rich, but not enough money to control malaria and TB which require inexpensive treatment. So they continue to kill the largest numbers. Lack of sanitation and clean drinking water transmit easily preventable deadly diseases especially to small children, while bottled water of various brands multiply for those who can afford. Private schools for rich kids often have fees that are higher than the annual income of an average Indian, while the poor have to be satisfied with schools without teachers, and enough class-rooms because the government feels itself constrained to spend.

The resulting composition of output produced by the market in the liberalised economic regime of high growth is highly energy, water and other non-reproducible resources intensive. We only have to think of the energy and material content of airconditioned malls, luxury hotels and apartments, air travels, private cars as means of transport. These become the symbols of 'world class' cities in a poor country, while by diverting resources they make a wasteland of our countryside where most live. This is the black hole of urbanisation with a giant appetite to gobble resources to help the rich by robbing the poor. Many are forced to migrate to cities. And it becomes another case of mutually reinforcing cumulative causation, migration—bigger cities—more depressed countryside and more impoverished agriculture, and yet more migration. The poor are forced to migrate to escape the wasteland of an increasingly impoverished agriculture, only to be pushed out of the city as unwelcome, illegal shanty dwellers and street hawkers, because a world-class city cannot tolerate the desparately poor!

The composition of output demanded by the rich is hardly producible by village artisans or the small producers. Naturally, they find no place either as producers or as consumers; instead, it has to be handed over to large corporations who enter in a big way into the scene. The cycle of high growth with rising inequality is now completed. The corporations are needed to produce goods for the rich, and in the process they make their high profits and provide well-paid employment for the rich in a poor country. The obliging economist or politician, usually an intellectual slave to the platitudes that go under the name of development discourse sees nothing wrong in this process. Their sermon goes that investments must flow to the most productive and profitable sectors for the efficient allocation of resources in a market economy. It is conveniently forgotten that the price mechanism guides, but the prices themselves are guided by the distribution of income in the society. Which sectors are most profitable and productive are determined largely by the pattern of income distribution ruling in a market system.

An increasingly unequal distribution of income might indicate a particular set of goods and lines of production as most profitable (like airconditioned malls, luxury apartments, private cars as modes of travel, etc.). However they would cease to be so with a more equal distribution of income in a poor country. The name of the game is to be a knowing or unknowing slave to economic platitudes, and talk of 'inclusive growth', while ignoring the link between greater inequality and higher growth. And yet, this is the link that binds the corporations with the government, and becomes the defining characteristic of India's recent high growth regime.

A common pattern of resource use dictated by a liberalised market and a corporate-led state begins to emerge. This is most visible in the large development projects each of which displaces thousands. Hydroelectric power from the big dams is transmitted mostly to corporate industries, and a few posh urban localities, while the nearby villages are left in darkness. Peasants even close to the cities do not get electricity or water to irrigate their land as urban India increasingly gobbles up these resources. Take the case of water use. According to the Comptroller and Auditor General report released to the public on 30th March 2007, Gujarat has increased the allocation of Narmada waters to industry five-fold last year, eating into the share of drought–affected villages. Despite many promises made to villagers by different governments, water allocation stagnated at 0.86 MAF (million acres feet), and now even this is being cut. Water companies and soft drink giants like Coca Cola sink deeper to take out pure ground water as free raw material for their products. Because peasants cannot match their technology or capital cost, their land in surrounding areas are left starved of water. Iron ore is mined out from distant tribal lands where people would hardly ever use iron beams or any other metal for their mud houses or roads. Common lands which traditionally provided some supplementary income to the poor are taken over systematically by the local rich as well as the corporations with active connivance of the government. While natural resources like land and water are being handed over under various guises mostly to a few corporations turning the Indian countryside to a wasteland for the poor, the rich and the powerful celebrate it as the progress of the whole country. And yet, it is nothing less than the internal colonisation of many of our poorest citizens. The manifest crisis engulfing Indian agriculture is a pointer to this process, with more than a hundred thousand suicides by farmers over the last decade according to official statistics. We are indeed colonising successfully our own agriculture, where most of our fellow citizens live.

The large corporations and the rich citizens of India who mostly benefit from this process of destructive creation of corporate wealth find that their interests increasingly coincide. A new coalition cutting across traditional Right and Left political division is being formed in the process. The name of the game is 'progress through industrialisation'. In effect, this leads to ganging up against the poor by the rich and upper classes who believe it their birthright to have all the industrial luxuries in the name of economic progress. The meagre livelihoods of the poor have to be destroyed, the small and marginal peasants' lands have to be snatched, consent has to be forcibly manufactured, if and where necessary at gunpoint, from the adivasis, so that their thousand-year-old habitats can be handed over to large private corporations in the name of public interest by a democratic government. Such practices are extensive particularly in the resource-rich states of Orissa, Jharkhand, Chhattisgarh and Madhya Pradesh, but even the Marxist government in West Bengal is not lagging far behind. The Adivasis who constitute only 8 per cent and Dalits who account for another 16 per cent of India's total population together accounted for an overwhelming 55 per cent of the people displaced in the name of economic progress in recent years. In this central part of India, where these states have parts of their land mass, in some 160 districts covering nearly one-fourth of the land area of the country, extremist Left-wing movements have gathered momentum. It would have been surprising if it did not. When people are preached continuously about the eventual benefits of industrialisation, but are left with nothing but destruction of their livelihood, resistance cannot be unexpected. The governments, at the federal as well as at the state level, irrespective of their political colour consider it the 'greatest security threat' to the country. However, they do not quite explain what the dispossessed rural poor should do when all the security of their livelihoods is snatched in the name of high growth.

The middle-class opinion makers, learned economists, democratic politicians, legal experts, and the media persons unite to restrict their liberal talk carefully to 'fair compensation' for the dispossessed. They are at a loss about how to create alternative dignified livelihood due to such large scale displacement and destruction. Even discussion about compensation is one sided, and focuses usually on ownership and, at best use rights to land property. However, the multitude of the poor who eke out a living without any title to landed property like agricultural labourers, fishermen, or cart-drivers in rural areas, or illegal squatters and small hawkers in cities seldom figure in this discussion about compensation. And yet, they outnumber by far, perhaps in the ratio of 4 to 1, those who have some title to property. In the meantime, the state acquires with single-minded devotion land, water and resources for the private corporations for mining, industrialisation or Special Economic Zones in the name of public interest. It destroys in the process livelihoods of numerous poor people with or without titles to property, presumably these poor people do not count in defining 'public interest'. None stops to ask why the poor who are least able, should bear the burden of 'economic progress', which constitutes a rapidly growing basket of goods and services as gross domestic product without any relevance to their lives. But rich India of a mostly urban, smooth-talking upper middle class pleased with their lifestyles as never before, needs these goods and services, and helps corporate billionaires to shine by multiplying their number and wealth at a furious rate.

The process of internal colonisation of the poor, of the Dalits and the Adivasis and of other marginalised and forcibly dispossessed groups, has set in motion a relatively little noticed social process, not altogether unknown as the relation between an imperialist 'master race' and the colonised natives. As the privileged thin layers of the society distance themselves from the poor, the speed at which the secession takes place is celebrated as a measure of the rapid growth of the country. Thus, India is poised to become a global power in the twenty-first century, with the largest number of homeless, undernourished, illiterates. Over them rules an unbridled market whose rules are fixed by the corporations aided by state power. The ideology of progress through dispossession of the poor, preached relentlessly by the united power of the rich, the middle class and the corporations colonise directly the poor, and has begun to colonise indirectly even our minds. The result is a sort of uniform industrialisation of the mind which sees no alternative. And yet, no matter how powerful this public relations campaign is, the combined power of the corporations, the media, and the politicians, is still defenceless in a way against the life experiences of the poor. If this process of growth continues for long, it would produce its own demons. No society, not even our mal-functioning democratic system, can withstand beyond a point the increasing inequality that nurtures this high growth. The dissent of the poor must either be suppressed with increasing state violence against the poor flouting every norm of democracy, and violence will be met with violence to engulf the whole society. Or, an alternative path to development that deepens our democracy with popular participation has to be found. Neither the rulers nor the ruled can escape for long this challenge thrown up by high growth.

References for Sources of Data and Other Information

1. India Development Report, edited by R. Radhakrishna, Oxford University Press, 2008.
2. Alternative Economic Survey, India 2006–2007, by Alternative Survey Group, New Delhi, Dannish Books, 2007.
3. Government of India, Economic Survey, 2006–2007, New Delhi, Ministry of Finance, 2007.
4. 'Revisiting Employment and Growth' by C. Rangarajan, Padma Kaul and Seema, *Money and Finance*, September 2007.
5. 'Service-led Growth' by Mihir Rakshit, *Money and Finance*, February 2007.
6. *'Inclusive Growth in India'*, by S. Mahendra Dev, New Delhi, Oxford University Press, 2008.
7. *Green Left Weekly* issue no. 710, May 2007.

3

Economic Growth A Meaningless Obession?*

We are living in India at a time when the media is transmitting continuously confusing, even conflicting, economic signals. If we restrict ourselves to the English language print as well as electronic media, our comfort level is likely to be high. The economy is growing at a high rate, the stock market is booming, our foreign reserve is at a comfortably high level, freer trade is bringing to our doors a variety of goods and services that would have been unimaginable a couple of decades ago as a mark of the benefits of globalisation. What is more, we are told repeatedly that India is poised economically and politically as an emergent world power.

We are told by the ruling political establishment, and reported prominently in the media, that this growing international stature of India has been possible due to the process of globalisation. Despite its many shortcomings, we are told further, if less directly, that we need to play the game according to the global rules set largely by the United States. Our edge in information technology would place us economically in a position of advantage in an era of out-sourcing. Politically, our changed stance in international relations is signified by the nuclear deal this government insisted on, and our uncritical support for combating global

---

*Based on the author's B.N. Ganguly Memorial Lecture; CSDS, Delhi, November 2006, Published in Seminar, 269–January 2007.

terrorism, neglecting conveniently the question whether terrorism feeds on the very processes by which it is being fought.

If we are able to look a little beyond our middle class noses, beyond the world painted by mainstream media, the picture is less comforting, less assuring. Contradictory signals appear in the same media, even if they are usually given far less prominence than they deserve. These opposite signals have begun to clash with greater intensity, and the noise level is getting louder by the day. India is doing well in many ways, and yet a sense of unease is growing rapidly at the same time. Once you step outside the charmed circle of a privileged minority expounding on the virtues of globalisation, liberalisation and privatisation, things appear less certain.

A sense of unease mixed with growing popular despair, rage and resistance seems to be engulfing a large part of our countryside. Look at such an index of despair. Going by conservative official statistics, between 2001 and 2006 in the four states of Andhra Pradesh, Karnataka, Kerala and Maharashtra more than 9,000 farmers committed suicide. Look also at a similar index of rage. According to the estimate of the Ministry of Home Affairs, some 120 to 160 out of a total of 607 districts are 'Naxal infested'. Supported by a disgruntled and dispossessed peasantry, the movement has spread to nearly one-fourth of Indian territory. And yet, all that this government does is not to face the causes of the rage and despair that nurture such movements; instead it considers it a 'menace', a law-and-order problem affecting the foreign investment climate that is to be rooted out by the violence of the state, and congratulates itself when it uses violence effectively to crush the resistance of the angry poor.

These are unmistakeable symptoms of a process that I have come to believe is generic. The way we have been accustomed to think of urbanisation, industrialisation, and 'development' and have accepted unquestioningly the logic of globalisation and liberalisation through the market, will only intensify this process. The contradictory economic signals will grow louder until they overwhelm us completely. Not thinking afresh about development might seem convenient, even pragmatic for the time being, but in effect it will only make the problem less manageable later.

In the meantime, however, this apparent quest for higher economic growth in the name of development will serve the interests of large corporations, receive accolades from the IMF and the World Bank for our decision makers in power, and get high credit ratings from international financial firms, while the ground reality steadily worsens. For the sake of higher growth, the poor in growing numbers will be left out in the cold, undernourished, unskilled and illiterate, totally defenceless against the ruthless logic of a global market dominated by large corporate interests.

This is not merely an iniquitous process. High growth brought about in this manner does not simply ignore the question of income distribution, its reality is far worse. It threatens the poor with a kind of brutal violence in the name of development, a sort of 'developmental terrorism', violence perpetrated on the poor in the name of development by the state primarily in the interest of a corporate aristocracy, approved by the IMF and the World Bank, and a self-serving political class. After Singur, one cannot even say that the traditional Left has anything better to offer.

A massive land grab by large corporations is going on in various guises, aided and abated by the land acquisition policies of both the federal and state governments. Destruction of livelihoods in the name of industrialisation, big dams for power generation and supposedly irrigation without adequate supporting canal systems in many cases, modernisation and beautification of our cities by demolishing slums, etc., are all examples of how development can turn perverse and systematically against the poor people.

Until September 2006, the Board of Approvals Committee of the Ministry of Commerce had approved 267 Special Economic Zones (SEZ) projects all over India. Land area for each of these projects 'deemed foreign territories' ranges from 1,000 to 14,000 hectares. So far for only 67 multiproduct SEZ involving 1,34,000 hectares have been acquired, mostly by state industrial development corporations. Similarly, mining rights are being granted to the corporations mostly over tribal lands. The tribals are not allowed by their customary laws to sell land individually to preserve their community, but the state governments, aided and emboldened by federal government policies, are acquiring land to give away to corporations.

With its two faces, government has all along shown remarkable energy and efficiency when it comes to acquiring land forcibly from the peasantry, but remains reticent, bound by bureaucratic red tape when it comes to acquiring land for resettling the poor and displaced. Recall that the year 2006 almost began with the shooting down in cold blood by the police of thirteen tribals in Kalinga Nagar, Orissa, when they resisted their land being handed over to the Tatas for mining. The acquisition price of their land was reportedly about one-tenth of the price at which the government gave it to the Tatas, and even that price was well below the market price. Singur was a variation on the same theme, again with the Tatas and this time the CP(M) and not the Janta Dal (Biju) as the pair doing the tango.

The Panchayat Extension to Scheduled Areas or PESA Act of 1996 requires gram sabhas to be consulted for land acquisition. And yet, in Jharkhand, and in Orissa this has either been ignored systematically or, as a recent report from the field documents, the police surrounds the gram sabha meetings and threatens the ordinary members, forcing them to agree to the proposals of giving up their lands at throwaway prices (*Down to Earth,* 31 October 2006).

The Left Front coalition in West Bengal led by Buddhadeb Bhattacharya is in the distinguished company of Mulayam Singh in claiming that the exact nature of the land acquisition deal in Singur and Dadri respectively cannot be revealed to the public under the Right to Information Act because these are 'trade secrets'. Yet a local TV channel reported, uncontested by the government, that the West Bengal government gave Rs. 140 crore in compensation, while the Tatas will give only Rs. 20 crore for the land, without stamp duty and with provision of free water.

We are indeed living in a globalised age. With their global reach, the large corporations, national and multinational, have reached almost all politicians who differentiate themselves by their rhetoric, but not by their actions. Academics and media persons have joined the political chorus of presenting the developmental terrorism as a sign of progress, an inevitable cost of development. The conventional wisdom of our time is that, There Is No Alternative, the TINA syndrome in the development discourse.

There is a hidden script to this TINA syndrome. The ruling ideological design of development is that the corporations will deliver us from poverty by raising the rate of economic growth. The IMF, the World Bank, and the Asian Development Bank propagate tirelessly this ideology in various guises. Now we have Marxist politicians and the theoreticians propagating the same. Our one-time China-haters have become its greatest economic admirers in this process. 'China's path is our path' is a slogan that will suit equally well in New Delhi, Kolkata, Mumbai, Ahmedabad or Lucknow! And yet this so widely agreed upon model of development is fatally flawed. It has already been rejected and will be rejected again by the growing strength of our democratic polity, and by direct resistance of the poor threatened with 'developmental terrorism'.

Three different variants of this broad ideology that growth will deliver by trickling down can be identified from the various experiences in the contemporary developing world. In the first variant, some countries with significant deposits of valuable natural resources like oil enter into an implicit political arrangement with the United States (and increasingly with China). They ensure the supply of oil, receive petrodollars in return, and recycle them through multinational banks to engage multinational corporations for the development and modernisation of their economies. The US as the military superpower ensures that these regimes of questionable legitimacy, upholding such agreements, are kept in power, irrespective of whether it is a democracy or not. Saudi Arabia, and many other Gulf states are the prototypes for this model.

Some have speculated that Saddam Hussain in Iraq faced American aggression when he had the delusion typical of many dictators that he could wield independent power by refusing such an arrangement. This has been the operative model in many oil and natural resource rich countries, which an American academic recently described as 'the curse of natural resources'. However, he conveniently forgot to mention the role the US and multinational corporations play in perpetuating this curse. Understandably, the US gets worried when this model is rejected by Hugo Chavez in Venezuela, and now increasingly in Bolivia, Argentina Equador and Brazil.

In the second variant, massive commercial borrowing from international banks is done by a willing national government for the purpose of development. This is encouraged and usually coordinated by the IMF and the World Bank by engaging multinational corporations, leading to various expensive, ambitious giant projects, typically according to rules of consultancy and contract fixed by the World Bank or the Asian Development Bank. Almost inevitably the country is caught in a debt trap. Many countries of central and Latin America, with Argentina as a prime case before total collapse and Indonesia under the military dictatorship of Suharto, are examples of this variant of the development model.

On the surface the first and the second variant differ because in the former case the country is usually a net lender, while in the latter it becomes a net borrower. However, in both the first and second variant, a mutuality of interests and corruption binds together the multinational banks and corporations, led by the IMF and the World Bank and a willing domestic government, which depends either militarily or economically (often both) on outside support.

However, there is a third variant which differs in so far as it injects a strong element of statism in the developmental process. In this case state-led or state-sponsored corporations are created and nurtured to compete with multinationals under active government support, especially in the world market. At the same time the government tries to attract direct foreign investment, either through these corporations, or in areas where the government corporations are not the preferred option for some reason. Nevertheless, the government becomes a ruthless promoter of the corporate entities in search of higher growth, irrespective of how it affects the interests of the people.

This is a case of state-led corporatism, and today's China seems to fit this description reasonably well; whereas South Korea, despite the obvious differences in the political and geopolitical situations and dependence at an earlier stage on foreign borrowing, traversed a similar path. However, the reliance on developmental terrorism by the state on behalf of the corporations is not any less in this third variant of development, and a dictatorial form of government fits it rather naturally.

The Indian case would have been complicated by a functioning democracy, and the political compulsions of coalition governments at the Centre as well as in several states. However, there seems to be a remarkable degree of political convergence on the model of development; elections change governments without changing the model accepted for development. The first variant of a highly resource-rich country is clearly not available for India. The third variant of strong statism is also realisable only to a limited extent given the compulsions of democracy in a land of overwhelmingly poor people. Therefore, all governments that have recently been in power at the Centre as well as at the state level irrespective of their professed political colour, meander somewhere between the second and third variant.

In other words, our notion of how to develop has come to be based on a design of international borrowing with greater presence of multinationals, encouraged by the IMF and the World Bank. At the same time, attempts are being made at creating more favourable conditions for domestic private corporations through measures like special economic zones (SEZ), granting of indiscriminate mining rights on tribal land, corporate farming by subjugating poor peasants and so on.

However, these two variants of development are fundamentally incompatible in the Indian case. A policy of massive borrowing under the supervision of the IMF and the World Bank necessarily requires an extremely multinational corporate friendly economic climate. This would also clash with the independent growth of indigenous corporations, particularly when they both target the domestic market. The case of China is misleading in this respect in two ways. First, because the nature and extent of support the Chinese government can give to its state-sponsored corporations or to particular foreign investors, and differentiate among them, if necessary even in terms of a malleable legal system, is not possible for a government, particularly when it follows the path of borrowing heavily under IMF World Bank supervision. They have to largely comply with the intentions of those agencies.

Second, the single-minded ruthlessness with which the Chinese system can follow its objective of corporate-led growth, at times by changing laws or suppressing the rights of ordinary people, is fortunately not yet possible in our system despite conscious attempts by the government to label all such resistance 'Maoist'. And yet, the higher the growth rate achieved through this route of promoting corporations as the bulwark of growth, the greater would be the level of developmental terrorism, while we would be fed on a lie that higher the growth, the sooner the problem of poverty would get solved. We would also be told that efficiency promoted by liberalisation, reform and international openness would raise growth to solve the economic problems of the common people over time through greater integration with the world market.

It is worth explaining why this argument is false. Since globalisation tends to increase the relative importance of the external vis-a-vis the internal market, the thrust of the strategy is to exploit the greater dependence on the world market through exports and direct foreign investment and other capital flows. However, since the size of the total world market is beyond the control of any individual nation state, especially India, the case is presented for focusing on increasing the share of exports by the country in the world market.

On the economic front, this has to be achieved through greater international cost competitiveness, by measures like wage restraint, banning workers' right to strike, tax concessions, higher labour productivity through downsizing of the labour force, privatisation of state enterprises at prices favourable to the private corporations, cheap allotment of prime agricultural land to industrial houses in the name of industrialisation, mining rights on tribal land, and a host of similar measures. The basic economic theme unifying all these measures is the notion of 'internationally competitive cost effectiveness' that would be achieved by the corporations at home. In effect, it boils down to applying the logic of corporate management by treating the whole economy as a giant corporation which would increase its international market share by out-competing rival trading nations through cutting costs.

Politically it is dangerous to treat a country of India's diversity as a homogeneous corporate interest. The economic reasoning is flawed, because the micro-logic applicable to individual corporations, involves a serious macro fallacy. At the most obvious level, it ignores the uncomfortable fact that all countries cannot be winners at the same time in the zero-sum game for producing an export surplus through competitive cost cutting, because a larger share by some countries in the global market must mean a smaller share by others. As a matter of fact, India has been an import surplus economy with an excess of imports over exports of goods met through capital inflows, which has even been sufficient in recent years to build up a relatively large foreign exchange reserve. However, they are mostly short-term capital inflows and portfolio investments.

Such capital flows in the Indian context are not merely NRI deposits and a greater demand for stocks by registered institutional investors like international banks and mutual funds. It also comes from other less transparent sources as participatory notes (PNs), routed through registered financial bodies. The PNs now (October 2006) constitute over half (about 52 per cent) of total inflows. For the time being these inflows contribute significantly to the stock market boom, but can turn into outflows with even greater ease leading to a financial downturn, panic and crash. As already mentioned, instead of raising the money at home, a lenient attitude towards borrowing abroad has been a crucial element. The option of raising money at home through deficit financing was foreclosed through a Fiscal Responsibility and Budget Management Act in 2003, in line with the conventional wisdom of the IMF. So the government can now claim that it can only raise money through privatisation or inviting foreign capital. But the script of crippling the economic role of the government goes deeper.

Arguably, the present phase of globalisation began around the middle of the 1970s with the deregulation of major capital markets in the rich industrial nations. As a result, the volume of private trade in foreign exchange today, facilitated vastly by fast electronic transfers around the world, is a staggering daily volume of some 1.2 trillion (i.e. million million or 10) dollars. Less than two per cent of this is needed at the most of financing export and import, and even less for financing the current level of direct foreign investment.

The daily volume of private trade in foreign exchange can easily overwhelm the foreign exchange reserve of any central bank. The combined reserve of all the central banks of the world put together is less than a couple of days' total volume of private trade in foreign exchange. Theoretically speaking, the entire reserve of all the central banks in the world could be wiped out by hostile private trades in a few days. This predominance of private finance capital has become by far the single defining characteristic of the modern phase of globalisation.

No wonder, all individual governments feel vulnerable and India, with its almost insignificantly small stock market or a relatively soft currency, feels particularly vulnerable. The rupee and Dalal Street can be set in an uncontrollable downward spiral due to capital flights triggered off by the speculation of a few important private players in the foreign exchange market. Mercifully, the Indian capital market is still not totally free; bringing in finance is generally easier than taking it out, but this government considers it a priority to make the market freer through capital account convertibility.

Even in the present situation, if a few major foreign institutional investors turn hostile and take out a part of their financial investments from the Indian market, it would dramatically bring down the stock market and the exchange value of the rupee. Even worse, it might trigger off a panic among ordinary investors who would then follow like a herd of sheep to turn it into a full-fledged financial crisis. Therefore the government remains wary of sending unfavourable signals to the financial markets, and many developmental issues become subservient to this consideration.

The Fiscal Responsibility and Budget Management Act in the name of 'sound finance' is one of its important signals of comfort to the stock market. In these circumstances, the government with support from the media can pretend to be doing very well economically by keeping the large private players in the capital market happy through sending the right signals with enthusiastic indirect support of the IMF and the World Bank. When the IMF or the World Bank says economic liberalisation is good, privatisation is a must, but large government expenditures or fiscal deficits are bad in all circumstances, our governments take the soft option of falling in line. The move to make the capital account convertible, a favoured IMF recommendation, would only further tilt the balance in this direction.

Unlike a visible external debt trap, under globalisation the invisible trap of international finance requires maintaining a rising stock market through capital inflows from foreign financial institutions, induced by financial market-friendly policies approved by the IMF and the World Bank. Typically, however, the resulting policies are anti-poor.

This reasoning is not mere academic speculation and fits the facts. The stock market went up in a frenzied bubble (ultimately resulting in the Harshad Mehta episode) to show an approval of economic reforms in 1992. The stock market suffered a massive post-election crash in 2004 to register its nervousness about reform, until market-oriented politicians were put in charge of the coalition government's economic policies. In the Indian context, the anti-poor thrust of this style of economic management is shown up in election verdicts.

It is no accident that economic policy-makers playing by this script are repeatedly rejected by the people in the elections. The Congress-dominated coalition, which prided itself in 'reforming' the economy lost the general election in 2000. Manmohan Singh, who was credited with initiating reforms failed to win a seat in the Parliament. The BJP-led coalition, which saw India shining through the glasses of the stock market did no better in the general election of 2004. Particularly telling was its electoral disaster in Andhra Pradesh. The lesson of our democracy should be clear. Those who tie the well-being of the Indian stock market with the well-being of the people should not expect to win elections. And yet, by agreeing to a flawed model of development, all political parties are closing our electoral options.

The political challenge facing India is clear. It is not how to achieve still higher growth, but how to impart a greater democratic content to our growth by following a different course of development. Higher economic growth spreading developmental terrorism without democratic content has to be downgraded as meaningless, not even desirable. We must consider instead growth as an outcome of the process of involving the people through gainful employment and expanding their opportunities for livelihood. This requires focussing on employment generation, and judging growth performance in terms of its ability to generate productive employment to include even the poorest and most marginalised citizens in our society.

By this yardstick, the high growth performance of neither India nor China has been impressive in recent years. In India the rate of employment growth in organised industries has actually been lower in the recent high growth era than in previous decades when the economy grew more slowly. The reason for this dismal performance on the employment front is the emphasis in isolation only on labour productivity growth, which is an outcome of the obsession with cost-cutting corporate style of economic management in the name of efficiency and international competitiveness without taking into account its impact on employment growth.

It is time we got rid of this dangerous obsession based on the false premise that India's development can be led by corporate and international financial interests. Our focus must shift instead to a time-bound programme for full employment with growth as the consequence not the cause of full employment. It is possible to devise such an economic programme, not as a Utopia, but as reasonable economics feasible even within our political context (see, *Development with Dignity* by Amit Bhaduri, National Book Trust, New Delhi, 2005). The intellectual challenge, indeed the compulsion of our time is to be able to work at this alternative with honest courage, without excess baggage of the political ideology of either the Right or the Left.

4

Economic Theory and Ideology*

We all know markets involve various buying and selling activities organised under certain rules. By and large, economists study in great detail the properties of an abstract form of the market called perfect competition. Under highly unrealistic assumptions that make the perfectly competitive market an almost mythical form of idealised competition, it is shown that an equilibrium set of prices exists which simultaneously clears all markets by equating demand and supply. Moreover, these prices are shown to result in an efficient and (Pareto) optimum arrangement where no individual participant in the market can do better. So, this is an optimum state of affairs in accordance with the dictums of classical liberalism focused exclusively on the individual.

The mythical notion of perfect competition has created the powerful ideological metaphor of the 'invisible hand' of the market leading a society of self-seeking individuals to an optimum state. This would imply two things. First, selfishness without any concern for the collective becomes an unintended social virtue, because the society can reach an optimum through the individual's self-centred activities in the market. Margaret Thatcher, a former conservative prime minister of Britain famously echoed this sentiment by claiming that there is no society, only individuals! Second, because the unregulated competitive market is claimed to

* Lecture delivered in memory of Professor Dipak Banerjee on 6.1.2009, Presidency College, Kolkata.

achieve an optimum, any regulatory role of the government becomes redundant, even counter-productive in many instances. (This view too was made academically more respectable with the award of several Nobel Memorial prizes in economics). Aided by such theories, driving for a minimalist role for the state becomes the war cry of various versions of neo-liberalism.

Nevertheless, the virtues of even this mythical model of perfect competition remain flawed in so far as it does not guarantee that the distribution of income in the society would be tolerably acceptable to all its members despite the Pareto optimality! To appreciate its practical implications, remember demand depends on the purchasing power of the participants in any market. Thus an unequal distribution of income even under competitive conditions might mean millions of children dying from malnutrition, or from easily preventable and treatable diseases like cholera, malaria or TB. At the same time, a highly unequal distribution of income would create demand for most expensive treatments in state-of-the-art hospitals for the rich (and even for the treatment of obesity from plain overeating). This is indeed inherent in the logic of the market, because voting takes place in the market according to purchasing power. Thus a handful of rich would have many more 'votes' than millions of poor in determining what would be profitable to produce for the market. Greater scope for the market in India today means villages go without housing, sanitation and drinkable water, but selected areas of cities pride themselves with world class amenities of luxury hotels, apartments, and malls. The logic of the market glorified by neo-liberal economists and politicians drives this process of diversion of natural and other resources to benefit the rich in the name of efficient allocation of resources by the market.

Outside the charmed circle of a few theoretical economists it is seldom emphasised that, without additional stringent assumptions economic theory guarantees not even the local stability, let alone a sufficiently high speed of convergence to such a competitive equilibrium (For a non-technical version the reader may consult, 'The intrinsic limits of modern economic theory: the emperor has no clothes' by Alan Kirman, *Economic Journal*, conference, 1989, vol. 99, pp. 126–139). In simpler language this means that we have no idea in general about whether a market equilibrium is attainable, and how long it might take to converge (if it at all does) to the optimum state. And here lies a political trick that practical pro-reform politicians often play. A neo-liberal prime minister or his pro-market finance minister can always claim that economic reforms are working well, and are about to produce desired results, perhaps with some more reforms, but they cannot specify even in theory, let alone in actual practice, the time needed for achieving the desired results. Like a dictator, the competitive market is without accountability within any definite time frame, and can go on promising without delivering! However, political democracy unlike the market system has some built-in accountability and, there is usually some reckoning at the time of elections. I need only to remind you that market-based reformers repeatedly did badly on that count. The slogan of 'shining India' crashed in the last (2004) general election, and the present Prime Minister, widely considered a guru of India's market-oriented reforms, could not ever personally win an election. No wonder, come election time and the enthusiasm for reforms fades, gone election time and it is back in business justifying the quip, "the masses vote but the class rules".

It needs hardly saying that actual markets are far removed from the mythical state of affairs depicted by perfect competition. In a competitive market all individual participants are equally powerful in carrying out transactions. It is an error, deliberate or otherwise, to assume that the actual rules of the market, unlike that of perfect competition, are impersonal and anonymous. In contrast, actual market transactions are embedded in unequal power relations. For instance, a starving agricultural labourer wanting a consumption loan from his local moneylender is very differently placed from an Ambani or a Tata seeking loan from a bank. In this context it is especially important to remember that a small peasant negotiating individually with a giant corporation over his land sale would hardly have equal negotiating power. Since land and the associated natural resources like water, forest and minerals involve the livelihood of multitudes, it becomes in many ways analogous to selling labour power. There is an obvious danger in treating land and labour simply as commodities meant for exchange like other commodities. This was perhaps the reason why Karl Polanyi in his classic, *The Great Transformation* called them 'fictitious commodities'. When manipulated by grossly unequal market power relations, these fictitious commodities have wide repercussions on the citizens of a country, calling for counter-action by the state as a part of a grand 'doubt movement' between the market and the state. However, rather than being moderated, these embedded market power relations often tend to be exacerbated systematically by government policies in the name of market-oriented reforms. The rules are manipulated and bent to suit the rich and powerful. To take only one example, the World Bank and the IMF imposed on developing countries various market-oriented reforms, privatisation programmes and reduction in government activities as 'conditionalities' for loans. This usually had the implicit, and occasionally explicit support of the US government. And yet, when powerful market players in the US like large banks and financial institutions are threatened with bankruptcy due to their own greed and folly (as in the recent housing mortgage triggered crisis in 2008), all market-based rules and disciplines are questioned to justify a massive rescue operation by a government that had preached free market rules and policies as great virtues to others!

The most pervasive fallout of this market-centric ideology is the least noticed. It has created the tendency to treat the market, not a human institution but almost as the natural state of our economic and social existence. It has resulted in the greatest ideological displacement of our time. Through a chorus of pronouncements of interested politicians, academics, and corporate- controlled media, this has largely succeeded in crippling our traditional understanding of the state as a regulator and moderator of the forces of the market against the poor. Those who are powerful enough to manipulate the rules by which the market is organised, claim most loudly that the market can guide or even act as a substitute for our moral values. Thus making loss is considered a 'bad' thing in general, while making profit is treated as a good' thing irrespective of what is being produced, or for whom it is being produced. For example, there is continuous pressure for the privatisation of most essential utilities like water, basic health, and education which means in effect the poor have to buy these services in the market irrespective of their ability to pay. It is called public–private partnership by the World Bank these days where the public sector bears most of the risk and the private sector takes most of the profit. The use of the 'eminent domain' clause to transfer land from peasants to private corporation, or the rules for the Special Economic Zones make clear how the rules of the game can be changed to alter the very nature of the 'market'.

The logic of the market is let loose on the overwhelming majority of India's poor. Close to 42 per cent of the population is poor by internationally set definition of absolute poverty on a latest World Bank count, and over three-fourth of the population are poor with purchasing power of less than rupees 20 a day according to another source. It must be remembered that they have little voice in the market in terms of purchasing power, whereas a handful of rich people can dominate the market. Yet, by attributing an almost moral dimension to the functioning of the market mechanism the pro-market logic undermines our political democracy of one adult one vote, and the market continues to discriminate systematically against the poor by increasing inequality in the society through three major routes.

The high growth in output at an average rate of some 7 per cent over the last two decades has resulted in regular employment growth hardly exceeding 1 per cent. The rest of the average 6 per cent growth in GDP came from the growth in output per worker or labour productivity. In contrast, during the earlier decades, when GDP grew on an average at less than 4 per cent, regular employment grew at the annual rate of 2 per cent. The recent drive to increase labour productivity has an international aspect. Globalisation in trade means increasing the importance of the external compared to the internal market. Corporations can compete in the world market mostly by cutting costs to increase their international competitiveness while maintaining quality. Above all, this means shedding labour force through mechanisation to increase productivity, in addition to restraining wages through labour contracts unfavourable to workers. For instance, if the labour force in a corporation is downsized to half at the same wage, labour cost per unit of output would be also be halved. How this process is working in practice can be glimpsed from a few specific cases. Edward Luce of *Financial Times* (London) reported that the Jamshedpur steel plant of the Tatas employed 85,000 workers in 1991 to produce 1 million tonnes of steel worth 0.8 million US dollars. In 2005, the production rose to 5 million tonnes, worth about 5 million US dollars, while employment fell to just about half. Despite being two of the largest receivers of direct foreign investment and housing most of India's big corporate houses, Gujarat and Maharashtra were among the slowest growing states in terms of regular income generation (*Times of India* headlined this information on 7 July 2008 based on 61st NSS report). Employment in regular jobs increased far too slowly leaving most Indians in the Hell described by the great Italian poet Dante. On the gate of his imagined Hell is written, "This is the land you enter after abandoning all hopes."

At the same time, the government is unwilling to increase expenditure on social services to soften the ruthlessness of the market mechanism. Instead, it follows a policy of 'prudent' sound finance by not letting fiscal deficit increase too much. Thus the percentage of government expenditure on both health and education in this overwhelmingly poor country remained stagnant at slightly over 1 and 2 per cent of GDP respectively, and the poorest with no other alternative are hit hardest by such austerity of government policy. And despite much publicity, the fate of a truncated and bureaucratised Employment Guarantee Scheme, the Integrated Child Development Programme or, of the targeted Public Distribution System has hardly been better. The indirect adverse impact of such policies persists over time due to the ill health and ill education of the younger generations. The government continues to talk of India as an emerging global economic power, while the poor continue to suffer, leaving more than half the children grossly under nourished and without any education.

The apparent reasons given for nearly stagnant spending on social services are lack of 'money' and poor public delivery system of social services. However, the more compelling reason is the globalisation of finance that has made the government highly sensitive to the moods of the stock market and the financial sentiments of major players in that market. India has a relatively large foreign exchange reserve (It was close to 300 billion US dollars before the economic crisis in September 2008). However, unlike China which has been enjoying export surplus for years, our reserve comes mostly from capital inflows exceeding balance of payments deficits, like deposits from NRIs, portfolio investments by various international banks and financial institutions. These deposits are mostly footloose by nature, and can be withdrawn at relatively short notice if the mood of the financial market turns sour. The government tries to guard against this danger of possible large scale capital flight by being on the right side of the IMF and the World Bank because they have a central role in shaping international financial opinion for banks, credit-rating agencies, and other financial institutions. This means following their guidelines in formulating economic policies. Thus the government minimises its social welfare expenditure of all sorts, and the ruthless operation of the market against those with very little purchasing power continues unabated. The cost of this squeeze on public expenditure through lack of social security, education, health and nutrition is borne mostly by the poor who are excluded increasingly from the market due to lack of job opportunities. The poor in India face a double blind with the market and the state reinforcing each other's vicious ruthlessness towards the poor.

Land acquisition for mining, industrialisation and SEZ together has turned the indirect into a direct assault on the poor. The destruction of agriculture-based livelihood deepens the extreme despair in this already bleak situation. Farmers continue to commit suicide in thousands, at least one-fourth of land mass covering over 125 districts of the country in twelve states in witnessing steady growth of extremist (Naxalite) activities. The Adivasis (8 per cent) and the Dalits (16 per cent) accounting for almost 25 per cent of India's population remain among its poorest on almost all accounts. And yet, they have all along been the biggest victim of the form of developmental terrorism through land acquisition by the state. Of 25 million hectares used for all development projects since 1947 to 2000, nearly half used to be common land accessed by Adivasi communities and forest dwellers, the Dalits and the poorest in India for supplementing their meagre livelihood. The common land used for 'national' development deprived systematically these people of their livelihood. Thus at least 40 per cent of the displaced persons are Adivasis who constitute no more than 8 per cent of the population (Data collected by Dr. Walter Fernandes).

This provides the background to our process of economic expansion which benefits not more than 25 per cent of our population. It is being sustained by the rapidly growing purchasing power of this minority. It has led to a mutually reinforcing vicious mechanism by which higher growth leads to greater inequality, and greater inequality feeds on higher growth. Guided by market profitability, resource allocation become biased against the poor as the composition of incremental output through growth changes in favour of the rich who can pay. The poor become a low priority for the market as well as for the government in the name of economic development. To celebrate this as the regime of high growth and India's emergence as a global economic power is a cruel joke on the poor majority of this country. The joke has begun to turn a little sour even for the rich with the onslaught of the engulfing economic crisis, and that might not be a bad thing altogether if it forces a change in the direction of our economic policies.

5
Urban Water Supply Reforming the Reformers*

The World Bank has been promoting the public–private partnership model based on management contracts in developing countries. In such contracts, all the risks are borne by the government while the companies do not invest a penny. Investment and expenditure becomes the responsibility of the government, and the companies only provide 'super managers', with complete control over the management, finances and assets of the utility and get a fat annual fee. The adoption of the same model by the Delhi government for pursuing reforms in the water sector was met by protests. The now on-hold Delhi project is worth examining in some detail for the lessons it can teach us.

Amit Bhaduri and Arvind Kejriwal

We no longer live in the age of innocence. The old stereotypes about the public or the private sector no longer hold, as wishful thinking on both sides has repeatedly been dashed. Neither public nor private enterprises usually work reasonably well in providing basic utilities like water, transport, power, health or education. When the private sector works reasonably efficiently, say in providing education or health, by the very logic of the marketplace, it marginalises, even excludes the poor. This is not acceptable in any democracy, least of all in India with so many poor

*Published in *Economic and Political Weekly*, 31 December 2005.

people. The public sector, on the other hand, tends to be horribly inefficient in many instances. Those who are ideologically inclined to favour the private sector and the market take delight in pointing out that the role of the public sector, and of government subsidies, has often been to make the privileged even more so, through state action in the name of the poor. And when privatisation of basic public utilities is put into operation, the remedy usually is worse than the disease.

On the surface it would appear both the International Monetary Fund and the World Bank as well as many of our important bureaucrats, economic advisors and politicians, despite their close affiliation with and sympathy for these institutions have by now learnt this lesson. The buzzword these days, both in the Bank and in the corridors of power of the central and many state governments, is the innocuous slogan, 'public–private partnership' (PPP) through 'management contracts'. They sound too persuasive. Like family values, liberty and democracy, it would be politically incorrect these days to have doubts about the virtues of this partnership. But we feel compelled to spoil the party after examining the content of this partnership in the case of the water sector reforms in Delhi, and similar reforms that are now being contemplated in several major cities in this country in the water sector.

Reform Models: World Bank Style

The public sector has failed to provide water, especially to the poor, in large parts of the developing world. During the 1980s, development banks made loans available to them, but the public sector failed to deliver. Their failure led to the predictable reaction of privatisation policies that dominated the 1990s. The privatisation of water supplies and sanitation has taken various forms, and yet its constant feature is the transfer of control and management of operations to private companies. In short, all management-oriented reforms of the most essential of all public utilities are being driven by private profit motive, almost invariably under the tutelage of the World Bank in developing countries.

The precise form privatisation has taken was dictated by the private companies. The concession contracts were the favoured form in the 1990s. Under a concession contract, a company takes over the water utility, and all future investments become the company's responsibility. The revenues are collected, and retained by the company, but it shares some part of it with the government as a rentier. The concession contracts typically extend over long periods like 30 years or so.

The experience with these concession contracts has been dismal for most, if not all developing countries, with the companies forced to withdraw from many countries in the face of stiff public resentment, at times even leading to water riots. Almost invariably the companies failed to meet their investment commitments, especially in low-income areas, thus depriving poor people of their most basic need of water, whereas earlier, and despite the inefficiencies of the public sector, the latter did provide some water to the poor. For instance, in Delhi, it is a common sight in many low-income areas of the poor collecting water from leaking pipelines for their daily needs. The companies removed those inefficiencies to boost their profit, and plugged the leakages. At the same time, they found it unprofitable to make the necessary investment to enable the poor to access water legally. Even where the poor could access it legally, they could no more afford it, as the prices set were too high.

Model Currently in Favour

Over the last few years, since about 2000, companies have favoured the even less risky option of management contracts. Nice sounding phrases like 'public–private partnerships'

(PPPs) and 'private sector participation' (PSP) have been used and the word 'privatisation' has been consciously avoided, as it has been thoroughly discredited. And yet, when examined a management contract is an even worse kind of privatisation. In such contracts all the risks are borne by the government while the companies take the profits. All the investments and expenditure becomes the responsibility of the government. The companies simply provide 'super managers', with complete control over the management, finances and assets of the utility and get a fat annual fee.

This model is fatally flawed. And yet, in the last few years, various development banks led by the World Bank have been pushing this model aggressively, especially in several Indian cities. How bizarre and illogical this whole model is, can be seen by taking a look at the scheme of water sector reforms proposed for Delhi. In the last seven years, the Delhi government has been contemplating giving out management contracts to water companies, after spending crores of rupees on several consultants imposed on it by the World Bank. However, the disclosure of the documents related to this project by a Delhi-based group called Parivartan, which obtained them under the Delhi Right to Information Act, forced the government to retreat, and put it on hold. Nevertheless, the now on-hold Delhi project is worth examining in some detail for the lessons it can teach us for similar schemes in other cities in India.

Outline of the Delhi Project

Delhi is facing a growing water crisis. Large parts of Delhi go without water for days altogether. The Delhi government decided to relinquish its responsibility. It began by saying that it could not run the Delhi Jal Board (DJB) any more. Under the tutelage of the World Bank, approved by the then powers that be in the ministry of finance of the central government, it decided to hand over the management of water distribution to private multinational companies, in the name of a 'management model', presumably a prototype of pubic–private corporation for many public sector utilities.

Financial Side of the Model

The money to run day-to-day operations of a zone had to be provided by DJB , with no stipulated upper limit on the money that a management company could demand. DJB's job would be to provide that money, but little control over its actual expenditure. DJB would, in addition, provide adequate water after treating, to the companies at entry points of the water zones. In consequence, the companies would acquire, in effect, total control over the management and finances of DJB, without investing any money. Moreover, since the company would not be spending any money, it would have little incentive to show prudence in expenditure. It would be foolish in these circumstances to expect that the costs of operations would not go up. Here are some numbers we obtained from the documents.

Each company would send four employees to run a zone at a cost of $ 25,000 per month per employee to DJB! For 21 zones in Delhi, this comes to Rs. 105 crore per annum. In addition, according to an estimate, a company would need Rs. 25 crore to run a zone. For 21 zones, the cost comes to Rs. 525 crore against Rs. 163 crore in 2003–04. All this would be recovered by raising tariffs. The tariffs would have to be raised at least six times within two years, in addition to the increase that has already taken place.

We note in this context that the Puerto Rican government signed a similar management contract with a French multinational company Vivendi in 1996. By 1999, the operational deficit of their water utility went up to $ 240 million, which further increased to $ 680 million by 2001. Vivendi was asked to leave in 2001. Suez, another French multinational company, came in 2001. The contract required

Suez to reduce the deficit by $ 250 million every year. Rather than decreasing the deficit, the company demanded an additional $ 100 million saying that they had under-estimated expenses. Suez was asked to leave in 2003. Now, both Vivendi and Suez are coming to Delhi. Does this not sound like the chronicle of a crime foretold?

Truths and Untruths

Dreams manufactured by consultants at a high price have to be separated from the realities the citizens would face if the type of model they envisage gets implemented. The increase in expenditure would not lead to any improvement in water services. It is claimed that 24 hours of continuous water supply would be provided, by reducing leakages. This is a myth! The companies have been given bogus targets for leakage reduction. They have been asked to reduce leakage to 34 per cent in three years, though the leakage at the distribution end today is just 24 per cent according to the information provided to us by DJB under the Right to Information Act. Also, the water company's performance would be assessed, not on the basis of whether a consumer receives 24-hour water supply in his house, but whether there was 24-hour water supply at the main input point of the colony. Therefore, the companies would be at liberty to divert water from domestic to commercial consumers, who pay better prices. In Puerto Rico, the water companies cut off water supply to many residential areas, and diverted it instead to swimming pools, five-star hotels, amusement parks, etc. To price-ration out the poor is a game the market plays well, but this is a dangerous game to play with the most basic necessity, water.

Accountability of Companies

Water management companies would not, in effect, be accountable to anyone under this scheme. If a person were aggrieved with a company, she would have nowhere to go. The performance parameters of the scheme are left vague, while targets set are either bogus or inconsequential. The process of their enforcement is not defined anywhere. It is being said that penalties would be imposed on the companies if they failed to achieve annual targets. How much penalty? Who would impose penalty? How would that be done? The government had no answers. But the World Bank said in a press briefing that the total penalty on a company for all violations put together would not exceed 30 per cent of the management fee. This means that no one could touch 70 per cent of a company's management fee or its engineering fee. The company loses nothing if DJB fails, and it gains only a little, by way of small bonus, if it improves. Then why should a water company perform? Short of cancellation of the contract, the government will have no control over its day-to-day functioning. But water contracts are difficult to cancel overnight, because total disruption of water supply in a large city even for a couple of days would be intolerable. It could be a recipe for water riots.

What kind of 'reform' is this? DJB is in a mess today because DJB officials are not accountable to anyone. It will be in a bigger mess tomorrow because the private companies would not be accountable to anyone. So basically, we would shift from one unaccountable system to another at a much higher cost to the public.

Arrogance of Power

The World Bank is in the habit of forcing models of its choice on developing countries. Various 'concession models' of water privatisation in which the company shares a part of capital investments and gets a proportion of profits in return, were imposed in several countries in the 1990s. Though the Bank says that this model failed everywhere, yet it is now advocating its 'management model', the one described above, for Delhi. Why should a company perform in the new model? The Bank would be less than intelligent to expect that the same inefficient and corrupt government (or some of its officials designated as 'regulator'), which failed to make its water utility perform, would make the private company perform. The inherent contradictions are just too obvious. Yet, blinded by arrogance, the Bank wants us to accept its new model without transparent public scrutiny. But why did the Delhi government agree to be the Bank's next guinea pig? Is it just because the Bank agreed to a loan of Rs. 120 crore per annum for six years to the DJB (out of which Rs 105 crore per year would go straight as salaries to the managers of the water companies) at a rather high commercial rate of interest? This looks implausible, because the government could easily raise this amount at almost half the cost from the domestic market by issuing bonds. Why then was the Delhi government accepting the World Bank's bullying for such a small loan amount at such a high rate of interest to implement such a disastrous project? Thereby hangs another tale of how the Bank interacts with our elected governments.

A Tale of Two Institutions

The credit goes to the Delhi government led by Sheila Dikshit for having pioneered the Right to Information Act in Delhi, well before a similar act became operative throughout the country from 12 October 2005. The earlier Delhi Act and now the national act have allowed Parivartan to access legally, and examine many sensitive documents of about 4,000 pages up to 2002. We are discovering even more startling facts that pertain to later years, but let the story be told up to 2002.

A leading role in preparing the proposal was played by Price Waterhouse Coopers (PWC), a consulting firm for which the World Bank seemed to have a special soft corner. The selection process went like this. In the pre-qualification bid, the top six firms were to be shortlisted, and in the 10th position PWC did not qualify. In order to qualify, the Bank pointed out, a company must be registered to a developing country. Being registered in India, PWC made it to the shortlist. Next, following strictly the criteria and the sub-criteria of the Bank, technical and financial bids were called with a qualifying minimum marks of 75 per cent. With only 68 per cent marks, PWC failed the technical test again. The Bank now asked DJB to revise the sub-criteria, and also required it to answer why PWC got such low marks. The relevant files show that some of the more courageous officers tried to defend the sub-criteria arguing that they had been formulated according to the Bank manual. But the Bank did not relent, asked for the cancellation of old bids and called for fresh ones. DJB obliged, and, even then PWC lost. The Bank now asked for the marks given by the individual examiners. In the final twist of the knife, DJB surrendered by cutting out the low marks given to PWC by R.K.Jain, the chief engineer of DJB at that time. PWC finally qualified! An incredible aspect of this story of armtwisting of a democratic government by the Bank lies in the fact that the Delhi government, which spends annually more than Rs. 550 crore, accepted a meagre loan of 7.5 crore (2.5 million dollars).

The Road Ahead

It is silly to pose public opposition to this type of reform as 'anti-privatisation' or even anti-poor as some have done in the media. The issues involved are different, and must be faced candidly.

(i) When encountered with documented facts, the World Bank openly defended its method of imposition of this project by stating that they have full authority to choose consultants and shape the project, because the initial consultancy money (a meagre Rs. 7.5 crore mentioned above) was given by the Bank. Since the Bank is not accountable to the Indian people, but our governments are, the lesson has to be learnt. No democratic government should take a consultancy loan from the Bank on these terms. We might add, that this applies as much to water sector reform, as to the much talked about Bharat Nirman project. Preparing schemes through consultancy must rest with the experts in the country. In very specific cases, these experts might like to supplement their expertise with foreign consultants. But this must be done transparently, and decided by the group of experts unanimously.

(ii) It has often been said that the decision to go to war is too important to be left to the military generals. It has to be a political decision. Similarly, decisions on how to reform the most essential public utilities are too important to be left only to the technical experts. Their political implications, their impact on all sections of the society must be considered. This requires relying on experts in the country, and political accountability must be built into the project.

(iii) The essence of political accountability in essential public utilities is accountability to all sections of the people. It is not true that the water system in Delhi is not accountable, it is accountable only to a selected 1 per cent of the population. In the cantonment and where the 'representatives' of the people, but not the people themselves live. They get more water than they need, even for their lawns, while the poor struggle for hours for a bucketful. The issue is to widen the notion of accountability. For basic utilities like water, all those who benefit or suffer under a scheme must have a say in reforming the scheme.

(iv) Indeed, part of the 'expertise' in preparing a water reform project consists of hearing the voice of the poor. Rhetoric apart, this has not been done, and is not being done, not only in Delhi, but also in Karnataka, Madhya Pradesh and Tamil Nadu. The water reforms, aided by agencies like the World Bank, are being carried out without transparency, without any attempt either to involve the public or to be accountable to them.

(v) We must call the bluff, and force the powers that be, to behave more responsibly, and not allow things to happen in the name of mythically efficient private management companies chosen by the World Bank. This has to be changed by enhancing transparency and accountability. It is our right to demand relevant information under the new Act, and the duty of the government to provide it. But it is also the duty of a genuinely democratic government to be more proactive by dissipating important information voluntarily through the media, and through publication of 'white papers' on controversial issues like the nuclear deal, Enron, Sikh and Gujarat riots. Successive governments so far have tried their best to hide than to reveal. It does not speak well for our democracy, and the people's campaign over the water sector reform is a small step in our long march towards changing this state of affairs. We have, however, taken successfully that crucial first step. The loan application by the DJB to the World Bank has been unconditionally withdrawn at the time of writing (2005). It remains to be seen whether the lesson has really been learnt.

6

The Political Economy of Social Democracy*

The interplay of continuity and change in history is echoed in political movements that are part of that broader historical process. Tensions invariably arise in an attempt to combine the longer term radical objective of changing the society with the short-term goal of maintaining continuity in day-to-day politics. Thus, the short-term practicality of politics requires accepting, at least partly, the continuing circumstances which the movement purports to change in the longer run. This tension, and the dilemma that it generates, has been especially acute in the history of the social democratic movement.

Universal Suffrage and the Socialist Movement

The dilemma surfaced historically as universal suffrage became increasingly a possibility in many parts of Europe. The Reform Act of 1867 in Britain—the very year of the publication of the first volume of Marx's 'Capital'—accepted an electoral system that recognized partly the right of the working class to vote. Although it did not mean 'parliamentary democracy' in the modern sense of the term, it did indicate an emerging trend. That trend gathered momentum through successive electoral reforms in 1884–5,

---

* This is a revised and extended version of the paper, 'The Economics and Politics of Social Democracy', in Pranab Bardhan, Mrinal Datta–Chaudhury and T.N. Krishnan (eds.), *Development and Change; Essays in Honour of K.N.Raj*, Delhi, Oxford University Press, 1993.

1918 and 1928. As a matter of fact, already in 1868, about half of the adult male population in Britain enjoyed voting rights. And, by the end of the decade of the 1880s, both in France and in Bismark's Reichstag (though not in the more important Prussian Parliament) universal male suffrage had been achieved.[1] The growing tendency towards greater political democracy was becoming the 'ground reality' in western Europe. And, socialists of all description came increasingly under the pressure of evaluating its political consequences for the socialist movement, especially in relation to their strategy for capturing state power. Social democracy, it might be said, was born at that historical juncture.

However, this apparent tendency towards greater political democracy was too close to the time to be interpreted unambiguously. Both the socialist Left and the conservative Right interpreted it with almost equal scepticism. Marx's own understanding of the process of capitalist development had inclined him to argue that universal suffrage which empowers the working class to vote, must turn out to be incompatible with private ownership of property. In his account of the 1848–50 working class upheavals in France, he argued that the logic of universal suffrage would lead from 'political to social emancipation' (Marx, 1952: p. 62) of the workers ultimately through the social ownership of all the means of production. The scepticism of Marx, and of the revolutionary Left in general, about the ability of capitalism to accommodate political democracy was matched by the scepticism displayed by the conservative Right. In the House of Commons debates of 1866–7 conservative politicians like Cecil argued passionately against the impending electoral reforms that would empower (male) workers to vote. In their eyes, democracy would inevitably lead to socialism.[2]

Ironically, at a time when both the revolutionary Left and the conservative Right agreed in effect on their assessment of the irreconcilability of capitalism with universal suffrage, the political climate seemed to be changing precisely in that direction. For instance, unlike in earlier times when the propertied upper classes in Britain mobilised every force in their command to oppose successfully successive electoral reform and Chartism in 1839, 1842 and 1848, they failed to stall the reform of 1867 which empowered electorally a significant section of the British working class.

Nevertheless, so long as universal suffrage remained only a partially attained goal, the broad socialist movement of the time had no compelling ideological reason to get divided between a 'parliamentary' and a 'revolutionary' Left. The reason was simple: the revolutionary Left could view political mobilisation for universal suffrage as a way of 'unchaining class struggle,[3] while the parliamentary Left could pin their hope on achieving a commanding economic position for the working class through universal suffrage. This latter more moderate view was being articulated within the socialist movement by political thinkers like Bernstein and Kautsky. Bernstein characterised socialism as the economic system in which political democracy reaches its 'logical conclusion', while Kautsky emphasised the tactical importance of taking electoral advantage of the 'growing proletarianisation' of the capitalist society. The contest between revolution and reform in the socialist movement was clearly coming to a head.

Political and Economic Democracy

With the advantage of historical hindsight, we can identify the errors of oversimplification in the understanding of both the revolutionary and the reformist Left. The unfolding of events turned out to be more complex in two crucial respects. First, both sides turned out to have exaggerated the quantitative importance of the working class in the process of capitalist development, based on the Marxian model of capitalist development of the growing proletarianisation of the population. As a matter of fact, even at its peak, workers as a proportion of the total electorate hardly ever exceeded 40 per cent under industrial capitalism. For instance, it reached a peak 37 per cent in Germany in 1903 and 40.6 per cent in Sweden in 1952. And, only in Belgium, the first country in continental Europe to industrialise, it peaked at 50.1 per cent in 1912.[4] Since the numerical strength of the working class turned out to be insufficient even in the heartland of industrial capitalism, it was unclear how political democracy would place the working class in a position of command. To some, it appeared that the narrower economic interests of the working class had to be 'compromised', i.e. diluted through alliance with other classes (e.g. self-employed or small proprietors in agriculture and service). This was an ideological anathema to the revolutionary Left. Alternatively, the role of political democracy and majority rule had to be underplayed in the economic interest of the working class, as Lenin had done. Whichever way one looked at it, the ideological distance between the reformists and the revolutionaries in the socialist movement could only increase in these circumstances.

Second, the Marxian model of capitalist development had not merely been over-optimistic about the numerical dominance of the industrial proletariat. At the same time, in its prediction about the immiserisation of the working class through falling real wage, it had been over-pessimistic. And this was another obvious source of ideological confusion, particularly for the revolutionary Left. It was hardly convincing to argue that the working class would maintain its revolutionary zeal, while the standard of living was rising in a secular manner over time. However, the case was not much easier to argue for the revisionist Left either. Although workers' strikes aimed at the extension of suffrage had been quite successful, e.g. in Belgium and in Sweden, even more widely supported mass strikes directed at economic demands of the workers failed almost invariably all over Europe—in Belgium in 1902, in Sweden in 1909, in France in 1920, in Norway in 1921, and in Great Britain in 1926.[5] It was becoming apparent that despite the move towards universal suffrage, capitalism was less accommodative towards the economic compared to the political demands of the workers.

From the United Front to the Welfare State

The elasticity of capitalist democracies in meeting the political demands of the workers coupled with the fact that the working class could not dominate numerically the electoral politics in these countries, created a new political dilemma which was made even more acute by the apparent inability or unwillingness of these democracies in meeting the economic demands of the workers. The way out of the political dilemma, at least for the section of socialists who accepted parliamentary democracy as their framework for mobilisation, was to broaden their electoral base. This meant that 'class politics' based on the narrower interests of the industrial proletariat had to be transformed into some sort of 'coalition politics' based on the broader interest of a united front. This shift, often debunked by the revolutionary Left as a 'historical compromise' of working class interests, was an outcome of the accommodative capacity of capitalist political democracy. However, social democrats like Kautsky saw that the workers alone would not constitute the dominant majority of the electorate to take advantage of this accommodative political system. This caused a shift in the paradigm of socialist political thinking. Although earlier revolutionary socialists like Engels had also suggested on occasion the need to form united fronts, this was viewed entirely as a matter of political expediency. In contrast, the coalition politics of the united front proposed by the social democrats accepted the impossibility of capturing state power through the numerical dominance of the working class. As a result, they had to give up the idea of 'proletarian dictatorship' in favour of a more lasting political coalition between the industrial workers, and some other classes as electorally desirable. United front politics, from being a mere short-term tactic became an integral strategy not only for the capture of state power, but for its exercise over the longer run. The ideological break between the revolutionary and the reformist Left was now almost complete.

This rather pragmatic turn towards the strategy of coalition politics raised, however, an awkward economic question. Experiences, particularly during the first three decades of the twentieth century had shown that the political accommodation permitted by the capitalist democracies was not matched by its elasticity in terms of meeting the economic demands of the workers.[6] Therefore, coming to political power through coalition politics had to be justified also in economic terms. Although the revolutionary and the revisionist socialists differed openly about the method of capturing state power, they continued to agree on the basic socialist proposition that private ownership of property made capitalist democracies incapable of responding sufficiently to workers' economic demands. The way out was to commit socialist-led united fronts to economic programmes of 'socialisation of the means of production', involving large-scale nationalisation and public ownership of industries. However, this was happening around the time, when evidence was also filtering through about the discouraging performance of nationalised industries in the Soviet Union, as well as other economic and political malaise afflicting the Soviet system in general. It contributed to strengthening the doctrinaire enthusiasm for nationalising industries on the other.

More important however, were the rules of the game set by the property-owning democracies. While the rules of political democracy allowed the socialists to share or even control power, the rules of private property permitted the capitalists as well as small property-owners, e.g. peasants or the self-employed who could be partners in a political coalition, to react against socialistic economic measures which they found unacceptable. Thus, private industrialists could strike back against nationalisation or pro-labour laws by reducing private investment sharply which, in turn, would reduce demand and employment in the short run as well as slow down the expansion of job opportunities in the longer run. Moreover, it could even create panic or upheaval in financial circles, and in the stock exchange. This ability of industrial capital to hit back through precipitating an 'investment strike' acted as an impending threat to socialist policies. If trade unions and labour movements of an earlier era had provided a countervailing power to capital, such an 'investment strike' now provided capital's countervailing power against a socialist government's policies.

The limit of coalition politics was reinforced by the threat of an 'investment strike' against the background of the often disappointing experiences with the performance of nationalised industries. Together, they discouraged doctrinaire nationalisation policies. Another pragmatic turn in social democratic ideology came gradually; in their economic programmes, 'socialisation of the means of production' began receiving lower priorities compared to improving the immediate standard of living of the working class, and of other poorer sections who might support the politics of coalition. This meant a change of economic focus which, in the context of Sweden, Ohlin described perceptively as a shift of emphasis from 'nationalization of the means of production' to 'nationalization of consumption'.[7] It also meant reassuring the captains of industry and avoiding possible investment strikes by them.

From this emerged ideas of 'social partnership between the contending classes which, for example, Bruno Kriesky visualised in the case of Austria even before the Second World War. A cooperative 'welfare state' began to become an integral part of the social democratic ideology.

In search of its economic rationale, this nascent ideology of the welfare state turned often to an old under-consumptionist argument.[8] In essence, it claimed, that redistribution of income in favour of the poorer classes with a higher propensity to consume, would increase the purchasing power of the whole economy, and provide incentives to industry to expand employment and output. This was an appealing argument for socialists, especially in the context of the depressive economic conditions of the 1930s. Not surprisingly, in 1936 when the Popular Front in France came to power, it made much use of such arguments for justifying its pro-labour economic policies.[9]

In a way, this under-consumptionist argument which identifies the principal problem of capitalism as over-production in relation to its consumption expenditure, carries the justification for coalition politics, and social partnership among the classes, almost to its logical extreme: it claims that higher income for the poorer classes, even through redistributive taxes, is beneficial also for the capitalists in so far as it expands the size of the market by raising the aggregate level of consumption expenditure. And, in a parallel vein, it could also be argued that, an increase in the 'social component' of wages, e.g. better education, housing, health and communication facilities provided by the state, would raise consumption expenditure on other goods and services provided by the private industries, through reducing the proportion of their earning spent on these necessities by the poor.[10] Moreover, this would also carve out a special economic role for the state as the provider of these services. Thus, the rationale for the 'welfare state' could be found without much difficulty in terms of the under-consumptionist logic. And yet, these under-consumptionist arguments turned out to have been built on shaky foundations in the Great Depression of the early 1930s.

Full Employment Keynesianism

Whatever political gains the social democrats might have made through redistribution of income and extension of public services, came to be haunted by the experiences of the Great Depression. The labour unions had witnessed helplessly at that time the collapse of the welfare state under the weight of mass unemployment. So long as the fear that such a crisis could easily recur haunted historical memory, the gains of the welfare state, and of social democratic policies could not but seem extremely fragile.[11] The policies for demand management, derived from the theory of aggregate demand formulated independently by Keynes and Kalecki around the same time, showed a way of overcoming this fragility. At the same time, it provided the social democratic project for establishing the welfare state with an almost compelling intellectual coherence.

Keynes distanced himself from the narrow under-consumptionist position by pointing out that either consumption or investment could be raised to stimulate aggregate demand, and avoid disastrous economic depressions with mass unemployment. Contrasting his views from those of early under-consumptionists like Malthus and Sismondi, he writes, 'Practically I only differ from these schools of thought in thinking that they may lay a little too much emphasis on increased consumption at a time when there is still much social advantage to be obtained from increased investment. Theoretically, however, they are open to the criticism of neglecting the fact that there are *two* ways to expand output'.[12]

Kalecki pointed out more precisely the entire range of possibilities for managing demand.[13] Each of the three major components of aggregate demand—private consumption, private investment or government expenditure—could be manipulated through a different set of policies to influence the level of aggregate demand. To these 'three ways to full employment', must be added also the possibility of generating demand through a larger export surplus in an economy open to foreign trade.

Of all these different routes to demand management, by far the speediest and the most convenient way is to increase the level of government expenditure through deficit financing. Understandably, governments of very different political persuasion took repeated recourse to this method for averting serious unemployment. Thus, the share of government spending in GDP in major OECD countries rose from 18 per cent before the Second World War to 27 per cent in 1950, and to 37 per cent in 1973.[14] However, more important than the actual method of demand management was the confidence that governments acquired to fight economic depression. Keynesianism brought about this dramatic change in the climate of opinion with more or less continuous full employment set as an achievable goal under capitalism. Thus, following the publication of the Beveridge Report in 1942, the maintenance of 'a high level of employment' was recognised by 1944 as a primary objectives of the British government.

Opinions differ as to the contribution actually made by the Keynesian style demand management in the maintenance of high employment (Matthews, 1968). Nevertheless, no matter how one explains it, unprecedented prosperity with near full employment followed for roughly quarter of a century with a remarkable consensus of opinions about the conduct of economic policy. That consensus was centred on Keynesian demand management, covering a wide political spectrum across governments, economists and opinion-makers.

The advantage of this consensus for social democracy was tremendous. The economic role of the state in maintaining high employment through high state expenditure became the accepted norm for the conduct of economic policy across a wide political spectrum. It also meant an expanding role for the welfare state. This was rooted in the consensus view that cooperative capitalism among the contending classes is practicable, because both sides gain through the action of the state in maintaining high demand. More than two decades of sustained near full employment with high growth seemed to reinforce this view. It was the golden age of capitalism. Perhaps, it was also the golden age for social democracy.

From Welfare Keynesianism to Monetarism and Conservatism

Economic policy that deals successfully with the immediate problems of the economic environment is likely to change the environment in that process. In this respect, it is somewhat like the grand algorithm of evolutionary selection, where successful adaptation at each round of evolution might call for a different type of adaptation at the next round. In other words, it was not that the Keynesian theory of demand management was wrong: rather, its success in dealing with the problem of unemployment created new problems, requiring different solutions and institutions.

It is not even that these problems were altogether unforeseen. Already in 1943, Kalecki expressed his scepticism about the political sustainability of long periods of full employment.[15] As he saw it, a shift of power in favour of the workers generated through long periods of sustained full employment would create new problems of workers' 'indiscipline', as the fear of job-loss as a disciplining device in the labour market begins to erode. This problem would arise despite the fact that high employment and capacity utilisation might be good for both profit-and wage-earners, as maintained by the basic postulate of cooperative capitalism. Kalecki pointed out that workers' indiscipline threatens the very authority structure of economic decision-making under capitalism. As a consequence, the government supported by captains of industry would retreat from time to time from demand management, perhaps in the name of 'sound' public finance and balancing the budget, to precipitate 'political trade cycles' and impose discipline on the workers.

The idea of 'political cycles' is an astute variation on the classical Marxian theme of the maintenance of the reserve army of labour as an integral feature of capitalist development. However, it needs some crucial modifications to suit the circumstances of modern capitalism. To start with, it should be recognised that the authority structure of economic decision-making under capitalism is threatened not merely by the indiscipline of the workers. The growing presence of the state itself in economic activity—in several OECD countries, government expenditure exceeds 40 per cent of GDP—shifts the balance in favour of the government bureaucracy in decision-making. The demand for 'rolling back the state' through economic liberalisation, deregulation or privatisation, finds wide support from the captains of industry in these circumstances, especially because, a democratic government seeks legitimacy through maintaining some degree of neutrality between the contending classes. Viewed from this angle, the discontent with the 'welfare state' in business circles is not simply due to its perception that it strengthens the bargaining power of the workers, and encourages workers' indiscipline by reducing their fear of job-loss (due to unemployment benefit, social security, etc.). Perhaps even more fundamentally, it is an expression of dissatisfaction by the captains of industry with the neutrality of the state itself as an arbiter between the contending classes.[16] And yet, this very neutrality of the state is the central, unstated assumption underlying traditional Keynesian policies of demand management.

The precise economic consequences of workers' indiscipline in the political trade cycle was left somewhat ambiguous. Marx had postulated that the presence of a 'reserve army' of labour would prevent real wages from rising. That prediction, literally interpreted, had turned out to be false. Nevertheless its obverse implication that cooperative capitalism has a marked tendency to degenerate into conflictive capitalism over the distribution of income under conditions of low unemployment and increased bargaining power of the worker cannot be so readily dismissed.

Thus, workers' indiscipline can take the economic form of demand for higher money wages, out of line with labour productivity growth to threaten the economy with inflation, and a squeeze on profits.[17]

Some of these ideas got a sharper quantitative focus in Phillips' statistical analysis which showed that money wages generally tend to rise faster at lower levels of unemployment.[18] From this, one could also infer an awkward choice between the two economic objectives of maintaining higher level employment and a reasonable degree of price stability—the 'employment–inflation trade-off', as it came to be known in policy debates. The first cracks in the traditional Keynesian-style demand management seemed to have appeared.

A way out of this dilemma, especially attractive to the social democrats, was to press for a 'wage policy', or more generally an 'incomes policy' which regulated increases in both wage and profit income. It is often lamented that this policy was not usually successful in the major OECD countries. However, the political reason for its failure is not difficult to identify. Like demand management policies, it is premised on the role of the state as a neutral arbiter between the classes. And yet, unlike demand management which allows for cooperation between the classes through increasing the level of national income through expanding demand, any incomes policy would necessarily involve the state directly in the distributive conflict between the classes. And, the premise of the neutrality of the state is almost bound to be challenged by either or both the classes in these circumstances.

At a time when traditional Keynesianism was grappling rather unsuccessfully with the problem of employment–inflation trade-off, the Monetarist attack led by Friedman[19] changed the terms of the debate. Based on more recent statistical evidence, Friedman denied the possibility of any such trade-off in the longer run. His theoretical argument gave particular twist to an obvious fact. Everyone knows that workers are interested in their standard of living. Therefore, the increase in money wages under collective bargaining takes into account not only the unemployment rate, but also the rate of inflation.[20] While normally this might lead to some sort of official or unofficial indexation of money wage increase to the rate of inflation, Friedman's twist postulated that the increase in money wage compensates exactly the *anticipated* rate of inflation. As a result, so long as the inflation rate is correctly anticipated, the real wage does not change. Using conventional (neo-classical) theory, it can then be argued that the profit incentives to the firms also remain unchanged, because real wages remain unaltered, and firms have no incentive to change the level of employment of output.[21] Therefore, unless inflation is *unanticipated,* it does not affect the level of employment. Moreover, because workers come to anticipate correctly the going rate of inflation, in the longer run, a dent in unemployment can be made only by raising continuously the inflation rate, so that part of the rising inflation rate remains unanticipated. In other words, expansionary fiscal and monetary policy on which the Keynesian demand management relies for fighting unemployment, can work only by raising the inflation rate continuously.[22] Thus Keynesian demand management policies tend to get trapped into higher and higher rates of inflation without any trade-off against unemployment in the longer run.

Playing on the fear of inflation that may be caused by higher wage claims at sustained full employment, theoretical constructs such as the 'natural rate' of unemployment or the 'non-accelerating-inflation rate of unemployment' (NAIRU) justified, in essence, the need for maintaining a 'reserve army' of labour under modern capitalism. The old idea was recycled in new theoretical terms. It has been reinforced further by the monetarist view that, expansionary fiscal policies financed through budget deficit, necessarily magnifies manifold the total money supply in the economy to cause inflation,[23] quite apart from being ineffective in reducing unemployment in the longer run. Monetarists were clearly taking no chances, by attacking the earlier Keynesian consensus on full-employment policies, and the welfare state on all possible fronts.

The heart of the matter—at least in so far as the theoretical debate on the unemployment problem between the Keynesians and the Monetarists is concerned—revolves around the relative importance of the cost factors on the supply side proxied by real wage versus the demand side captured to aggregate demand analysis, in determining the level of employment. However, the resilience of Keynesianism stems from the fact that the analysis of aggregate demand pioneered by Kalecki and Keynes has a much wider political range than the conventional Keynesian policies of demand management suggest. This fact is seldom recognised even by the Keynesians themselves. Thus, although the theoretical schemes are different, many of the typical conservative monetarist policies could be derived also from simple extensions of the Keynes' theoretical framework.[24] Its theoretical generality becomes in a way the source of its political ambiguity.

Since the stimulation of private investment is a distinct route to demand management in a closed economy, measures aimed at achieving this become logically justifiable within the Keynesian framework. For instance, reduced taxes on corporate profits or restraint on wages has been considered helpful for improving the climate for private investment. Such measures constitute the case for a politically conservative style of demand management based on profit-led and private investment-driven economic expansion within the Keynesian intellectual tradition. Moreover, in so far as such private investment-led economic expansion also creates sufficient jobs with a relatively slow rise in real wages in relation to the growth in labour productivity, private profitability is increased, but, at the same time, the working class also gains in terms of higher real wages and expanding employment opportunities.

The original under-consumptionist thesis of wage-led and consumption driven economic expansion, which argued essentially that 'high wage' is beneficial to both the classes, finds its antithesis in this case of profit and private investment-driven economic expansion. Ironically, both can be interpreted as models of cooperative capitalism. And, both are based on the Keynesian theory which assigns centrality to aggregate demand in determining output and employment.[25] However, their policy consequences are almost diametrically opposite. While the under-consumptionist view, supplemented later by the need for higher public investment in case of serious short-fall in aggregate demand makes the case for the welfare state, the view of economic expansion driven by profit and private investment makes a case decisively in favour of private business.[26] And, Keynesianism in this wider sense, leaves ambiguous the economic basis of social democratic politics by accommodating different forms of cooperative capitalism. Helmut Schmidt, as the social democratic chancellor of the then West Germany articulated this conservative alternative by pointing out: 'The profits of the enterprises today are the investment of tomorrow, and the investments of tomorrow are the employment of day after'.[27] It symbolised complete reliance on private industry and investment to solve the problem on unemployment, rather than creating jobs through direct expansion of public investment. In a way, this view was also an intellectual watershed in social democratic thinking. It marks the beginning of a new conservative era, when it becomes increasingly difficult to distinguish social democratic from conservative economic policies.

Internationalisation of the Nation State

Theoretical ideas supporting 'conservative' and 'progressive' policies contest against one another in the larger democratic polity; and within each political movement that is alive. The long evolution of the socialist movement, from the time when universal suffrage became a distinct possibility, has been no exception to this. The interesting question, therefore, is not why these different political tendencies coexist in the social democratic movement, but why a particular tendency dominates at a particular historical juncture. In short, what made conservatism so widely acceptable in recent times?

At the level of the relevance of theory, there can be little doubt that the Kalecki–Keynes model of the closed economy which had emphasised the critical role of the home market, had become increasingly obsolete as world trade, particularly among the industrialised countries, began to grow rapidly in the post-war years. In an economy increasingly open to foreign trade, the under-consumptionist argument of mass consumption-led growth through a 'high wage' policy becomes less compelling. Because, in so far as higher wages through higher prices at home also leads to lower international price competitiveness, aggregate demand may actually decline, if the resulting deterioration in trade balance outweighs the increased demand for consumption at higher wages. As a result, the increased relative importance of the 'foreign' compared to the 'home' market would dampen enthusiasm for promoting aggregate demand through 'high wage' policies. In that case, a basic tenet of welfare capitalism has to be given up. In contrast, both conservative Keynesianism and Monetarism, which for different theoretical reasons agree on the virtues of a 'low wage' policy for propelling economic expansion led by profit and private investment, would find that policy compatible with increasing openness in trade.[28]

Growth in international trade under contemporary capitalism has been linked intimately with the internationalisation of production by the multinational corporations. Some claim, as high as 40 per cent of the trade in manufacturing is accounted for by intra-firm trade among the subsidiaries of these corporations.[29] As a result, attracting direct foreign investment of the corporations assumes special significance for improving the trade performance of a nation and alleviating its balance of payments problems. Since foot-loose corporate investments would tend to choose the most profitable locations, a 'race to the bottom' follows among the nations by reducing competitively corporate tax rates and restraining wages. This only reinforces the conservative perspective of a growth process driven by profit and private investment on the one hand, and led by export promotion on the other.

Traditional Keynesianism which assigned to the national governments the specific economic role of demand management, and situated itself almost self-consciously in the context of the nation state, finds it naturally difficult to counter these powerful economic tendencies to internationalise the nation state. However, even more than the multinationalisation of production the tendency towards the integration of the world capital markets can be singled out, perhaps, as the most important aspect which makes autonomous conduct of economic policies by the nation state, not only difficult, but also exceptionally risky. On a very rough estimate, the daily transactions in the foreign exchange markets exceeding at present one trillion dollars per day, outweigh the total foreign exchange reserves of all the central banks put together. Only a very small fraction, of these daily transactions, is related directly either to foreign trade or direct foreign investment. Most of the transactions remain purely 'financial' in nature; they are in nature; they are sales, purchases and recontracting of existing financial claims in the secondary markets by various private traders in the foreign exchange market. They generate highly volatile short-term capital flows. Since this involves speculations about the strengths and weaknesses of various currencies almost on a moment-to-moment basis, each national government finds itself constrained to follow policies that would not 'disturb' the private traders and set off speculation against its currency. The most obvious victim of this, has been Keynesian expansionary policies to fight unemployment, which relies traditionally on government spending through deficit financing or taxation.[30] These policies are usually perceived as leading to a worsening of the climate for private investment in financial assets. In addition, they usually create at least temporary difficulties for the balance of payments through partial spill-over of the higher aggregate demand into imports. Consequently, they run the risk of triggering off adverse speculation against the national currency.[31] Even financing government expenditure through 'borrowing from the market' may not be a viable option: persuading the market to hold more government securities would raise the rate of interest on government bonds, and create additional debt servicing burden for governments with large overhang of public debt.

The result of global financial integration has been visible in an almost total paralysis of social democratic policies in promoting the vision of 'welfare capitalism' and fighting unemployment through public expenditure. The fear of inflation at home has been reinforced by the apprehension of 'disturbing' the international capital and foreign exchange markets. And, the captains of industry, multinational corporations and financial institutions in their common dislike of surrendering their authority structure of economic decision-making to the government, have made out a strong case that the only viable option in these circumstances is a process of economic growth that is driven entirely by private investments, profits and export promotion.[32] In this way, the most conservative aspect of Keynes' theory has been combined with the political orthodoxy of Monetarism, to create a powerful counter-ideology against traditional social democracy.

The collapse of the former Soviet Union, and the end of competition between the two systems has removed almost the last traces of resistance to this ideology. The end of the Cold War did not signify just a decisive victory for western democracy and the market economy over the authoritarian political system of the command economy. It also encouraged the captains of industry to reject ideologically almost all forms of economic cooperation between the classes. Gramsci had pointed out that successful capitalism is based on cooperation and co-opting, in so far as the capitalists elicit consent of the workers by offering material concessions combined with implicit threats of coercion.[33] And, for the political legitimacy of the capitalist system eliciting such consent of the workers through material concessions had been strong so long as socialism posed a serious challenge as the alternative economic system. When this challenge collapsed finally, so did the need to legitimise capitalism through material concessions to the workers. This is reflected in the almost festive mood with which the 'rolling back' of the welfare state is greeted in business and academic circles these days. And this refusal even to legitimise the economic system throws up the most direct conservative challenge against all social democratic policies. While modern social democracy has been premised on the fundamental postulate that cooperative capitalism is the most legitimate system, this postulate is now under challenge. However, if the system really loses its legitimacy in the eyes of some of the major contending classes,[34] cooperation runs the danger of degenerating into conflict and disintegration of social cohesion. This danger of abandoning the social democratic ideal of cooperative capitalism should not be minimised, either by modern social democrats or by their political opponents. It is time that the debate turns towards the problem of how to restore cooperation, not how to destroy it.

Notes

1. See Stone (1983), p. 45–53 for further details.
2. Hobsbawm (1969), p. 125 provides more for details.
3. Marx (1952), p. 47.
4. Przeworski (1985), p. 24.
5. Ibid, p. 12.
6. Przeworski (1985), in particular has emphasised the role of this factor in the development of social democratic politics.
7. Ohlin (1938), p. 5.
8. Thompson (1963, p. 206), quotes an interesting resolution of 1817 by the Leicester framework-knitters which puts quite succinctly the under-consumptionist argument: 'That if liberal wages were given to the Mechanics in general throughout the Country, the Home Consumption of our Manufactures would be immediately more than doubled and consequently every hand would soon find full employment.'
9. Colton (1969) and Kalecki (1936).

10. An increase in the 'social component' of wages may be helpful in coalition politics in so far as it also raises the standard of living of some other partners in coalition politics who are not industrial wage-earners.
11. Glyn (1995).
12. Keynes (1936), p. 325: emphasis in original.
13. Kalecki (1944).
14. Maddison (1991).
15. Kalecki (1971).
16. The emphasis put on 'labour market flexibility' in almost all propgrammes of liberalisation can be explained in these terms. It reduces workers' indiscipline and bargaining power through increasing the fear of job-loss on the one hand, and on the other, by cutting down the welfare measures for the unemployed, it also reduces the economic role of the state and gives back the initiative to the employers. Labour market flexibility is given such high priority, because it kills two birds with the same stone!
17. Wage in relation to labour productivity, i.e. the concept of 'efficiency wage' is particularly helpful for analysing how both the cost of production and the distribution of income are interrelated. A rise in the efficiency wage, measured as the ratio of wage to labour productivity, raises the cost of production, while raising the share of wages in manufacturing industries.
18. Phillips (1958).
19. Friedman (1968).
20. This was the 'augmented' Phillips curve which included the actual rate of inflation also as an explanatory variable. Many empirical works had introduced this modification prior to the work of Friedman, who later replaced the *actual by the anticipated* rate of inflation, to give the argument a twist.
21. In textbook terms, firms attain their inflation, to give the argument a twist of output and employment when the real wage rate equals the marginal product of labour. Therefore, there is no incentive for the firms to change their output or employment level so long as the real wage remains the same. Whether employment is determined by aggregate demand or by profit-maximising equilibrium is not merely a matter of theoretical debate (Benassy, 1986; Bhaduri, 1983, 1991; Malinvaud, 1977). It involves the important policy issue as to whether higher employment can be achieved only by expanding demand, without reducing the real wage. Keynes (1936) himself was ambiguous on this point.
22. In order to depress the real wage which is essential for higher employment according to both pre-Keynesian 'classical' and modern neo-classical theory, see also the preceding footnote.

23. Because budget deficit creates high-powered money on which the money multiplier works. This view is better at explaining how *potential* money supply increases, but not necessarily how an increase in *actual* money supply takes place. The latter depends also on the demand for money, i.e. how a part or the whole of that potential money supply gets injected or transmitted into the economy. This debate revolves around the exogeneity versus the endogeneity of money supply.
24. Bhaduri and Marglin (1990).
25. Ibid.
26. If the state has any economic role, it is only to support private business by improving the 'climate for investment', as conservative politicians often asset.
27. *Le Monde*, 6 July 1976.
28. See Bhaduri and Marglin (1990) for elaboration.
29. European Commission, (1995), p. 2.
30. Even in the case of government expenditure financed fully by taxes, there would be an expansionary impact through the 'balanced budget multiplier'. It arises because the government spends the entire tax revenue, part of which would have otherwise been saved, if it were left with the tax-payers.
31. A contrary scenario can be derived from the arguments of Flemming (1962) and Mundell (1961, 1963). Expansionary fiscal policies raise the interest rate, if domestic monetary policy is not sufficiently accommodative. The higher interest attracts capital inflow and strengthens the domestic currency in this first round. See also Bhaduri and Matzner (1990) for a related discussion.
32. There is an obvious 'fallacy of composition' in this strategy. Not all countries can achieve export surplus at the same time.
33. Gramsci (1971).
34. This could probably happen in countries which fail to achieve expansion led by private investment and export surplus, while giving up traditional Keynesianism of the welfare state, and suffering high unemployment.

References

1. Benassy, J. P. (1986), 'Theories of Unemployment' in *Macroeconomics: An Introduction to the Non-Walrasian Approach.* London, Academic Press.
2. Bernstein, E. (1961), *Evolutionary Socialism.* New York, Schocken.
3. Bhaduri, A. (1983), 'Multimarket Classification of Unemployment: A Sceptical Note', *Cambridge Journal of Economics,* Vol. 7, pp. 235–41.

4. Bhaduri, A. and E. Matzner (1990), 'Relaxing the International Constraints on Full Employment', *Banca Nazionale del Lavoro Quarterly Review,* No. 172, pp. 49–62.
5. Bhaduri, A. and S.A. Marglin (1990), 'Unemployment and the Real Wage: The Economic Basis for Contesting Political Ideologies', *Cambridge Journal of Economics,* Vol. 14, pp. 375–93.
6. Bhaduri, A. (1991), 'Keynesian and Classical Unemployment: A False Distinction', *Economic Applique,* Vol. 44, pp. 43–9.
7. Colton, J. (1969), 'Politics and Economics in the 1930s: The Balance Sheet of the Blum New Deal' in Charles K. Warner (ed.), *From the Ancient Regime to the Popular Front.* New York, Columbia University Press.
8. Flemming, J.M. (1962), 'Domestic Financial Policies under Fixed and under Floating Exchange Rates'. *IMF Staff Papers,* Vol. 9, pp. 369–79.
9. European Commission (1995), *A Level-playing Field for Direct Investment World-wide,* COM (95) 42 (mimeo).
10. Friedman, M. (1968), 'The Role of Monetary Policy'. *American Economic Review,* Vol. 58, pp. 1–17.
11. ——— (1975), *Unemployment versus Inflation.* London, Institute of Economic Affairs.
12. Glyn, A. (1995), 'Social Democracy and Full Employment'. *New Left Review,* No. 211, May–June, pp. 33–55.
13. Gramsci, A., Q. Hoare and G. Nowell Smith (eds.) (1971), *Prison Notebook.* New York, International Publishers.
14. Hobsbawm, E.J. (1969), *Industry and Empire.* Pelican Economic History of Britain, Vol. 3, p. 125, Pelican, Hammondsworth, Middlesex, England.
15. Kaldor, N. (1955–6), 'Alternative Theories of Distribution'. *Review of Economic Studies,* Vol. 23, pp. 212–26.
16. Kalecki, M. (1936), 'The Lesson of the Blum Experiment'. *Economic Journal,* Vol. 48, pp. 26–41
17. _______ (1944), 'Three Ways to Full Employment', in Oxford Institute of Statistics (ed.), *Economics of Full Employment.* Oxford, Blackwell.
18. ——— (1971), 'Political Aspects of Full Employment (Originally published in 1943)' in *Selected Essays on the Dynamics of the Capitalist Economy.* Cambridge, Cambridge University Press.
19. Kautsky, K. (1971), *The Class Struggle.* New York, W.W. Norton.
20. Keynes, J.M. (1936), *The General Theory of Employment, Interest and Money.* London, Macmillan.
21. Maddison, A. (1991), *Dynamic Forces in Capitalist Development.* Oxford, Oxford University Press.
22. Malinvaud, E. (1977), *The Theory of Unemployment Reconsidered.* New York, John Wiley & Sons.

23. Marglin, S.A. and A. Bhaduri (1990), 'Profit Squeeze and Keynesian Theory' in S.A. Marglin and J. Schor (eds.), *The Golden Age of Capitalism: Reinterpreting the Postwar Experience*. Oxford, Clarendon Press.
24. Marx, Karl (1952), *The Class Struggle in France, 1848 to 1850*. Moscow, Progress Publishers.
25. Mathews, R.C.O. (1968), 'Why Has Britain Had Full Employment Since the War?' *Economic Journal*, Vol. 78, pp. 411–19.
26. Mundell, R.A. (1961), 'Flexible Exchange Rates and Employment Policy', *Canadian Journal of Economics and Political Science*, Vol. 27, pp. 509–17.
27. ——— (1963), 'Capital Mobility and Stabilization Policy under Fixed and Flexible Exchange Rates', *Canadian Journal of Economics and Political Science*, Vol. 29, pp. 475–85.
28. Ohlin, Bertil (1938), 'Economic Progress in Sweden', *The Annals of the American Academy of Political and Social Science*, Vol. 197, pp. 1–7.
29. Phillips, A.W. (1958), 'The Relation Between Unemployment and the Rate of Change of Money Wage Rates in the United Kingdom; 1862–1957', *Economica*, Vol. 25, pp. 283–99.
30. Przeworski, Adam (1985), *Capitalism and Social Democracy*, Cambridge, Cambridge University Press.
31. Sachs, J. and C. Wypolsz (1986), 'The Economic Consequences of President Mitterand', *Economic Policy*, pp. 261–321.
32. Stone, N. (1983), *Europe Transformed, 1878–1919*. New York, Fontana.
33. Thompson, E.P. (1963), *The Making of the English Working Class*. New York, Vintage Books.

7

The Rise of Monetarism as a Social Doctrine*

This paper was written in the early days of neo-liberalism when Monetarism was the new high fashion, embraced by politicians and academia. It explains the political economy of Monetarism and, is being reprinted here as a historically relevant piece.

Amit Bhaduri and Josef Steindl

Introduction

It is hardly worthwhile to discuss the contents of monetarism. The really interesting question is how this ideology steadily gained ground to become the creed of the ruling circles in some countries and at least of very influential circles in others.

It should be noted at the outset that monetarism—in present-day practice, if not necessarily in theory—is associated with *restrictive* monetary and fiscal policy.[1] Our basic observation is that such restrictive policies have always been supported by banks and financiers (the City, Wall Street) more than by any other group in the economy. It is they who have consistently clamoured for high interest rates and for restrictive budgetary measures. The specific monetarist theory has found a home in those circles more than anywhere else.

---

* Published in *Thames Papers in Political Economy*, London, Autumn, 1983.

Cui bono?

The question immediately arises as to why this should be so. What interest is served by following restrictive monetary and fiscal policies? The answer comes most naturally on ideological grounds. Monetarism attributes to the control of money supply and to the banking system the central regulatory role, a strategic position almost comparable to the central planning office in a socialist state. This cannot fail to flatter the bankers' vanity. But more than being merely flattering to 'high finance', monetarism articulates an ideological attack against the Keynesian doctrine. Monetarism intends to displace Keynesian policies which threaten the social power of the banking system by relegating it to one of the instruments of government policy in maintaining full employment. It is by no means necessary to recall the 'euthanasia of the rentier' which bodes ill for the banks also, but it is quite sufficient to state that Keynesian policies entail an enormous strengthening of the national government's hand in the conduct of banking policy. This cannot find favour with the banks, unless they feel confident that the economic policies of the national government would be run more or less exclusively in the interest of 'high finance'.

Faced with the historical experience of the interwar years, J.M. Keynes, although in principle a liberal, was driven to support national economic policies designed to defend the level of home employment against depressive influences coming from the outside world. Such defensive national policies might involve devaluation, protectionism, exchange control, etc. These essentially entailed severe restrictions on the international role which the City had enjoyed under a gold exchange standard with the pound sterling as a reserve currency.[2]

Let one of us (J.S.) indulge here in a historical reminiscence. Kalecki used to interpret the events in Britain around

1931/32 in terms of a shift of power from the City to industry. The interest of the City was overruled by abandoning the Gold Standard, adopting a floating exchange rate and establishing the Exchange Equalisation Account. Industry got protection again and free trade was rejected in a major turn about of British economic policy. This change was connected with a decline in the international status of the city as the financial centre of the world. Kindleberger (1973) maintains that the City was neither able nor willing to plug the holes that had appeared in the network of international finance and thus prevent the snowballing effect which led to the breakdown of the entire structure in 1931. With this tarnishing of the international image of the City, the centre of gravity of British economic policy shifted to home-front in favour of domestic industries. This provided the necessary socio-political base for the acceptance of Keynesian policies.[3]

In order to answer the question 'Whose advantage?', it is worth stressing that a high interest rate policy is generally beneficial to banks under normal circumstances, i.e. as long as they do not become the victims of a financial crisis.

It is true that those financial institutions which have a lot of long-term investment committed at low interest and are forced to borrow short at very high interest tend to lose money on that account. In more extreme cases, they may even face financial ruin, as is apparent from the threat of bankruptcy which hangs over the head of many American thrift institutions at present (i.e. 1982). But, by and large, commercial banks neither in the US nor in the UK, although some in Germany, have been locked in such a situation of borrowing short at a high rate and lending long at a low rate. Long-term government bonds are not a large part of the financial portfolio of the commercial banks either in the US or in the UK nowadays (of the order of one-tenth perhaps), so that this consideration is not of overriding practical importance to them. In addition, new credit instruments have emerged which facilitate long or medium term lending at variable interest rates determined by a spread over the interbank lending rate (for example, LIBOR, i.e. the rate which the London banks charge each other for short-term money). The share of outstanding debt of developing countries carrying such floating interest rates is estimated to have increased from about 28 per cent in 1973 to nearly 60 per cent in 1980.[4] Increasingly, longer term loans are being committed only on the basis of floating interest and the practice today extends in large measure even to newly issued industrial bonds. Such new credit arrangements have helped to insulate the banks against the only disadvantage which an increasing level of interest rates may have for them.[5] Otherwise, high interest means increased earnings on loans advanced by banks, while small saving deposits usually do not get a proportionate rise in interest payments and demand deposits get none.

These general arguments find some empirical support in the fact that the British banks have done particularly well at a time when industry has withered away under high interest rates (as can be seen in Table 7.2).

The Shift of Power

The rise of monetarism from a local sect to world wide eminence has been preceded by a shift of power from industry to the banks. Perhaps this shift was nowhere as clearly marked as in Britain.

All existing evidence regarding the scope of operation of traditional financial centres like the City or Wall Street tends to suggest that such a process of shift in relative power has indeed been steadily taking place over the last two decades or so.

Table 7.1 gives an indication of the extent to which the City has managed to extend its scope of operation during

Table 7.1: U.K. Banking Sector's Assets
(Total Lending £ m)

	Public Sector Total	Index	Private Sector Total	Index	Overseas Sector Total	Index	Total Assets Total	Index	GDP GDP	Bank Assets as per cent of GDP
1970	7.474	100	10.786	100	15.471	100	33.727	100	43.530	78
Proportion	22		32		46		100			
1979	17.305	232	53.602	497	128.678	832	199.585	592	163.647	122
Proportion	9		27		64		100			

Source: CSO, Annual Abstract 1981.

the 1970s. It shows that overseas lending has increased more than eight-fold, lending to private domestic customers has increased five-fold and lending to the public sector has increased only two–fold. The total assets of the UK banking sector were 78 per cent of the GDP in 1970 and 122 per cent in 1979. This illustrates the tremendous increase in the relative power and control wielded by the City. At the same time, the much faster growth of overseas operations allowed the banks to enjoy a certain degree of independence both from the national government and from the domestic public sector.

Table 7.2 shows the ratio of undistributed income of financial companies to that of industrial and commercial companies. This ratio is seen to rise steadily in 1960–78 and then to jump to extraordinary proportions in 1979 and 1980, the years of domination by monetarism when the banks continued to prosper while industry decayed.

As Table 7.2 shows, the undistributed profits of the British banking sector as a percentage of those of the industrial-commercial sector rose spectacularly from 7 per cent in the early 1960s to 28 per cent in 1980. In the absence of access to similar data from many other OECD countries, it is hard to judge how 'special' is the British case. Nevertheless, since the British banks' fortunes were connected with the rise of the Euro-market and the transfer of oil money, and since other countries' banks shared this experience, we may guess that a similar shift in the distribution of profits has taken place in other industrialised countries, although it has probably gone nowhere as far as Britain. It has to be pointed out here that a traditional divergence of interest exists between banks and industry in Britain owing to a general reluctance on the part of industry to indebt itself and borrow from banks (Samuels, Groves and Goddard, 1975). It is arguable that to a large extent this peculiar alienation has also been caused by the long-standing

Table 7.2: U.K. Profits: Industrial and Commercial as Compared to Financial Companies

(£ m., annual averages)

Undistributed Income*	**1960–64**	**1965–72**	**1973–78**	**1979**	**1980**	**1981**
1. Industrial and Commercial Companies	2468	3523	12251	19795	15238	16268
2. Financial Companies	169	391	1664	3687	4290	3327
3. Financial in p.c of Industrial Commercial	7	11	14	19	28	20
Undistributed Income plus Dividends**						
4. Industrial and Commercial Companies	3584	5021	14108	24099	19306	20333
5. Financial Companies	337	642	1998	4175	4882	3999
6. Industrial–Commercial	9	13	14	17	25	20

* Before providing for depreciation, stock appreciation and additions to reserve, net of taxes.

** Dividends are net of tax after 1973; the data before and after 1973 are therefore not comparable.

Source: CSO Economic Trends, Annual Supplement 1982 Edition and July 1982.

international position of the London-based banks, who often find their foreign business more profitable than lending to domestic industries.

The relative independence of finance from domestic industry in Britain owes a lot to the old tradition of the City as an international financial centre. Indeed in the two historical reserve currency countries—the UK and later the US—the City and Wall Street could play their international financial role without necessarily being constrained by the growth of domestic industries.[6] In contrast, the transnational banks from countries like Germany and Japan, where industries have been reconstructed in the post-war period largely so as to poise them favourably in terms of international competitiveness, have had their operations grow more in line with the interests of their transnational corporate business.[7]

The Sources of the Banks' Prosperity

In attempting to understand the reason behind the shift in power from industry to the banking system which has been taking place over the last two decades or so, it is essential to consider both the national and the international dimension of the problem. Undoubtedly these two aspects have tended to reinforce one another in facilitating the process of shift of power in favour of the banking system, but for the sake of clarity in exposition, we wish to separate them here.

On the *national level,* the long post-war prosperity of capitalism saw a renewed growth of rentier interests. It resulted in significant accumulation of personal savings held in the form of financial assets in accumulation of personal savings held in the form of financial assets in most OECD countries (Steindl, 1982). Alongside grew the public debt which, in large measure, only reflected the growing rentier interest. As inflation tended to erode the real value of accumulated savings and the real interest rate, the rentiers interest in trying to find compensation in the high interest rate of a 'dear money' policy become more pronounced. In so far as such a policy is normally also favoured by the banks, as we have seen above, the rentier becomes a natural political ally of the banks in his insistence that inflation is a more serious problem than unemployment.

In its *international aspect,* it hardly needs to be stressed that finance is a surface phenomenon reflecting the underlying relations of economic power between nations. The unchallenged 'reserve currency' status of the dollar under the Bretton Woods System merely reflected the new hegemonic role of America in the international capitalist system. Both as an international unit of account and as a store of value, the dollar played the role of international money for more than a quarter of a century. And it was the store of value or reserve currency status of the dollar which also allowed America to buy freely in the whole world with her paper liabilities which the foreigners willingly held as assets and considered as good as gold. Thus, under the reserve currency status of the dollar, America was able to finance not only some of her worldwide military expenditure, but also a large flow of private foreign investment into Europe. American multinationals could take over European firms, while the Europeans had to be satisfied with an equivalent dollar holding in exchange.[8] It needs to be stressed that these financing operations were increasingly routed, not through official transactions among central banks (as visualised under the Bretton Woods System), but through transactions conducted by large international commercial banks whose dollar claims became the basis for loans denominated in dollars. The result was the birth and growth of a massive *Eurodollar market,* where expatriate dollars, detached from their national monetary base, were held in commercial banks located outside the United States. It is hardly necessary to add that the motive for the expatriation of banking business from the US (as well as from other countries where the same happened) was strengthened by the desire to escape from national monetary controls and national taxation.

In time the Eurodollar market developed into an international commercial money market, comprising not only dollars but all other major convertible currencies as well, all of which were also detached from their national monetary base. The total value of such expatriate currencies held in the commercial banking system is estimated (November 1981) at 1.35 trillion US dollars—a 3.353 per cent increase from the 39 billion US dollars recorded in 1965, the earliest measure of the Euromarket's size.[9] And, even as early as 1973, just before the quadrupling of the oil price, the volume of the commercial banks' transactions in such expatriate foreign currency exceeded total value of foreign exchange transactions by all central banks and monetary authorities taken together (Engellau and Nygen, 1979).

Such phenomenal growth of the Eurocurrency market dramatically altered the balance of power, at least temporarily, between the international commercial banking system and the national monetary authorities and their central banks. Like multinational corporations in their field, international commercial banks emerged as a main focus of financial power, largely independent of the control of national monetary authorities.[10] The Keynesian view of the economic autonomy of the national government in the conduct of economic policy and maintenance of full employment at home became almost anachronistic in this context. As economic power continued to shift steadily in favour of large commercial banks, a new economic ideology, as an antidote to Keynes, was called for.

Superimposed on this trend of growing independent financial power of international commercial banking has been, since the quadrupling of the oil price in 1973, the emergence of a class of international rentiers from the OPEC countries.[11] Not only did it vastly augment the deposit base of the large commercial banks, where most of the petromoney was held in short-maturing deposits, but it also made the entire international payments system crucially dependent on the commercial banks. The non-oil developing countries' current account deficits were increasingly met through commercial borrowing and the commercial banks' usual ability to create credit was applauded as an international virtue in the name of 'recycling' on a global scale (see Table 7.3).

A remarkable feature about Table 7.3 is the heavy reliance of non-oil developing countries on borrowing from international capital markets which finance approximately half of their financial requirements. Mostly the credit came directly from commercial banks which accounted for over 70 per cent of total borrowing during 1976–81. (Table 7.3, row 2 ÷ row 1). Well over half of such credit from commercial banks during 1978–81 was publicised Eurocurrency lending (Table 7.3, row 2 ÷ 3) which typically requires syndication of credit. Nevertheless, Table 7.4 also shows the somewhat self-contained nature of Eurocurrency lending in spite of all the attention paid to the global recycling phenomenon. It will be noted (from Table 7.4 row 1) that non-oil developing countries together account for about one-third of total Eurocurrency bank credit, while industrialised countries still have the major share (50–60 per cent).[12]

In light of the above evidence on international bank credit, it would be rash to maintain that the present system of international banking is crucially dependent on the market for non-oil developing countries in general. Instead, the broad picture that emerges is the *crucial dependence of a few borrowers among* non-oil developing countries on the international banking system (see Table 7.4 row 2 and 3). It is on these selected few countries—less than a dozen in number, all belonging to the middle to high income group

Table 7.3: Role of private credit in current account financing of non-oil developing countries (1973–1982)

(In billions of US dollars)

Year	1973	1974	1975	1976	1977	1978	1979	1980	1981	1982	Cumulative Total 1973–81
0. Total to be financed (i)	21	39	44	46	41	55	71	91	100	101	508
1. Borrowing from international markets (banks and bonds) (ii)	11	16	16	23	18	34	44	50	52	N.A.	264
2. Credit from commercial banks (iii)	N.A.	N.A.	N.A.	18	18	23	37	34	37	N.A.	N.A.
3. Publicised Eurocurrency lending to non-OPEC developing countries (iv)	N.A.	N.A.	N.A.	N.A.	N.A.	14	27	24	33	N.A.	N.A.
4. Total publicised Eurocurrency lending (v)	N.A.	N.A.	N.A.	N.A.	42	70	83	77	133	N.A.	N.A.
5. Per cent share of non-OPEC developing countries in publicised Euro lending	N.A.	N.A.	N.A.	N.A.	N.A.	20	33	31	25	N.A.	N.A.

Table 7.3: Sources and Notes

(i) Row (O) is the algebraic sum of current account deficit and reserve accumulation giving ex-post financial requirement. Current account deficit is the net total of balances on goods, services and private transfers, as defined in IMF *Balance of Payments Yearbook*. Source of Row (O): World Bank (1982), Appendix B, Table 25.

(ii) Row (1) estimates finance raised through bank loans and issue of bonds. The latter item of bond issues is only around 10 per cent of the total for developing countries (1979-80). See, *Economist* (1982a, p.83) on the relative composition of bonds and bank loans, estimated from three different sources namely, OECD, the World Bank and Morgan Guaranty Co. Row (2) is compiled from IMF and B.I.S. sources.

(iii) Source: *First Chicago World Report (1981)*. Reported in R.W. Lombardi 'Multinational banking and the Third World'—International Herald Tribune (1981 b, p. 85).

(iv) Source: Morgan Guaranty Co., *World Financial Markets,* various issues. Morgan Guaranty estimates are somewhat lower than estimates by OECD and the World Bank (see *Economist*, 1982d for comparison); also International Currency Review (1980), No. 6, p. 9 using Morgan Guaranty estimates (for 1978-80).

(v) Sources same as note (iv) above.

Table 7.4: Eurocurrency bank credit concentration

Shares of certain groups of recipients in total Eurocurrency bank credit in per cent

	1973	1974	1975	1976	1977	1978	1979	1980	1981	Average 1973–81
1. Share of non-oil developing countries (i)	19	21	39	38	32	38	43	31	26	32
2. Concentration according to region: Share of Central and Latin America (ii)	N.A.	N.A.	58	59	55	55	55	56	N.A.	N.A.
3. Concentration according to countries: Share of 8 major borrowing countries (iii)	N.A.	N.A.	53	54	52	53	56	55	N.A.	N.A.
4. Concentration according to countries: Share of 9 Newly Industrialising countries (iv)	N.A.	N.A.	69	67	63	65	71	74	N.A.	N.A.

Table IV: Sources and Notes

(i) 1981 figure relates to January to November. Source is *Morgan Guaranty and Co.* Morgan Guaranty data relate to non-OPEC developing countries, which corresponds fairly closely to non-oil developing countries data in this context.

(ii) Source: *BIS, IMF and Morgan Guaranty Co.*

(iii) Sources as in note (ii) above. Includes 4 countries, namely, Brazil, Mexico, Argentina and Chile in the Americas, and Korea (South), Philippines. Thailand and Malaysia in Asia. The 4 Asian countries account for about 10–12 per cent of total Eurocurrency bank credit, while the 4 countries in the America account for 43–45 per cent on an average.

(iv) Sources: *BIS, IMF and OECD.* These 9 countries are: Brazil, Mexico, Argentina, Korea (South) (as in note (iii) above) as well as Greece, Spain, Portugal, Yugoslavia and Taiwan; they are on a comparable per capita income level.

among developing countries and most of them trying to industrialise typically through what are called 'open trade and investment policies'—that international banks' loans have been showered on an unprecedented scale during the last decade or so. At the same time, poorer non-oil developing countries have not had any significant access to large commercial loans. In the pattern that increasingly emerged in recent years, the domestic savings of OECD countries and the liquid surplus of OPEC merged to result in a powerful rentier interest that got tied to the smooth operation of international commercial lending. On the receiving side of commercial loans were some OECD countries with serious balance of payments problems, a few socialist countries as well as a handful of selected developing countries belonging to the middle-income group.

Commercial banks' dependence on their clients either as lenders or as borrowers has not been one sided, which ensured them a position of relative autonomy. In particular, the relative importance of OPEC deposits in the total deposits of commercial banks has not shown any clear tendency to increase over time. The OPEC's share in total deposits has remained relatively stable around 10 to 12 per cent throughout the period 1975–80.[13] As a consequence commercial banks have not increased their dependence of OPEC depositors; instead, they have increasingly relied upon international re-lending of domestic savings of OECD countries.[14] The fact that only a few selected developing countries in the middle income range (led by Brazil and Mexico) have been the main borrowers implies that commercial banks' dependence on their borrowing clients in the developing countries has been highly specific. It would be wrong then to presume either a *general* dependence of developing countries on commercial banks or of the banks on developing countries' capital markets. More exactly, a few selected middle-income developing countries depend heavily on commercial borrowing,[15] while rentiers both from

OECD and OPEC depend on profitable deployment of their financial savings through 'recycling' carried out by commercial banks.

Escape from National Control

Given the concentration of international commercial banking in the traditional financial centres, large banks have increasingly shown a tendency to become more independent of their home governments and domestic industries. The development of Euromarkets, in allowing commercial banks to operate extensively in *foreign* currency, has also meant that the traditional business of international liquidity creation has largely got detached from the control of national monetary authorities. In a fundamental sense, therefore, restrictive national monetary policies do not any longer affect so severely the international commercial banking system, the banks can reap the benefits of a high interest policy without having to surrender to the control of central banks. The special attraction of monetarism for commercial banking lies precisely in this paradoxical fact that a restrictive national monetary policy is largely ineffective in curbing their international operations. And, evidence seems to suggest that a 'dear money' policy hits domestic industries, while international commercial banks do not seem to suffer particularly from it (see Tables 7.1 and 7.2).

In the ultimate analysis, the social position of industry rests on its being a provider of jobs. It is evident that this function is inadequately fulfilled today by industry in spite of abundant support from the state. In most industrialised countries, basic and traditional industries mainly play the role of petitioners vis-à-vis the government, in some countries one might even say, of old age pensioners in constant need of support. The state subsidises industry even in the case of multinationals who sell their location by auction among the countries who desire their presence. In contrast, as representatives of the mythology of self-reliant private capitalism, the banks have been presenting a better image until recently. Their social influence rests on their nearly unilateral power to grant or withhold credit, to shift funds from country to country and to influence the rate of exchange in a manner which is largely independent of particular national governments' policies. Even the United States government and the Federal Reserve find themselves largely ineffective in regulating such international banking operations. The recent attempts by the Federal Reserve to gain some control of the Eurodollar market by imposing minimum reserve currency requirements (initiated in April 1980) have been almost scornfully rejected by the central banks in other countries in an attempt to protect the interest of international commercial banking located in their respective countries.[16] Banking seems to have become internationalised and independent both from domestic industries and from national governments to an extent where even the most powerful of national governments can exert little control over international banking operations. Nevertheless, there is a reverse side to this picture that is now becoming increasingly apparent. The international lending structure, particularly the Euro-market, is exposed to considerable risks which need not to be dwelt upon here. In the event of large scale defaults the banks would have nobody to turn to but the monetary authority and the government of their home country. This implies serious qualifications to the above statement about the freedom of international banks. Their independence has a limit in the consideration they have to show to their home government and central bank, in order to facilitate intervention on their behalf in case of need. The bond to the home base can never be broken completely.

These considerations touch on the inner contradictions in the position of the banks. There seems to be a good deal of 'double-talk' in their embrace of monetarism. They praise the restrictionist policy at home in so far as it gives them high interest and high margins, but they escape the restrictions on volume by seeking expansion abroad. The dramatic expansion in the volume of international credit has largely resulted from fierce competition among banks. But the paradoxical outcome of the ensuring recycling process carried out by international banks during the last ten years or so is only now becoming apparent. Most of the handful of developing (and some socialist) countries to which the banks lent heavily (see Table 7.4) resulted in a sort of *borrower's debt-trap,* where they cannot avoid increasing recourse to borrowing, if only to service their outstanding debt. The mirror image of this is the situation in which the banks now find themselves. The fear of technical default by a few of these heavily indebted borrowers can set in motion a chain reaction of defaults, the risk of which has been further aggravated by the 'cross default' clause of the usual syndicated lending. A dear money policy encouraged by monetarism and recent devices such as floating-interest loans which shifted the burden of debt-servicing to these borrowers have only contributed further to the fear of widespread default which the international banking system must try to avoid in its own interest (*Economist,* 1982b, pp. 21–24). As a result, banks now find themselves in an uncomfortable *lender's trap,* where they have to keep on lending, rescheduling and rolling over their debts to already heavily indebted borrowers who probably can never pay back. And such debt-rolling must continue to keep the present fragile structure of international finance from crumbling.

It is in this context that we must judge the recent deviations from more orthodox monetarism. The tight money policy is now being relaxed by the Fed and the Bundesbank, followed by several other central banks, and, interest rates have also begun to decline.[17] While these developments may be connected in an obvious way with the compulsions of electoral processes in these countries, it appears to be more than a merely temporary manoeuvre. Restrictive monetarism has begun to become irreconcilable with the uncomfortable position in which the banks have landed themselves. The insolvency of many of their debtors makes it necessary for central banks to intervene as lenders of the last resort and the Bank of International Settlements has already felt compelled to create at least some modest facility to bail out banks in difficulty. Neither the necessity to inject money into the system to unfreeze bad loans nor the strain of high interest on debt servicing can be overlooked by the bankers any more, while such demands also cannot easily be reconciled with the tight money policy.

It may be concluded that tight money policy cannot continue unless the central banks refuse to intervene effectively, as they did in 1931, which would inevitably have the same consequences it had then (Minsky, 1982). This is not to say that trouble could not arise even if the central banks are prepared to advance credit in so far as a financial crisis may be an international currency problem as well, it would require a coordinated international action of monetary authorities to deal adequately with it.

The precarious position of the banks is only the logical consequence of their policy, and that of the US government allied to the Fed. The harm done to both the developing countries and to industry in advanced countries by the high interest policy and the long-lasting refusal of the US government, upheld still at Toronto, to expand lending facilities of the IMF would certainly have come back with a vengeance to the banks if the US had maintained its position.[18] But then, as Keynes (1972. p. 156) once said: "Banks and bankers are by nature blind." It might be added that some governments, with their monetarist spectacles, have hardly better sight.

Summary and Conclusions

The ascent of monetarism to worldwide influence can be explained as a social and political phenomenon. Without going into the broader political aspects of monetarism, this paper concerns itself with the question of how monetarism has been able to gain so much power despite the evident damage it is doing to industrial capitalism. Monetarism, seen as the ideology of the banks and of the rentiers whose interests are defended by the banks, serves as an antidote against Keynesian ideology which assigns to the banks the role of instruments of the government's full employment policy and therefore deprives them of their autonomous power and influence on policy. Moreover, the high interest rates which usually result from monetarist policies are in most cases directly beneficial to the banks as long as there is no danger of a financial crisis. The gradual rise of monetarism since the early 1960s can be explained by the increase in the banks' influence and power which resulted from the expansion of their business, chiefly through operations in the Euromarket. By 1981 the volume of the Euromarket had expanded to forty times its size in 1965. The lending was not confined to less development countries, 50 to 60 per cent was lent to industrial countries. The sources of the banks funds were both the financial surplus of the OPEC countries and the savings of the industrial world. The Euromarket thus constitutes a network of financial relations extending over all parts of the world.

A major attraction of the Euromarket is the escape route it provides from national monetary controls. The large transnational banks, in their support of monetarism, play an ambiguous role: they favour tight money policy which keeps interest high; but at the same time through their participation in the Euromarket they escape the tight credit policy imposed by the monetary authorities. Historically the basis for such a successful policy of expansion of banking business was provided first by the expansion of trade and investment, and subsequently by the recycling of petro-money. Since both these favourable conditions have vanished the reverse side of the monetarist medal has become visible. Owing to the protracted recession, to which tight credit policy has largely contributed, the safety of the banks' customers is threatened, both in industrial and in less developed countries. At the same time, the complicated network of international lending increases the dangers implicit in the instability of the banking system. As a result the position (and the point of view) of the banks has undergone a fundamental change: their interest is now in easier money, because they want more liquidity, so that their customers, threatened with insolvency and forced to borrow, can at least service their debt. This explains the turnabout of the Fed's policy since August 1982 when interest rates were permitted to decline in US followed by those in Europe.

The conclusion is that monetary policy has been of singular short-sightedness, because it has disregarded the interests of the banks' customers (in industrial and less developed countries) until their economic plight reacted back on the banks. With a recession lasting longer than expected and the fear of growing insolvencies a return to a high interest policy is not likely.

Notes

1. Historically it was not always the case. In 1929 the photo-monetarists Foster and Catchings were inveighing against the Federal Reserves's policy of stopping the stock market boom by tight credit policy (Tavlas and Aschheim, 1981). This stance of bygone times is still reflected in Milton Friedman's monetary history (Friedman and Schwartz, 1983).
2. A recent issue of the *Economist* recaptures this change of mood: "In the particular circumstances of 1931, it is easy to accept the macro-economic argument that devaluation was a better short-term remedy than yet another attempt to drive down wages and salaries. There was then a downward spiral of expectations of lower prices and costs," (See reference 1, p. 14). The *Economist* then tries to make out

that a depreciating sterling is no alternative (to wage cut) today. Indeed, a stable and highly valued sterling serves the interest of the City, and that is our point.

3. Or, in particular, that aspect of Keynesian policy which argued for the economic autonomy of the state in managing demand through public works to provide a sufficient market for domestic industries so as to maintain in full employment.
   The attitude of Keynes was evident already in his opposition to the return to gold (1925), a policy which meant putting the interests of the City above the interest of industry.
4. Its consequences has been not only to increase the general debt service ratio (i.e., interest and amortisation payments as percentage of exports of goods and services) for the borrower developing countries, but to increase the particular component of interest payment ratio disproportionately. Thus the group of middle-income net oil importing developing countries which account for most of the commercial debt had an almost four-fold increase in their interest payments ratio between 1973 and 1982 while their overall debt–service ratio during the same period doubled. See World Bank (1982), Table 33 in particular.
5. The corresponding reduction in bond prices is likely to affect far more adversely thrift institutions with long-maturing portfolios.
6. In the case of American banks, during the 1960s their expansion into Europe was linked to take-overs and opening of subsidiaries by American multinational corporations. But we suspect that, once the Eurocurrency market assumed its vast size, even American banks could begin to operate relatively independently of their corporations. In the case of Britain, this is a more clearly established pattern.
7. This impression distinctly emerges from an as yet unpublished survey of 84 transnational banks (with 3,941 foreign entities) conducted by the UN Commission on Transnational corporations. See its forthcoming report on *Transnational banks: operations strategies, and their effects in developing countries.*
   With regard to Germany, however, it must be added that the Bundesbank has an exceedingly strong position of power and that it has pursued time and again since 1967 restrictive policies to the detriment of employment and of domestic industry, contributing very largely to the weakness of private investment in all that time. This happened although Germany, unlike for example Italy, has not been under the compulsion of a chronic and serious balance of payment problem.
8. United States' balance of payments figures for the period 1960–67 suggest that America ran an average annual export surplus of goods and services of the order of 6 billion dollars. But US grant and aid

plus net transfer on official exchange account (annual average 5 billion) and foreign private investment (annual average 3 billion) resulted in an overall payments deficit.

9. This figure was reported in *International Herald Tribune* (1981 a). (See article by Cari Gecoirtz, 'Euromarkets: a gawky adolescent begins to settle down', p. 15).
10. The main reason for this is the Euromarket of expatriate dollars, Deutsche marks, Swiss francs, sterling, guilders, French francs, yen, Belgian francs and various smaller convertible currencies as well as composite units such as Units of Account. European Currency Units and Special Drawing Rights, which form a varied currency base of commercial banking operations, detached from national monetary bases.
11. Mainly 'low-absorber' OPEC countries (i.e. Saudi Arabia, UAE, Kuwait, Qatar) who accounted for 33.6 billion out of a total OPEC surplus of 34.1 billion dollars in 1977. (See, *World Financial Markets,* September 1976 and June 1977). On an average till the end of 1980, OPEC invested around 40 per cent of their financial surplus in Euromarkets according to U.S. Treasury and Bank of England data.
12. A more exact percentage break-down based upon Morgan Guaranty data is the following:

Year	**1970–73**	**1974–76**	**1977–79**	**1980–81**
Industrialised countries Non-	66.2	48.0	38.5	57.8
OPEC developing countries	19.4	30.9	37.8	28.3
Others	14.4	21.1	23.7	13.9

13. The data relate to banks reporting to the Bank of International Settlements (BIS)

	1975	**1976**	**1977**	**1978**	**1979**	**1980**
Ratio of OPEC's deposit in total bank deposit	0.11	0.12	0.12	0.10	0.11	0.12

Source: BIS

14. See *International Herald Tribune* (1981 a).
15. For example, three Latin American countries (Brazil, Mexico and Argentina) accounted for 78 per cent of gross commercial lending to Latin America at the end of 1979, which amounts to 51 per cent of their total lending to non-oil developing countries. Similarly, almost the entire commercial lending to Asia is concentrated in a few countries (South Korea, Indonesia, Malaysia, Philippines and Thailand).
16. See *International Currency Review,* (1980), where the letters written by several Central Banks to Fed are quoted in part. Thus, the Bank of England wrote: "These proposals appear to us to carry with them an implication that the U.S. authorities consider it necessary to extend

their regulatory jurisdiction into the affairs of non-American banks. We would find this a troublesome principle and one which, if generalized, could materially damage effective international cooperation in this field. We feel sure that these concerns could also be shared by a number of other major countries to whose banks these proposed regulations would apply" (p. 16) – letter dated 11 January 1980. Soon the same point was repeated by Deutsche Bundesbank as well as the Bank of Japan in their letters to the Fed.

17. This was written soon after the Fed changed their stance in August 1982.
18. The Administration has in the meantime consented to an increase of the quotes by about 50 per cent. The effect of this on the lending capacity of the IMF will not be felt immediately because of procedural delays.

References

1. *Economist,* (1981), 5–11 September,London.
2. *Economist,* (1982 a), 20–26 March, London.
3. *Economist,* (1982 b), 16–22 October, London.
4. Engellau, P. and Nygen, B. (1979), *Lending Without Limits,* Secretariat of Future Studies, Stockholm.
5. Friedman, M. and Schwartz, A. (1963) *A Monetary History of the United States,* Princeton University Press, Princeton, N.J.
6. *International Herald Tribune,* (1981 a), Special Supplement on Euromarkets, November.
7. *International Herald Tribune,* (1981 b), Special Supplement on International Finances, March.
8. *International Currency Review,* (1980), Vol. 12, Nos. 4 and 6, London.
9. Keynes, J.M. (1972), *Collected Works,* Vol. IX, Macmillan, London.
10. Kindleberger, C.P. (1973), *The World in Depression* 1929–39. Allen Lane, London.
11. Minsky, H.P. (1982), 'Can it Happen Again? A Reprise'. *Challenge,* July–August.
12. Samuels, J.M., Groves, R.E.V. and Goddard, C.S. (1975) *Company Finance in Europe,* The Institute of Chartered Accountants in England and Wales, London.
13. Steindl, J. (1982), 'The Role of Household Saving in the Modern Economy', *Banca Nazionale del Lavoro, Quarterly Review,* March.
14. Tavlas, G.S. and Aschheim, J. (1981) 'The Chicago Monetary Growth Rate Rule: Friedman or Simons Reconsidered', *Banca Nazionale del Lavoro, Quarterly Review,* March.
15. World Bank, (1982), *World Development Report,* Oxford University Press, Oxford.
16. *World Financial Markets,* Morgan Guaranty Trust, various issues.

8

Labour-Market Flexibility and Economic Expansion*

Introduction

The major economies of Western Europe have been facing almost chronic unemployment, often hovering around double digits, for nearly two decades now. This is especially true of Germany, which acted as the economic powerhouse in the consolidation of the European Union. It is all the more paradoxical that advanced market democracies can live with high unemployment placing relatively little emphasis on this problem, except perhaps at times of elections. A deep change in the climate of opinion has occurred in striking contrast to the post–Second World War years, when the pursuit of full employment was the agreed policy objective of almost all shades of political opinion. History is seldom mono-causal; several causal factors and processes usually coincide at a particular juncture of time to bring about such a dramatic change in the climate of opinion.

To a significant extent, this change of opinion began as a reaction against the Keynesian style of demand management in pursuit of high employment, which gradually lost ground for several interrelated reasons. First, the Keynesian argument was almost self-consciously set in the context of an economy closed to international trade and

---

*From: *Wages, Employment, Distribution and Growth* (eds) E. Hein, A. Heisse and A. Truger. Palgrave, Macmillan, 2006, pp. 9–19.

capital flows. The intention might have been to emphasise the importance of domestically oriented economic policies for fighting unemployment. The disastrous consequences of 'beggar-my-neighbour' policies of trying to export unemployment through competitive devaluation of the national currencies during the interwar period [until the (stand-still) agreement of 1936] was still fresh in memory. At the same time, the prestige of the City as the financial centre of the world was in jeopardy, and its views propounding the virtues of 'sound finance' was in ruins. It was rather natural in that context to look inward for a solution to the problem of unemployment which relied more on domestic industries, and less on 'high finance' (Bhaduri and Steindl, 1985).

Second, although the contest between the competing systems of capitalism and socialism was most visible in the arms race during the Cold War, its ideological dimension was essentially economic. The socialist system appeared capable of providing full employment through deliberate state policies, although much of it was neither satisfactory to the employees nor socially useful. (A common joke of the time in these countries was, 'they pretend to pay, we pretend to work.') The capitalist market economies, where the level of employment depended largely on the decision of private business, had the opposite problem. The employment it provided had to be necessarily gainful; that is profitable for the private employer, even if private and social gain differed. But the level of economic activity was prone to cyclical fluctuations, at times resulting in severe unemployment. Given this visible difference between the two systems, even initiatives like the Marshall Plan tended to be influenced, at least partly, by the economic competition between the two systems (Hobsbawm, 1994). It was around this time that the welfare state also found wider political acceptance. Its theoretical rationale derived from Keynesian demand–management policies, whereas the rising real wage with near-full employment, leading to rapidly improving standards of living for the working population under this new style of economic governance in most Western democracies, posed a counter-challenge to the socialist ideology.

Third, the very success of demand management, high employment and rising consumption, which had ushered in a 'golden age' of welfare capitalism through rapidly expanding domestic markets for nearly a quarter century, came to be troubled by its own contradictions (Marglin and Schor, 1990). Years of high employment had reduced the fear of job-loss for the workers leading to higher wage claims. It was in this context that the experiences of the two major oil price shocks of the 1970s served as almost the watershed years. They made it clear that the burden of such shocks could no longer be passed on easily to the workers. The model of cooperative capitalism of the welfare state was giving away to the model of conflictive capitalism, in which conflict over the distribution of income tended to manifest itself through inflationary or stagflationary price rise (Rowthorn, 1977). Even more problematically, the fiscal policy of the state itself got entangled in this distributive conflict, as both workers and their employers tended to pass on the additional tax burden to one another (Bhaduri, 1986: ch. 6). Understandably, targeting inflation rather than unemployment became the new focus of policies under these changed circumstances, and new economic doctrines, at time reviving old ideas that had been pushed aside by the success of Keynesian economic policies, returned in academic circles and policy discussions under the broad heading of Monetarism. Ironically, Monetarism reinvented the Marxian idea that a 'reserve army' of labour is needed to keep a check on the real wage. Kalecki 1943, (reprinted in 1971) had already foreseen towards the end of the Second World War that 'political trade cycles' would be imposed deliberately, particularly in the name of sound finance (read, no deficit financing) to inflict unemployment from time to time on the workers, in order to keep control over the workers. These ideas returned in the orthodox monetarist framework of economic theory as the 'natural rate' of unemployment (Friedman, 1968), or as the non-accelerating inflation rate of unemployment, NAIRU (Layard, Nickell and Jackman, 1991). They all had a common theme in so far as they propounded the view that, keeping inflation and inflationary expectations under control requires accepting a certain, it may even be a fairly high rate of unemployment. In particular, it requires giving up demand management policies intended at keeping the rate of unemployment lower than that 'natural' or NAIRU rate. Since deficit financing by the government had been the most potent instrument used for demand management, unsurprisingly it came under special attack. The doctrine of the virtues of a balanced budget, and the evils of a fiscal deficit by a self-seeking government in the name of 'public choice theory' were propounded as general truths, applicable to almost all countries under all circumstances.

The wider process of globalisation that gathered almost irresistible momentum with the deregulation of national capital markets since the mid-1970s in OECD countries also contributed to this change in the climate of opinion to a significant extent. The greater economic opening-up in goods and services trade means an increase in the relative importance of the foreign or external market compared to the domestic or internal market. It encourages countries to stimulate demand through export surplus, rather than through demand management by the fiscal policies of the government. As a result, each country tries to be more price competitive compared to its rivals, by cutting unit cost through wage 'flexibility' on the one hand, and raising labour productivity on the other. Yet there is an obvious 'fallacy of composition' in this strategy; because all countries cannot achieve export surplus at the same time as the export surplus of some must be matched by the import surplus of others. But even for any particular country, which does manage to achieve an export surplus in this zero-sum game, such policies may turn out to be counter-productive if the contraction in the size of its internal market more than outweighs the expansion of its external market.

The danger of over-contraction of domestic demand from such policies is serious in many countries. Wage restraint depresses consumption by the working people, while labour productivity growth brought about by the corporations through the downsizing of the domestic labour force reinforces this depressive effect. Analytically, this may be identified as the wage-or consumption-led regime in which the depressive effect on consumption of wage restraint and downsizing outweigh its possible stimulating effect on investment and export (Bhaduri and Marglin, 1990). And yet, this danger of a sharp decline in domestic demand tends to be overlooked in policy discussions, not due to ignorance, but for reasons that are considered unavoidable, because the benefit corporations in the current phase of globalisation.

Successive waves of deregulation and liberalisation of capital markets since the mid-1970s have unleased private trade in foreign exchange on an historically unprecedented level. In comparison to its daily volume of some 1.2 trillion dollars (BIS, 2001, 2002), the total foreign exchange reserve of all the central banks is insignificantly small, while foreign trade and investment together do not account for even 4 per cent of it. The economic policies of national governments seem overwhelmed by the power of the financial markets. In particular, this has generally meant that expansionary fiscal policies for fighting serious unemployment through budget deficits are generally not favoured options by financial markets; and therefore by national governments. Similarly, easy money policies with lower interest rates are not favoured either, in so far as they stimulate consumption and investment expenditure (for example hire–purchase, inventory accumulation, housing and so on), and tend to strain the current account of the balance of payments through lower borrowing cost. Moreover, financial markets often read the lowering of the interest rate as signalling the government's intention of embarking on expansionary fiscal policies. The fear that private capital would vote with its feet in the foreign exchange market by crossing borders on a massive scale has crippled fiscal and monetary policies required to fight growing unemployment.

However, there has been a significant difference in this respect between the United States and Europe. Due to the reserve currency status of the dollar, the United States manages to run growing current account deficits and a relatively free national demand-management policy, while the rest of the world, especially Japan and Germany and increasingly China as important export surplus countries, continues to finance the US import surplus in the form of capital inflow into the USA. This is no longer because of the international 'store of value' property of the US dollar; these export-surplus countries are almost locked into this arrangement, because economically they have come to depend too heavily for their export surplus on the US market for maintaining demand, while politically they perceive their national defence capability as being dependent on the USA (except China).

The consequence has been a peculiar paradox about national employment policies which is seldom commented upon. The current strength of the euro has been bought at the cost of restrictive fiscal policies imposed by the Maastricht 'stability pact', and even more restrictive monetary policies pursued by an independent European Central Bank. But if the euro becomes an international 'store of value' through its strength replacing largely the dollar, capital inflows to the USA would be sharply reduced, reducing in turn the export market, particularly for the large export surplus nations like Germany. Japan (or China). As a result, they would face an even more serious unemployment problem. Thus, with the present international financial arrangements and policies, the paradox is that the euro and the yen seem doomed to remain 'strong' currencies without becoming alternative international stores of wealth. Consequently, the privilege to run large trade deficits continuously by issuing paper liabilities accepted by the rest of the world—the privilege based on the international store of value status of a currency—which England had before the First World War, and the USA has enjoyed since the Second World War, is denied to these countries. The wisdom of following restrictive monetary and fiscal policies that inflict high unemployment also needs to be examined in the light of this paradoxical international financial arrangement.

Theories and Counter-theories for Economic Policies

The macro-economic perspective justifying restrictive monetary and fiscal policies is neo-liberal in its essence. Since its general philosophy is to roll back the economic role of the state, it is natural that it would view adequate employment creation as the job of the private sector, and not of the state. At best, the role of the state is seen as creating the 'right' climate for the private sector by increasing its profitability, so that it offers sufficient employment. In this respect it has three distinguishing characteristics contrary to the Keynesian theory.

First, unlike Keynes and Kalecki, who identified the lack of effective demand in the product market as the central cause of unemployment, these theories locate the central cause of unemployment in the labour market. In terms of policy, this means demand management in the product market becomes less important than correcting the malfunctioning of the labour market. This de-emphasises the role of demand management on the one hand, and brings to the forefront the importance of labour–market 'flexibility' on the other.

Second, even the branch of theory relatively sympathetic to the Keynesian view (for example, the neo-Keynesians), tends to make a distinction between the 'short run' and the 'long run'. It is claimed that there may be insufficiency of demand in the product market in the short run, but somehow the demand problem is resolved in the long run by the market. This is starkly visible in almost all versions of neo-classical long-run growth theory which assumes away the demand problem as a short-run phenomenon.

Third, and perhaps most basic to this neo-liberal way of thinking, is its foundation of 'methodological individualism'. It uses some procedure of optimisation by the individual agent as the central organising principle of macro-economic theory. Approaching macro-economic problems exclusively in this way has many serious ramifications, and in so far as the unemployment problem is concerned perhaps its most serious consequence is to blur the distinction between 'voluntary' and 'involuntary' unemployment. Thus, all unemployment, even mass unemployment, begins to look voluntary in this framework, because it has to be explained through some optimising decision by the individual worker, but not by a failure of the system which requires intervention. This then becomes attributable to the imperfect functioning of the price mechanism for giving wrong signals to the worker. In some cases government interventions, mostly related to the welfare state, are supposed to distort the signals carried by wages. An important case in point is the criticism levelled against social safety nets like unemployment benefits provided by the government. A widely prevalent view, propagated by the media as well as some academic economists, is that it raises the 'reservation wage' so much that the worker chooses voluntarily to be unemployed. Another version with a similar thrust is to claim that the worker refuses to take up employment at the prevailing wage, either because (s)he is misinformed and spends all his or her time in search of a better job, or waits until the wage rate becomes higher. For a non-economist with some common sense these theories lie only a little distance away from the view that some are unemployed because they are lazy or unreasonably ambitious who do not know their 'market worth'. In this framework either the jobless worker becomes responsible for his or her own situation; or the blame is put on government intervention.

Neo-liberalism relying on the market rather than the government to deal with problems like unemployment has a different kind of advantage which is seldom recognised. Nothing in economic theory specifies how long it might take to reach 'equilibrium', through the market mechanism, even under the most idealised circumstances of perfect competition, when the competitive equilibrium has all the desirable properties of so-called Pareto-optimality by the 'fundamental theorem' of welfare economics. In democracies, the government and the politicians in power remain accountable to their people at regular time intervals through the elections, but the market mechanism has no such definite time horizon for showing results. And, this ambiguity helps in sustaining the market ideology in so far as it can always be claimed that, given 'sufficient' time and 'sufficiently' wide-ranging pro-market reforms, the desired results would materialise without having to specify how long is sufficiently long. The market mechanism, like a dictator, can always promise without actually delivering!

The virtues of sticking adamantly to pro-market policies as the solution to the unemployment problem get further strengthened by the role of the media. The enormous power wielded by electronic media and television images in shaping public opinion was noticed by perceptive commentators even in the very early stage of current globalisation (see for example McLuhan, 1960). It helps in spreading a sort of a popular culture in economic policy, policies that can be easily comprehended by 'practical' men and women. In this respect, most appealing is the analogy with the individual. Since spending beyond means is considered bad for the individual, a budget deficit of the government is also considered bad; because the demand for apples can be raised by lowering its price, the demand for labour can also be raised by lowering the wage rate; hard work helps, so a corporate manager helps the economy by downsizing its labour force. Underlying these pronouncements, popularised by the media, is the foundation of 'methodological individualism.' Unfortunately, politicians become victims of it, even if some of them understand better, because political expediency often demands that they do not swim against the current of popular 'understanding'.

Nevertheless, this popular culture of viewing macro-economic policies exclusively through the neo-liberal glass of methodological individualism goes against the very logic of having macro-economics as a distinct branch of enquiry. The latter is justified, precisely in those situations when the analogy with the individual is misleading. And, serious unemployment is perhaps the most important example of such a situation, as the Keynesian theory demonstrated. The common mistake in all arguments based on methodological individualism is to fall into the fallacy of composition. Thus, cutting wages may improve the profit margin for one firm, but the total volume of sales in the economy is likely to suffer. Downsizing the labour force may reduce unit cost for one firm, but when followed by many firms it may reduce total employment and the volume of sales in the economy. Even export surplus for one country must be balanced by the import surplus of another; so the strategy of export-led expansion cannot work for all. These familiar examples show why the argument that holds for the individual part may fail to hold for the whole system. Keynesian macro-economic theory is based precisely on this premise, and the macro-economic policies to fight unemployment follows from the fundamental insight that, unlike in the case of the individual, the macroeconomy is characterised by a circular flow from expenditure to income. Expenditure by creating demand may determine output and employment in situations of serious unemployment and excess capacity.

Policies for High Employment

It is against this intellectual background that we need to reconsider policies for attaining and sustaining higher employment. However, at the very outset of this policy discussion it is worth pointing out that many different types of projects may be devised for generating employment. By and large these projects would be country-specific, dependent on geography, stage of development, degree of openness, and so on. The purpose of economic theory in this context is not to list a set of such projects irrespective of the situation specificity, but to indicate the direction in which an employment generating and employment-sustaining programme can become feasible.

The problem of servicing debt exists, but it is far from clear why a government cannot take recourse to further borrowing to service its debt, so long as its higher spending is effective in raising the employment level and the rate of growth. The well-known result that so long as the growth rate exceeds the interest rate in real terms, the debt to income ratio tends to stabilise, might be invoked in this context to serve as a guide. On the whole it seems misplaced to argue that a growing debt-servicing burden necessarily strains the credibility of a government under all circumstances. A government's economic credibility might indeed suffer more due to persisting high unemployment and low growth. Therefore, the real issue to be faced is whether government spending can be effective in raising productive employment opportunities and growth prospects.

This is indeed the crux of the problem, and needs to be decomposed in two parts. First, to the extent the economy faces insufficiency of demand with excess capacity, the traditional Keynesian remedy should be reasonably effective provided it fits the composition of demand, governed mostly by income elasticities. In that case, until it really begins to overheat the labour market, even the financial markets might not react unfavourably. Anyway, with considerable excess capacity, inaction is no solution in the face of growing unemployment.

The second part of the problem is to devise suitable programmes for government spending. Going against received wisdom, it needs to be pointed out that extensive labour training schemes of various sort cannot be of much help. Because, although it might improve labour productivity, without strong demand-side policies such training would only raise the bar for entering the labour market. Thus, while the better trained persons would probably have a higher chance of getting a job, macro-economically it would not be a very effective policy for the entire labour force. It would be rather like changing the positions of the candidates in a long queue for a fixed number of jobs, without being able to shorten the length of the queue.

A better policy with respect to training might be to have a government and private sector forum to agree on the types of training needed in view of both the composition of demand and cost-effectiveness. The training programmes would be partly financed by the government on the understanding that the private firms would simultaneously provide on-the-job training as the rest of the financing.

Second, instead of large centralised projects, it might be better to decentralise them. This would at least have the advantage of identifying the regions in which government spending has been relatively more effective in fighting unemployment, and would thus introduce an element of competition into the allocation of public funds.

Finally, in the post-industrial societies with aging populations, there might be considerable scope for creating innovative services for the aged. Note that better care of the aged is a demand that cannot be easily saturated, and therefore provides a longer-term perspective on the directions of training and public spending. For financially sustaining these programmes, the government and beneficiaries might share the costs through voluntary schemes of using part of pension and insurance funds. It is the increased quality and productivity of labour in these so-called non-tradeable areas of services, directed at the domestic rather than the external market, in which the future for a better quality of life with higher employment in post-industrial societies may well lie.

Beyond this suggested long-term path of development of the service industry, the problem of labour-market flexibility also has another long-run aspect which is overlooked in current policy discussions. Higher labour productivity tends to reduce prices by reducing unit costs in the more competitive industries. For given money wages, this raises the product wage rates in these industries, normally implying an increase in the overall real wage rate. Therefore, unless labour productivity rises more or less in line with increasing real wage, the share of wages in income would tend to increase over time. However, the observed relative stability of the wage share over the longer run suggests that productivity growth itself adjusts to rising real wages, just as the wage claims of workers have to adjust to the growth in labour productivity. In the long run, therefore, a two-way relationship seems exist between the growth rate in wage and in productivity which might be a central driving force of 'endogenous' growth, making technology appear as 'neutral' to distribution in successful market economies (Bhaduri, 2007). In this virtuous circle of positive feedbacks or cumulative causation, growth in productivity tends to raise the real wage rate by lowering unit costs and prices due to competition among firms, while rising real wages induces firms to increase productivity for maintaining their profit margins. Viewed from this longer-run perspective, artificially imposed wage restraints might well weaken this complex positive feedback mechanism between productivity and real-wage, to weaken economywide increasing returns. This process has been recognised as a potent dynamic force in the successful development of capitalism, at least since Adam Smith identified division of labour as a main source of the wealth of nations. To ignore this dynamic force propelling long-term growth in the name of labour-market flexibility might turn out to be counter–productive, and not a sign of wisdom for the longer term successful management of capitalism.

References

1. Bank for International Settlements (2001), *Central Bank Survey of Foreign Exchange and Derivatives Market Activity in April 2001,* preliminary global data, press release (9 October).
2. Bank for International Settlements (2002), 'Quarterly Review of International Banking and Financial Markets Development', *Statistical Annex* (March 2002).
3. Bhaduri, A. (1986), *Macroeconomics: The Dynamics of Commodity Production,* London, Palgrave Macmillan.
4. Bhaduri, A. (2007), 'Endogenous Economic Growth: A New Approach', *Cambridge Journal of Economics,* 30: 69–83.
5. Bhaduri, A. and Marglin, S. (1990), 'Unemployment and the Real Wage: The Economic Basis of Contesting Political Ideologies', *Cambridge Journal of Economics,* 14: 375–95.
6. Bhaduri, A. and Steindl, J. (1985), 'The Rise of Monetarism as a Social Doctrine', in P. Arestis and T. Skouras (eds.), *Post-Keynesian Economic Theory,* Weatsheaf, Sussex (Reprinted in chapter 7 here).

7. Friedman, M. (1968), 'The Role of Monetary Policy', *American Economic Review,* 58: 1–17.
8. Hobsbawm, E. (1994), *The Age of Extremes; A History of the World, 1914–1991,* New York, Pantheon Books.
9. Kalecki, M. (1971), 'Political Aspects of Full Employment' [1943], in M. Kalecki, *Selected Essays in the Dynamic of the Capitalist Economy,* Cambridge, Cambridge University Press.
10. Layard, R., Nickell, S. and Jackman, R. (1991) *Unemployment, Macroeconomic Performance and the Labour Market,* Oxford, Oxford University Press.
11. Marglin, S. and Schor, J. (eds.) (1990), *The Golden Age of Capitalism,* Oxford, Oxford University Press.
12. McLuhan, M. (1960), *Explorations in Communications,* Ontario, University of Toronto Press.
13. Rowthorn, R. (1977), 'Conflict, Inflation and Money', *Cambridge Journal of Economics,* 1: 215–39.

9

Joblessness*

Abstract: The paper is divided into three parts, and a summary at the end. Part one explains how policies conditioned by historical circumstances moved away from the objective of high employment. Part two deals with the theoretical controversies in support or against particular policies. Part three sets out the basics in theory needed for a high employment policy. The paper concludes with a summary suggestion of some operational steps and observations. While the first part of the paper covers the same ground as Chapter 8, the part dealing with the operational aspects of an employment policy traverses new ground.

Key-words: Unemployment, Budget Deficit, Globalisation, Decentralisation, Domestic and Foreign Markets.

JEL Classification: E24, E61, E62, E66.

Historical Background

It is somewhat paradoxical that market economies, even under the system of representative political democracy, can live with high unemployment, and place relatively little emphasis on this problem, except perhaps at times of elections. Various plausible explanations can be offered, and perhaps they all contain some elements of truth. After all, the deep change in the climate of economic management, in sharp contrast to the post-WWII years of policies in pursuit of full employment in advanced market economics, is

---

* *Brazilian Journal of Political Economy, vol. 25, no. 2(98),pp.45–59, April-June/2005.*

unlikely to be the consequence of any single cause. As historical narratives often remind us, changes in history are seldom mono-causal; instead, they are usually the result of several factors and processes coinciding at a particular juncture of time.

The climate of opinion against the Keynesian style of demand management in pursuit of high employment advanced gradually for at least three interrelated reasons. First, the Keynesian argument was almost self-consciously set in the context of an economy closed to international trade and capital flows. The intention may well have been to emphasise the importance of domestically oriented economic policies for fighting unemployment. After all, the disastrous consequences of 'beggar-thy-neighbour' policies of trying to export unemployment through competitive devaluation of the national currencies during the inter-war period was still fresh in memory, while the prestige of the 'City of London' in propounding the virtues of 'sound finance' was in ruins (Bhaduri and Steindl, 1985). It was rather natural in that context to look inward for a domestic solution to the problem of unemployment.

Second, although the contest between the competing systems of capitalism and socialism was most visible in the Cold War arms race, its ideological dimension was essentially economic. The socialist system appeared capable of providing full employment through deliberate state policies, although much of that employment was neither satisfactory to the employees nor socially gainful. (A common joke of the time in these countries was, "they pretend to pay, we pretend to work".) In the capitalist market economies the level of employment depended largely on the decision of private business, posing an opposite problem: although the jobs it provided had to be gainful to the private employer, even if private and social gain differed, the level of economic activity was prone to cyclical fluctuations, at times resulting in severe and persistent unemployment. Given this known difference in the performance of the two systems, even initiatives like Marshall Plan tended to be influenced at least partly by the economic competition between the two systems (Hobsbawm, 1994). It was also around this time that the welfare state found wider political acceptance, with its theoretical rationale in Keynesian demand management policies. The rising real wage with near-full employment, leading to rapidly improving standards of living for the working population under this new style of economic governance in most Western democracies could be posed as a counter-challenge to the socialist ideology.

Third the very success of demand management, high employment, and rising mass consumption, which had ushered in a 'golden age' of welfare capitalism through rapidly expanding domestic markets for nearly a quarter century, came to be troubled by its own contradictions (Marglin and Schor, 1990). Years of high employment had reduced the fear of job-loss for the workers, and increased workers' wage claims. Against this background, the experiences of the two major oil price increases of the 1970s made it clear that the burden of such shocks could not be passed on easily to the workers. The model of cooperative capitalism of the welfare state was giving away to the model of conflictive capitalism, in which struggle over the distribution of income tended to manifest itself through inflationary or stagflationary price rises (Rowthorn, 1977). Even more problematically, the fiscal policy of the state itself got entangled in this distributive conflict, as both the workers and their employers tended to pass on the additional tax burden to one another (Bhaduri, 1986; ch. 6). Understandably, targeting inflation rather than unemployment became the new focus of policies. New economic doctrines, at times reviving old ideas that had been pushed aside by the success of Keynesian economic policies, returned in academic circles and policy discussions under the broad heading of Monetarism. Ironically, monetarism revived the Marxian idea that a "reserve army of labor" is needed to keep a check on the real wage. Kalecki (1943, reprinted in 1971) had already made use of a similar idea towards the end of the Second World War to predict that "political trade cycles" would be imposed deliberately, particularly in the name of sound finance (read: no deficit financing), to inflict unemployment from time to time in order to keep control over the workers. These ideas returned in the orthodox monetarist framework as the 'natural rate' of unemployment, NAIRU (Layard, Nickell and Jackman, 1991). The common theme underlying these policies held that keeping inflation and inflationary expectations under control requires accepting a certain, even fairly high, rate of unemployment. In particular, it requires giving up demand management policies intended to keep the rate of unemployment lower than that 'natural' or NAIRU rate. Since deficit financing by the government had been the most potent instrument used for demand management, unsurprisingly it came under special attack. The doctrine of 'public choice' theory proclaimed the virtues of a balanced budget and the evils of a fiscal deficit by a self-seeking government. These were held as general truths, applicable to almost all countries under all circumstances.

These theories and policy perspectives directed against the welfare state and Keynesian policies were embedded in the wider process of globalisation that had been going on mostly through gradual expansion in post-war international trade. However, they gathered irresistible momentum with the deregulation of national capital markets, from mid-1970s in the OECD countries. The greater economic opening in the trade of goods and services meant an increase in the relative importance of the foreign or external market compared to the domestic or internal market. It encouraged countries to stimulate demand through export surplus, rather than through demand management by government fiscal policies. As a result, each country try to be more price competitive than its neighbours by cutting unit cost through wage restraint and labour market flexibility, on the one hand, and by rising labour productivity on the other. Yet there is an obvious 'fallacy of composition' in this strategy: all countries cannot achieve export surplus at the same time, as the export surplus of some must be matched by the import surplus of others. Moreover, even for any particular country that *does* manage to achieve an export surplus in this international zero sum game, such policies may turn out to be counter-productive if the contraction in the size of its internal market more than outweighs the expansion of its external market.

The danger of contraction of domestic demand from such policies is serious. Wage restraint depresses consumption by working people, while labour productivity growth brought about by corporations through downsizing of the labour force reinforces this depressive effect. The overall consequence might be a decrease in the size of the domestic market despite an increase in the external market through export surplus. Analytically, this may be identified as the wage-or-consumption-led regime, in which wage restraint and downsizing have depressive effects that outweigh their possible stimulating effect on investment and export (Bhaduri and Marglin, 1990). Nevertheless, the danger of a sharp decline in domestic demand tends to be overlooked for reasons that have become almost the defining characteristic of the current phase of globalisation.

It is well known that the deregulation and liberalisation of capital markets since the mid-1970s has phenomenally increased the volume of private trade in foreign exchange. With a daily volume of some 1.2 trillion dollars, such trade far exceeds the total foreign exchange reserves of all the central banks put together. Foreign and investment combined account for less than four per cent of private trade in foreign exchange. Thus, in formulating their economic policies, national governments feel obliged to abide by the sentiment of the extremely powerful financial markets, particularly because finance can move across borders at a moment's notice. Expansionary fiscal policies for fighting unemployment through either (a) deficit spending or (b) imposing higher taxes on the rich to expand government programs, are generally not favoured by the financial markets. In this context, tax cuts remain almost the only option for stimulating demand, which might, of course, cause larger budget deficits. Similarly, so-called 'easy money' policies, in which low interest rates aim to boost economic activity, are often seen as suspect, as signals of the government's intention to embark on expansionary policies which might, in turn, lead to trade deficits or capital outflows.

The typical consequences of abiding by the sentiments of the financial market have been over-sensitivity to inflation, insistence on the independence of the central bank, and a near-paralysis of fiscal and monetary policies. Variations on this policy package are found in some developing countries, but also in developed countries. They tend to deliberately keep the domestic interest rate high for attracting short-term capital inflows, even if it discourages investment at home. Note the general point that all such policies have the same economic consequence of reducing the relative importance of the domestic compared to the external market.

Multinationals tend to erode further the space left for national economic policies. Governments in developed economies tread softly in so far as taxing corporate profits are concerned. Not only are footloose corporations capable of shifting to low-tax locations, but they can also make use of transfer pricing: out-sourcing through various practices of intra-firm trade to show profit at more convenient points. And, though intra-firm trade, (estimated conservatively at 40 per cent of all manufacturing trade) appears as international trade, national governments have little control over it. Governments in developed countries try to deal with multinationals by forming supra-national arrangements about uniform taxes, competition policies, etc. However, among the developing countries, typically a 'race to the bottom' takes place. As countries hope to improve their trade balance by becoming part of intra-firm trading networks, the link to such networks may indeed be the most tangible benefit of FDI, though the level of technology or skills transfer varies across country and sector, and remains a topic of controversy.

Theories and Counter-theories on Unemployment

This alternative perspective, marked by its neglect of domestic demand and the domestic market, and which aspires to replace the Keynesian consensus, is neo-liberal in essence. Contrary to the Keynesian view that markets fail seriously—as when insufficient domestic demand inflicts serious unemployment—and thus need to be managed through public action, neo-liberalism emphasises the opposite point of view. It wants to roll back government, on the assumption that the market by and large performs better than the state. The extreme view is to claim that markets never fails. Put differently, it is claimed that market outcomes with available information cannot be improved upon by government intervention, a view associated with the so-called 'new classical' school of economic theory and 'efficient market' hypothesis for financial markets. A more moderate view is to suggest that the markets fail only because the price mechanism does not function properly at times, mainly due to incomplete information, e.g. information being asymmetrically distributed. This view, associated with various versions of 'neo-Keynesianism,' leaves some room for government action through correcting the price mechanism. Nevertheless, in so far as unemployment is concerned, both schools share a common economic philosophy that, conforms to the 'neo-classical' view of unemployment. This view more or less rules the current academic and policy orthodoxy, and has three distinguishing characteristics contrary to the original Keynesian paradigm.

First, unlike Keynes and Kalecki, who identified the lack of effective demand in the market for goods and services as the *central* cause of unemployment, these theories look directly at the labour market to explain unemployment. Thus the causation runs directly from the labour market, and not indirectly from the product market, to unemployment. In terms of policy, this means demand management in the product market becomes less important that correcting the bad-functioning of the labour market.

Second, even the branch of neo-classical theory sympathetic to the Keynesian view (e.g. the neo-Keynesians), tends to make a distinction between the "short run", when there may be insufficiency of demand in the product market, and the 'long run', when the demand problem is resolved by the market. This kind of dichotomy between the short and the long run is most starkly visible in nearly all versions of neo-classical long run growth theory.

Third and perhaps most basic to this neo-classical way of thinking, is the philosophy of 'methodological individualism'. It uses some procedure of optimisation by the individual agent as the central organising principle of macro-economic theory. Approaching macro-economic problems exclusively in this way has many serious ramifications, and with regard to the unemployment problem, perhaps its most serious consequence is to blur the distinction between 'voluntary' and 'involuntary' unemployment. All unemployment, even mass unemployment, begins to look voluntary in this framework, because it has to be explained through some optimising decision by the individual worker. The problem then becomes attributable to high wage demanded by the workers or, to imperfect functioning of the price mechanism for giving wrong signals to the unemployed worker. In some theories, government interventions, mostly related to the welfare state, are supposed to distort the signals carried by wages in the labour market. In this framework either the jobless worker becomes responsible for his or her own situation; or the blame is put on government intervention. Needless to add, this serves well the neo-liberal cause.

A basic attraction of this neo-liberal theory stems from its implicit policy implication because, the market ideology has a very different kind of advantage over the government. It is seldom mentioned explicitly, but follows from the present body of theoretical knowledge on the subject. Even under the most idealised circumstances of perfect competition—when the competitive equilibrium has all the desirable properties of Pareto optimality by the so-called 'fundamental theorem' of welfare economics—nothing in economic theory specifies *how long it might take to reach that equilibrium.* This ambiguity helps is sustaining the market ideology. In democracies, the government and the politicians in power remain accountable to their people at regular time intervals through elections, but the market mechanism has no such definite time horizon for showing results. It can always be claimed that, given 'sufficient' time and 'sufficiently' wide-ranging pro-market reforms, the desired results would materialise, without having to specify how long is sufficiently long. In this respect, the market mechanism, like a dictator, can always promise without actually delivering!

The enormous power wielded by the electronic media and television images in shaping public opinion was noticed even in the very early stages of globalisation by perceptive commentators (e.g. McLuhan, 1960). In particular it helps in spreading a sort of a popular culture of economic policy, which is the lowest common denominator of economic theory, and can be easily comprehended by men and women of 'practical affairs'. In this respect, easiest to comprehend is the analogy of the individual. Since spending beyond one's means is bad, a government budget deficit is considered bad; since the demand for apples can be raised by lowering their price, the demand for labour can also be raised by lowering the wage rate; since hard work helps one to get ahead, so a corporate manager helps the economy to get ahead by downsizing its labour force. Underlying all of these popular pronouncements in the media is the neo-liberal foundation of 'methodological individualism'. Unfortunately, even politicians who know better often feel helpless, because political expediency demands that they do not swim against the popular current.

This popular culture of viewing macro-economic policies exclusively through the lens of methodological individualism goes against the very logic of Keynesian-style demand management, which followed from a demonstration of the misleading nature of the analogy of the individual. The macro-economy is characterised by a circular flow of expenditure and income where, unlike in the case of the individual, expenditure, i.e. expenditure and demand determines income and output in situations of mass unemployment.

The Basics of Policies for High Employment

It is against this intellectual background that we need to reconsider policies for attaining and sustaining higher employment in developing countries. At the outset it is worth pointing out that many different types of projects may be devised for generating employment. By and large, these projects would be country-specific, dependent on geography, stage of development, degree of openness, etc. and general prescriptions like labour or local resource intensive technology are hardly helpful. The purpose of macro-economic theory in this context is not to list a set of such projects irrespective of their country-specificity, but to indicate how to devise a programme for generating and sustaining high employment in developing countries.

The preceding discussion already pointed that the responsibility of maintaining high employment has gradually passed from the government to the market. This view is reinforced further in developing countries in two ways. First, the 'less-government-more-market' economic philosophy propounded generally by the Bretton Woods institutions operates with full force through 'conditionalities' imposed on developing countries experiencing balance-of-payments difficulties. Second, it is further reinforced by the governments in developing countries themselves, in so far as they often find it politically expedient to escape accountability by attributing the problem to the market and to the Bretton Woods institutions. The result is a set of 'market-friendly' policies for employment generation which may or may not produce the desired results within any given time horizon. In either case, the market cannot be held responsible for delivering within a given time period.

In the context of the unemployment problem, the most important feature of market-friendly policies has been to look upon wage simply as the major element of production cost for private employers, and not as an important factor in determining the size of the total domestic market. The result is to focus exclusively on the labour market, instead of paying sufficient attention to the fact that no cost-cutting measure can succeed in isolation without sufficient demand. The various measures that are undertaken—wage restraint, downsizing of the labour force, change in labour laws that makes it easier to hire and fire employees, revision of pension fund laws in favour of the employer, curbing workers' rights to strike, etc.—are like designing a more and more efficient private boat without enough water, in the public river of effective demand for it to float!

The dependence on the private sector to solve the employment problem is also a slippery path, especially in the context of globalisation. The more a developing economy tries to integrate with the world market, the stronger the pressure becomes for reducing unit cost through the labour market for achieving international competitiveness, or for attracting foreign direct investment and other forms of capital flows. This dependence impacts employment policies adversely in two different ways.

First, labour productivity growth that makes more goods and services available for domestic use is not pursued as a desirable objective in itself; instead, its desirability is judged in terms of enhancing international competitiveness. Note also that more goods and services would be available in the aggregate from higher productivity *only* if higher productivity does not quantitatively outweigh a decrease in employment; whereas unit cost would decrease and enhance competitiveness so long as productivity per worker rises irrespective of the level of employment. Thus, the exclusive focus on competitiveness and profit separates the productivity objective from the employment objective, making, for example, the down-sizing of the labour force attractive in terms of unit cost, but not necessarily in terms of either aggregate supply *or* demand. Moreover, if demand fails to expand sufficiently fast to absorb both productivity and labour force growth, the result would be growing unemployment, and various scenarios of jobless growth.

Second, the preoccupation with cost reduction leads to a focus on micro-efficiency at the level of the enterprise, but downplays macro-inefficiencies that result, such as serious unemployment due to insufficient demand. This has led to a blurring of the distinction between good management of an enterprise or household , and sensible management of the economy as a whole. The former usually takes the market size for a product as broadly given (with some product differentiation, related to new products, etc.) by the income of the actual and potential customers. The typical objective of any particular enterprise is to increase market emphasise, **share** rather than the total market **size** through competitive micro-efficiency; whereas it is precisely the purpose of macro-management to ensure that the overall market size expands at a sufficient pace to absorb both the growth in the labour force and its productivity. There are, however, two rather special circumstances in which this enterprise management view might succeed: either by stimulating exports, or by raising private investment sufficiently through these micro-incentives of cutting costs.

In the former case, the micro-efficiency paradigm could increase the international market share of the country concerned in a successful scenario of export-led growth. But it must be remembered that this is an international zero sum game, and there must be winners as well as losers in this game. It cannot help all developing countries, especially the most disadvantaged among them that suffer from acute technological backwardness, limited diversification of exports, etc. In the latter case, the micro-efficiency paradigm might stimulate sufficiently the profitability of private investment to expand demand, and therefore the size of the market, through the multiplier in a scenario of investment-led growth (Bhaduri and Marglin, 1990). Investment-led growth is an unlikely outcome, and is more a logical rather than a real possibility. Because measures such as lower wage reduces total consumption expenditure to depress investment despite higher profitability; whereas higher labour productivity without a proportionate increase in the wage rate, raises surplus and potential profit per worker, but does not create an adequate market to dispose off the surplus (Bhaduri, 1986). The central point to remember is that micro-efficiency in cost reduction has to result in sufficient expansion of macro-demand. The frequently made policy mistake is to think that this is an automatic outcome.

The pitfalls in this process are indeed many. For instance, exports not only need to expand, but must exceed imports sufficiently to produce the necessary export surplus; otherwise demand would not expand sufficiently. Therefore, this strategy can work only for those countries that can achieve a sufficient export surplus, while other countries with corresponding import surplus depressing their demand would face a serious problem. For this reason, trying to promote exports with very high levels of imported content typically fails in many developing countries.

There is no certainty either that private investment on a macro scale would be sufficiently stimulated through micro efficiency at the enterprise level. Private investment in fixed capital needs to take a long view of the prospects for profit. Therefore, it tends to respond sluggishly in general to an increase in current profitability. More important, however, is an inherent coordination problem. Unless many firms become simultaneously convinced that their profit prospect has increased over a relatively long time horizon, aggregate demand will not increase sufficiently through private investments. On the other hand, each individual firm will hesitate to move first, so long as other firms remain passive in their investment demands. Thus, relying exclusively on micro-efficiency at the enterprise level to solve the unemployment problem becomes fraught with many difficulties. In general, the more severe the problem of unemployment is, the more difficult becomes the problem of coordination, and of convincing the private investors that the climate for investment has indeed improved.

Given these difficulties, perhaps the most obvious starting point for breaking the inertia of low employment is through the budgetary policy of the government. Current orthodoxy in economic theory, greatly helped by the Bretton Woods institutions in the developing countries, takes the view that budget deficits are undesirable in general, and insists that the fiscal deficit of the government, estimated with or without interest payments on outstanding public debt, must not exceed a certain percentage of the GDP. There are two common objections against running large deficits. The first stems from the burden of servicing this debt; the second from repeated recourse to large deficit as a 'soft option' by an irresponsible government with dangers of inflation (see chapter 10 for elaboration in the Indian case).

The first objection has greater force if the debt is external, and needs to be serviced in foreign exchange by a developing country. A high level of external debt squeezes import capacity, and carries in addition the danger of precipitating a financial crisis, if for some reason foreign lenders try to withdraw their credit in a panic. However, with internal debt these objections are less serious, and often invalid. When an economy is growing and the government remains credible, there is no obvious limit to the extent a government can borrow further to service its debt. It is rather one-sided to suggest that only the level of public borrowing, and no other indicator, like growth or employment level, affects the credibility of the government. Thus, in the face of serious unemployment the central issue is not whether the government should run a large deficit to finance its employment-generating strategies, but whether such a strategy would be effective and financially sustainable. Three conclusions regarding the government's budgetary policy follow: (a) More caution should be applied in contracting foreign debt, and premature capital account convertibility; (b) a bureaucratic limit on the extent of the permitted budget deficit is unfounded in macro-economic logic; and (c) close examination is needed not of the deficit, but of whether the deficit can be effective in fighting unemployment and sustaining a high level of productive employment.

The second objection, about government budget deficit as a dangerous soft option, is mostly ideological. It follows from a general mistrust of the government, which is often, but not always, justified. The government, like the market, often fails, and fails miserably. The way to approach this issue is to consider whether some correction mechanism would be in place in case of serious and continuous failures by either institution. As already pointed out the market mechanism is not self-correcting in the sense of being 'close' to equilibrium within any given time horizon; nor does it have any in-built mechanism to correct income distribution or promote development and high employment. Thus, it might be rational to accept a solution that improves upon what the market might attain within some given time frame.

However, it must also be remembered that the experiences of bureaucratic central planning showed how disastrously things could go wrong with no self -correcting mechanism in place. This is especially true without the economic accountability of the government in the absence of political democracy. In the light of experience, a pragmatic compromise between these two most essential institutions, the state and the market, seems unavoidable.

A more balanced approach that adopts a less ideologically coloured position would be to let both these essential institutions develop in a historical 'double movement' of mutual checks and balances (Polyani, 1944). In this process, each would have to restrain the other from becoming over-dominating. By and large, this seems to have happened in most cases of successful development of the market economies. Employment policies, like any others, need to be devised without upsetting this dynamic balance. Thus, when the market fails visibly to cope, as in the case of serious unemployment, the state has to initiate actions, and not leave matters to market incentives. Conversely, when the state over-reaches and tries to create socially unproductive employment in an unsustainable manner, the market has to reassert it ability to restore the balance. There is clearly no once-and-for-all answer in this complex game of balancing that is valid under all circumstances. It is more correct to view this process as a 'challenge and response' between these two major and equally essential institutions.

Both for immediate employment creation, and for its longer run sustainability through growth, it must be remembered that the notion of a resource constraint for the economy as a whole is different from that of the financial budget constraint facing an individual unit. With serious unemployment, excess capacity and inventories, the economy is not constrained by finance, but by how well it can make use of these underutilised resources. In these situations, it makes little sense to restrain the government from deficit financing by some inflexible rule in the name of 'sound finance' . It also seems rather besides the point to talk of the 'independence' of the central bank to follow a tight money policy. It would be wiser instead to start from the real economy and arrival at more flexible monetary and financial policies. The mistake of monetarism has typically been to start the other way round.

In particular, if excess capacity exists in the relevant domestic capital goods industries with unemployment, useful economic and social infrastructural investments can be undertaken through budgetary or financial support from the government. It is not wise to wait for domestic or foreign private investment to solve the problem of growing unemployment or deepening recession, because the more persistent and serious the problem, the more difficult it becomes to turn around private expectations. As a matter of fact, in many developing countries public investment would act as a catalyst to 'crowd in' rather than 'crowd out' private investment first by increasing the size of the domestic market and second, by providing better infra-structural facilities to raise profitability. Needless to add, the impact of these investments on employment would be positive, and stronger if some of its construction components can be made labour-intensive.

Nevertheless, the fundamental Keynesian insight that higher expenditure by the government would activate underutilised recourses to generate more income and saving to finance the higher level of government spending has to be applied with some caution to suit the conditions of particular countries. So long as basic wage-goods are not in cripplingly short supply or, as a second best option, can be imported, identifying the broad direction for starting a public investment programme is easier. Widespread poverty, or at least concentrated pockets of poverty, presents an opportunity for policy makers to devise useful public works through guaranteed employment schemes at some minimum wage for a certain number of days per year. The minimum wage would have to be paid for empolyment on demand, and a degree of self-selection to attract mostly the poor and needy is built into the scheme.

However, despite the self-selection mechanism, these schemes tend to be wasteful in different ways. Policy packages that are often chosen by a remote, non-accountable centralised bureaucracy often turn out to be useless, because they fail to be sensitive to local needs. Very often, they also suffer from 'giantism', i.e. unnecessarily big and technologically complicated projects which a centralised bureaucracy can handle more easily, but in which the unutilised and relatively unskilled labour cannot contribute effectively. A large percentage of the funds also tends to leak out in administering these public works, with the result that only a small fraction usually reaches the needy poor for whom it is intended in the first place. On the other hand, a large machinery for supervision increases the leakage by raising administrative cost, but without it, there is the danger of non-performance, inefficiencies and corruption.

The way out of this dilemma is to take recourse to decentralisation as far as possible with two added provisions. First, while the decentralised local bodies would have control over the use of the funds, there must be transparency of their budget through a legally recognised right to information which has to cover both the central bureaucracy and also the decentralised local bodies choosing and implementing the projects. The free availability of information naturally must apply both to the available funds and their disbursements. Second, to sustain such programmes over time, attempts should be made to move increasingly towards the principle of '(s)he who benefits should (partially) pay'. This has to be based on two different pillars. The first is the pro-private sector policy. It would extend the schemes to specified types of capital formation on private property, chosen on the basis of their desirability by the local community, and having some social benefits or positive externalities—e.g. small irrigation, land improvement, linked pathways through private land, etc. These would benefit directly one or more private owners, but also indirectly the larger community. They should also have the potential for sustaining employment at the local level, even when undertaken on private land or property provided approved by the whole community.

The second pillar of this policy would be to ensure that the private owners who belong to the local community, and voluntarily participate to benefit directly, have to bear a part of the cost—e.g. in terms of paying part of the minimum wage bill, or in paying a lump-sum to the local body as capital gains on completion of the projects. Additionally, while such payments would be to the local entities for their own use, they must be based on transparent rules. This would reduce both the cost to the local bodies and the need for supervision as the beneficiary himself or herself would be interested in the quality of the work done. In other words, it would be a way of subsidising socially useful capital formation through private incentive at the local level without losing sight of the public employment objective. Within limits, the above argument may also be extended to the use of some social infrastructural facilities like secondary schools and vocational training centres, where the beneficiaries should bear part of the cost, which could be on a progressive scale decided by the local bodies.

It has often been suggested that better training schemes raise the aggregate level of employment. Experiments with various 'voucher schemes' to determine the type of training demanded by the voucher-holders have been tried on a limited scale to make these schemes more responsive to individual needs and preferences by creating miniature local markets, in which the vouchers act as 'votes' for choosing the particular training schemes. The schemes devised to mimic the market mechanism often turn out to be flawed, in so far as the schemes with maximum votes do not always turn out to be either very useful for the community or for getting jobs (Lepenies, 2004). The reason for the latter is that training facilities by themselves usually cannot generate more employment on the macro-scale, because they are pure supply-side policies. There must either be latent demand already in the market for those skills, or conscious demand-side policies must complement them. Training either raises the bar on entry to the labour market, or it becomes like shuffling the long queue for jobs, where the better trained are placed in the front without shortening the queue.

The connecting thread in this argument so far has been to point out the importance of domestic demand-led growth with adequate policy space for government action as the essential prerequisite for high employment policies in developing countries. Although larger-sized countries have the advantage of a larger domestic market, this perspective on policy is also useful for the smaller countries. However, large and small are rather relative terms in this context, especially because the size of the market depends both on population and on per capita income. Therefore, regional cooperation, based on the guiding principle that the domestic policy space should not suffer, is to the advantage of all irrespective of size. This would be a feasible proposition only if democratic rights are observed. And, in the international context, the defining characteristic of any civilised democracy is the protection of minority rights, i.e. the right of the smaller or poorer nations, rather than the brute force of majority rule by the larger nations. The current process of globalisation has generated discontent and disenchantment precisely because it has failed in this respect.

Concluding Observations

The basic elements of a policy for generating and sustaining high employment may now be summed up briefly.

(a) *A minimum-wage employment guarantee scheme:* This will kick-start the programme in face of serious unemployment, especially in rural areas.

(b) *Decentralisation of activities and administration:* This should take place through local bodies with gradual extension to private properties based on the principle of '(s) he who benefits should (partially) pay'.

(c) *Transparency regarding the allocation and use of funds:* Ensuring this requires recognising the right to information at all levels with respect to funds.

(d) *Domestic demand-led expansion:* This is the cornerstone of this strategy, which means placing due emphasis on the domestic market, rather than being preoccupied with the external market. In this sense, it is not an export-led growth strategy, because most developing countries cannot achieve an export surplus in an international zero-sum game. Nor is it an import substitution policy, because that too is motivated largely by considerations of the external market and foreign exchange. Our emphasis instead is on changing the composition of investment to promote and sustain employment. It is decentralised Keynesianism, less reliant on a centralised bureaucracy.

(e) *Ensuring that the objective of productivity growth is not separated from employment growth:* This separation typically happens if productivity growth is considered only as an instrument for enhancing competition or generating profit. But it is forgotten that higher productivity along with higher employment makes more goods and services available for the domestic market, and the poor.

(f) *An environment of sufficient growth:* Only a sufficiently expanding market can accommodate both labour productivity and labour force growth. While government policies can influence to some extent that rate of expansion of the market through its monetary and fiscal policies, it is important not to follow policies exclusively in search of productivity growth, since the latter makes sense only if productivity is considered a weapon for international competition. It is more important to recognise that, specially in poor countries with various types of technological backwardness and handicaps regarding international marketing, increased productivity is desirable to augment the availability of output from the supply side, to be matched by an increased level of demand through higher employment.

(g) *Increase the social content of wages:* Decentralised public works leading to more economic and social overhead and infrastructural facilities helps in increasing the social content of wage and earnings from self-employment, especially of the poor people. Local bodies should try to ensure that this becomes a reality. This would help in reducing the need for an increase in private wages and make such employment generating schemes more self-sustaining.

The Role of the Informal Sector in Employment Generation: Some Observations

Many developing countries are facing the serious problem of rapidly expanding cities and mega-cities with deteriorating infrastructure due to the massive influx of jobseekers in the urban sector. This has meant, on the one hand, more and more resources going into the cities in a desperate attempt to cope with the problems of urban infrastructure, with an attendant lack of resources being used to improve rural infrastructure. The result has been a steadily growing urban-rural divide, and a phenomenal growth of the so-called informal sector. It is not merely the direct pull of higher expected earning in urban employment that leads to in-migration into cities (Harris and Todaro, 1970), but also the indirect pull that operates because the urban centres are generally far better equipped with economic and social overheads. This can be looked upon as the 'social content' of wage or earning, and an objective of decentralised public works would be to reduce the gap in the social wage and earning.

Employment in the informal service sector has grown very rapidly in many developing countries. A high percentage of this employment is not wage employment but self-employment, and for these workers the separation of total earning between wage and profit income is rather meaningless. The entire self-employed category consists of a relatively small percentage of high-level professionals, and, often, a very large percentage of the poor who take refuge in it part or full-time both in the urban and in the rural sector, because they have no other opportunity for livelihood. In any employment policy, it is essential to consider this segment, typically with massive disguised underemployed. By and large, the productivity of these workers, at least in the short run, depends not so much on the capital equipment or skill they possess, but on the level and composition of demand, and on the infrastructural facilities that they can use (Reddaway, 1962; ILO, 1972). One of the advantages of decentralised demand-led policies, which would usually involve improving local infra-structural facilities especially in non-urban areas, is to be able to reach out to these people who are often among the very poor.

For generating and sustaining employment in the informal, less-skilled services several interrelated aspects need to be considered. First, and in a way most obvious, is the emphasis on better irrigation and water management, as well as communication. Apart from increasing the productivity and intensity of land use, better water management allows crop diversification to absorb considerably more labor per hectare of land, and better communication is a prerequisite for the commercialisation of agriculture, without which crop diversification cannot succeed. In countries that are not predominantly agricultural, or have natural limitations, conscious attempts have to be made to develop a symbiotic relationship between the organised and the unorganised sector through sub-contracting, out-sourcing, etc. For this relationship not to be exploitative, the government might have to use both regulations and incentives (e.g. tax break for such sub-contracting to informal units). At the same time, independent artisan producers and design and marketing support, channeled as much as possible through decentralised local bodies need receiving performance-related funds for this specific purpose from the government.

The way to visualise the strategic link between the general macro-economic policies for domestic demand-led expansion and the informal sector is to develop the notion of 'nodal points' of economic activities for employment generation partly through measures like regulated sub-contracting and partly by enabling local communities to market their product both for the community itself, and for urban centres and other areas. They would mostly have to work backwards from demand, somewhat like the 'accelerator principle' in economic theory. In the past, policies in this respect often failed in many countries, because more emphasis was laid on the supply side, without creating the necessary demand links, either from the local markets in the rural areas or from the organised industries or urban centres. The concept of a 'node' might be a helpful starting point, in so far as various types of demand from these different sources would have to converge for the transformation of the informal sector from mostly a 'refuse sector' of the poor and desperate job seekers into a genuinely dynamic sector of the economy.

References

1. Bhaduri, A. and J. Steindl (1985), 'The Rise of Monetarism as a Social Doctrine', in P. Arestis and T. Skouras (eds.) *Post-Keynesian Economic Theory*, Sussex, Wheatsheaf, 24–56.
2. Bhaduri, A. and S. Marglin (1990), 'Unemployment and the Real Wage: The Economic Basis of Contesting Political Ideologies'. *Cambridge Journal of Economics* (14) 375–93.
3. Bhaduri, A. (1986), *Macroeconomics: The Dynamics of Commodity Production*, London, Macmillan.
4. Friedman, M. (1968), 'The Role of Monetary Policy', *American Economic Review* (58) 1–17.
5. Harris, J.R. and M.P. Todaro (1970), 'Migration, Unemployment and Development: A Two-Sector Analysis', *American Economic Review*, 60: 126–142.
6. Hobsbawm, E. (1994), *The Age of Extremes: A History of the World, 1914–1991*, New York, Pantheon Books.
7. ILO— International Labor Organization (1972), *Employment, Income and Equality*, Geneva, ILO.

8. Kalecki, M. (1971), 'Political Aspects of Full Employment' in his *Selected Essays in the Dynamics of the Capitalist Economy*, Cambridge, Cambridge University Press.
9. Layard, R.S. Nickell and R. Jackman (1991), *Unemployment, Macroeconomic Performance and the Labour Market*, Oxford, Oxford University Press.
10. Lepenies, P. (2004), 'Exit, Voice and Vouchers: Using Vouchers to Train Entrepreneurs— Observations from the Paraguayan Voucher Scheme', *World Development*, 32: 713–724.
11. Marglin, S. and J. Schor (1990), *The Golden Age of Capitalism*, Oxford, Clarendon Press.
12. McLuhan, M. (1960), *Explorations in Communications*, Ontario, University of Toronto Press.
13. Polyani, K. (1944), *The Great Transformation*, New York, Holt, Rinehart and Winston.
14. Reddaway, W.B. (1962), *The Development of the Indian Economy*, London, Allen and Unwin.
15. Rowthorn, R. (1977), 'Conflict, Inflation and Money', *Cambridge Journal of Economics*, 1: 215–239.

10

The Politics of Sound Finance*

With the retreat of Keynesianism in the advanced industrial economies and the Fund-Bank backing a whole array of financial market friendly policies, including those based on the principle of sound finance, the United Progressive Alliance government is falling in line by being overly concerned about the perception of private foreign investors. In this context one needs to consider what strategic interests are being served by the implementation of the Fiscal Responsibility and Budget Management Act. The paper relates aspects of Keynesian economics to Indian politics since liberalisation.

The Retreat of Keynesianism

The climate of opinion in almost all the advanced industrial countries of Europe has turned decisively by now against the Keynesian style of demand management in pursuit of contra-cyclical stabilisation and the high employment objective. In the US its acceptance had always been less enthusiastic, and the doctrine lost intellectual respectability even more easily. The process began in the late 1960s, and a decisive turning point came with the 'stagflation' of the 1970s following the two oil shocks. Nevertheless, such dramatic changes in the intellectual climate seldom have a single cause. In this case, three reasons come immediately to mind. First, the Keynesian argument was almost self-

* Published in *Economic and Political Weekly*, 4 November 2006

consciously set in the context of an economy closed to international trade and capital flows. The intention might have been to emphasise the importance of domestically oriented economic policies for fighting unemployment. After all, the disastrous consequences of 'beggar-my-neighbour' policies of trying to export unemployment through competitive devaluation of the national currencies during the inter-war period was still fresh in memory, while the prestige of the City of London for propounding the virtues of 'sound finance' was in ruins [Bhaduri and Steindl, 1985; Chapter 7 of this volume]. It was rather natural in that context to look inward for a domestic solution to the problem of unemployment. However, the global setting changed vastly by late 1970s. Not only had the volume of international trade grown, but even more significantly the 'dollar standard' agreed at the Bretton Woods had collapsed to usher in a new regime of flexible exchange rates and deregulation of capital accounts. It was easy to claim in these circumstances that the Keynesian theory is outdated.

Second, although the arms race was the most visible aspect of the contest between the competing systems of capitalism and socialism in the Cold War years, its ideological dimension was rooted in economics. The socialist system appeared capable of providing full employment through deliberate state policies, although much of it was neither satisfactory to the employees nor socially gainful. (A common joke of the time in these countries was, "they pretend to pay, we pretend to work".) In the capitalist market economies the level of employment depended largely on the decision of private business with an opposite problem. The employment it provided had to be necessarily gainful to the private employer irrespective of whether private and social gain differed. However, the level of economic activity was prone to cyclical fluctuations, at times resulting in severe and persistent unemployment. Given this visible difference in the performance of the two systems in terms of employment, initiatives like the Marshall Plan were influenced by the economic competition between the two systems [Hobsbawm, 1994]. It was also around this time of post-war reconstruction that the welfare state found wider political acceptance, with its theoretical rationale provided by Keynesian demand management doctrine. And, over time under this new style of economic governance with a rising real wage at near-full employment, leading to a rapidly improving standard of living for the working population, most Western democracies could be posed as a counter-challenge to the socialist ideology.

Third, there was also an ironical side to it. The very success of Keynesian demand management with high employment and rising mass consumption, which had ushered in a 'golden age' of welfare capitalism, came to be troubled by it own success [Marglin and Schor, 1990]. Years of high employment had reduced the fear of job-loss for the workers, and increased workers' wage claims. Against this background, the experiences of the two major oil price shocks of the 1970s made it clear that the burden of such shocks could not be passed on easily to the workers. The model of cooperative capitalism of the welfare state was giving away to the model of conflictive capitalism, in which conflict over the distribution of income tended to manifest itself through inflationary or stagflationary price rise. Even more problematically, the tax policy of the state itself got entangled in this distributive conflict, as both the workers and their employers tended to pass on the additional tax burden to one another. Understandably, targeting inflation rather than unemployment became the new battle cry of economic policies. New economic doctrines, at times reviving old ideas that had been pushed aside by the success of Keynesian economic policies, returned in academic circles and policy discussions under the broad heading of monetarism. A central idea was the 'natural rate' of unemployment [Friedman 1968], or its modified version of the non-accelerating inflation rate of unemployment (NAIRU). The underlying common message of these theoretical constructions was that, keeping inflation and inflationary expectations under control requires accepting a certain, at times fairly high rate of unemployment. In particular, it requires giving up demand management policies intended at keeping the rate of unemployment lower than 'natural' or NAIRU rate.

The new terminology of monetarism revived in a way the Marxian idea that a 'reserve army of labour' is needed to keep a check on the real wage rate. Kalecki (1943, reprinted in 1971) had already made use of a similar idea towards the end of the Second World War to predict that, in order to keep control over the workers, 'political trade cycles' would be imposed deliberately in the name of sound finance (read, no deficit financing) to inflict unemployment from time to time. Since deficit financing by the government is the most potent instrument for demand management, unsurprisingly it came under special attack. The doctrine of the virtues of a balanced budget, and the evils of a fiscal deficit by a self-seeking government were propounded in the name of 'public choice theory' as general truths, applicable to almost all countries under all circumstances. The International Monetary Fund (IMF) and the World Bank, known for their adherence to economic doctrines that restrain the economic role of the government, predictably found 'sound finance' a particularly welcome idea to impose on developing countries.

The emerging policy perspective directed against Keynesian welfare statism was embedded in a wider process of globalisation that had been going on mostly through gradual expansion in post-war international trade. However, it gathered irresistible momentum with successive waves of deregulation of the national capital markets since the mid-1970s in OECD countries. These two aspects of greater economic openness due to globalisation, in trade and, in finance undermined Keynesianism in different ways.

The greater economic opening up in goods and services trade means an increase in the relative importance of the foreign or external market compared to the domestic or internal market. Stimulation of demand through an export surplus rather than fiscal policies requires each country to be more price competitive compared to its rivals, by cutting unit cost through measures like wage restraint, flexibility in labour contracts, and higher labour productivity through downsizing the labour force. And yet, there are obvious 'fallacies of composition' in this strategy. First, all countries cannot achieve an export surplus at the same time. Even if a particular country manages to achieve an export surplus in this international zero sum game, such policies may still turn out to be counter-productive, if the contraction in the size of its internal market more than outweighs the expansion of its external market. Wage restraint would depress consumption by the working people, while labour productivity growth brought about by the corporations through the downsizing of the labour force reinforces this depressive effect. The overall consequence might turn out to be a decrease in the size of the domestic market despite an increase in the external market through an export surplus in the wage-led regime, in which, the depressive effect on consumption of the wage restraint and downsizing outweigh its possible stimulating effect on investment and export [Bhaduri and Marglin, 1990].

The second aspect of openness resulting from financial deregulation of capital markets since the mid-1970s increased phenomenally the volume of private trade in foreign exchange. In comparison to its daily volume of some 1.2 trillion dollars, the total foreign exchange reserve of all the central banks together barely amount to a couple of days' volume of private trade. Foreign trade and investment together do not account for even 4 per cent. In formulating their economic policies, national governments can no longer ignore the sentiments of the private traders in the financial markets. Since expansionary fiscal policies for fighting unemployment through a budget deficit, or higher taxes on the rich to expand government programmes are generally not favoured by financial markets; instead regressive tax cuts, stimulation of the stock and real estate market through monetary or tax policies have become preferred options for managing demand. Politically it makes a mockery of the original Keynesian and social democratic vision of cooperative capitalism, in which a neutral state is supposed to follow more even-handed policies towards capital and labour. The typical consequences of abiding by the sentiments of the financial market have been over-sensitivity to inflation and a tight money policy to discourage capital outflows through insistence on greater independence of the central bank, and most importantly, a near-paralysis of expansionary fiscal policies through higher government expenditure under the false pretence that wage restraint, labour market flexibility and labour training can substitute for demand management policies.

The Indian Case

What goes under the names of IMF 'conditionalities' and the Washington "consensus" bears unmistakeable resemblance to the array of financial market-friendly policies mentioned above. Not surprisingly, the IMF and the World Bank as leaders of multinational banks and financial institutions encourage developing countries to pursue these policies under normal circumstances. And, when developing countries in balance of payments difficulties turn to them for assistance, these policies are imposed. Viewed from this angle, the Fiscal Responsibility and Budget Management (FRBM) Act of 2003 has implications that might have been less obvious at first sight. Note that the Act was not crisis-driven, but strategy-driven. It was enacted at a time when the Indian economy was not facing any particular international payments crisis; instead our foreign exchange position was comfortable and the stock market was booming. So we need to consider what strategic interests of the Indian economy would be served by this Act.

The Act, by crippling government action certainly does not serve the interests of the poorer section of the Indian population. It is a cruel joke in the present Indian context to talk of intertemporal optimal choice involving successive future generations when about half of our children remain undernourished, with India heading in the 21st century as the country with the highest number of illiterates and homeless. By virtue of this Act, directly the central and indirectly the state governments are restrained from spending in social sectors like basic education and health. In particular, it starves the recent Rural Employment Guarantee Act, constrains even minimal social security in the unorganised sector, all justified under the banner that a prudent government has no money! It is simply anti-poor in the name of financial prudence. This is particularly unfortunate at a time when the excess demand from higher government spending can be met to a significant extent through utilisation of existing excess capacity in many of the critical construction materials and wage goods sectors, and a comfortable reserve of foreign exchange has accumulated to smooth over particular supply-side bottlenecks. The standard Keynesian argument has a very good chance of succeeding in rural India in these circumstances in expanding productive employment. However, this cannot happen unless government spending is genuinely decentralised by giving financial autonomy to the gram sabhas to decide on the local investments, and panchayats to execute the spending. For this purpose the nationalised banking system can provide support under greater transparency of the Right to Information Act [Bhaduri, 2005]. Yet, almost no serious initiative is in sight except tall political talk: instead, we hear of road maps for liberalising the capital account, special economic zones, privatisation of basic services in the name of public-private partnerships, and restricting the scope of the Right to Information Act.

Even in a hypothetical scenario not favourable to employment expansion, greater spending would lead to some increase in prices. Mostly wage goods prices would increase. In effect, however, it means from the rest of the society a redistribution of income in favour of the poorest sections among the unemployed who starve today without an employment guarantee scheme. Should not the government try to strengthen system in rural areas, giving more teeth to the Right to Information Act? What we are seeing instead is that, both the central and the state governments are unduly cautious in expanding the employment guarantee scheme for the poorest. So we must return to the question: what is the economic strategy behind this Act, enthusiasm about which is shared by this and the previous coalition government, i.e., all political parties in the parliament?

The imprint of rising financial interests on India's development strategy has been unmistakeable in recent years. While economic policies are increasingly being formulated as never before with a view to the sentiments of the financial markets, the dominant English language media shaping Indian middle class opinion, behave as if the daily fluctuations of the stock market are the barometer to judge the health of the real economy. Since the Indian stock market is pathetically small in relation to the vast global trade in foreign exchange, the rupee and Indian stocks can easily be set into an uncontrollable downward spiral by a few large international players speculating against some Indian stocks or the rupee, while the increasing quantitative importance (about 52 per cent of inflows) of anonymous 'participation notes' (PN) might leave the origin of such a crisis unnamed.

Things have been gradually developing in this direction over several years under the guise of economic reforms. It is no longer about dismantling the police inspector raj, or improving the efficiency of the public sector. Indeed, one of the factors behind the drive to privatise public enterprises and public provision of basic services has been to generate the resources to narrow the fiscal deficit. Clearly, the game has changed. Recall how the Dalal Street nose-dived immediately after the 2004 general elections results, because a few large, mostly foreign institutional investors began to withdraw from the Indian capital market under the fear that a coalition government supported by the Left will be unfriendly towards private businesses. However, as soon as the United Progressive Alliance government named its top economic team, a trio of the prime minister, the finance minister and the deputy chairman of the Planning Commission, all known for their extreme pro-market, pro-finance and pro-corporation outlook, the stock markets began to shine again in no time. Nothing had changed about the ground realities of the Indian economy in those few weeks, except international finance capital needed assuring political signals. In the process, the future course of economic policies for the country got set.

The confidence that the team of economic policy-makers enjoy with the IMF and the World Bank is a critical part of the story, because those two institutions are in a pivotal position to influence the perception of private foreign investors like multinational corporations, banks and other financial institutions. This is the name of the game that is being played under the name of sound finance.

References

1. Bhaduri, A. (2005), *Development with Dignity,* New Delhi, National Book Trust.
2. Bhaduri, A. and J. Steindl (1985), 'The Rise of Monetarism as a Social Doctrine' in P. Arestis and T. Skouras (eds.), *Post-Keynesion Economic Theory,* Sussex, Wheatsheaf, pp. 24–56.
3. Bhaduri, A. and S. Marglin (1990), 'Unemployment and the Real Wage: The Economic Basis of Contesting Political Ideologies', *Cambridge Journal of Economics,* 14: 375–93.
4. Friedman, M. (1968), The Role of Monetary Policy', *American Economic Review,* 58: 1–17.
5. Hobsbawm, E. (1994), *The Age of Extreme: A History of the World, 1914–1991.* New York, Pantheon Books.
6. Kalecki, M. (1971), 'Political Aspects of Full Employment' in his *Selected Essays in the Dynamics of the Capitalist Economy,* Cambridge, Cambridge University Press.
7. Marglin, S. and J. Schor (1990), *The Golden Age of Capitalism,* Oxford, Clarendon Press.

11

Reflections on the Role of the State in Economic Development (with Special Reference to Large Predominantly Agrarian Economies)*

Defining the Problem

The state can be involved in economic development (or underdevelopment) in so many different and complex ways that it is necessary first to demarcate somewhat precisely the problem under discussion. Precision in this context means simplification, but hopefully not over-simplification to the point where it can become misleading.

It is useful to begin with a tangible and not too ambitious index of economic development. For that purpose, we shall assume that increase in per capita income is the main index of economic development. Despite the fact that the 'quality of life' is not determined entirely, or, at times even primarily by the level of income, the emphasis on per capita income with some attention to the pattern of income distribution is probably the best workable index that we have of economic development in the very poor countries. It bears emphasis that, when the overall labour productivity and per capita

---

* From: *The State and the Economic Process:* edited by C.W.M. Naastepad and Servaas Storm Edward Elgar, Cheltenhorm, U.K., 1996, pp. 51–66. The paper is based on a lecture in memory of Sukhamoy Chakravarty in the Hagne.

output are exceedingly low, neither significant redistribution nor environmental consideration alone can go very far in raising the quality of life. On the whole, therefore, it seems worthwhile to begin by focusing attention on per capita income or output as the strategic variable underlying economic development, with respect to which the role of the state may be discussed.

It is a matter of the simple arithmetic of weighted averages to decompose statistically per capita income into its three major components:

(a) the participation ratio, i.e. the ratio of active to total population;

(b) the occupational distribution, i.e. the distribution of the active population among (say) the three major sectors of the economy, namely, primary (agriculture), secondary (industry) and tertiary (services); and finally

(c) the sectoral productivity of labour, i.e. output of value added per worker in each of those sectors.

Together they yield the identity[1]

$$y = k\sum_j x_j w_j, \sum_j w_j = 1 \qquad (1)$$

where y = per capita output;

k = participation ratio;

x_j = labour productivity in sector j;

w_j = proportion of labour employed in sector j (i.e., occupational distribution);

and j = a (agriculture), i (industry) or s (services)

This arithmetical truism decomposes the factors on the supply side influencing capita output as the index of economic development. Consequently, the role of the state influencing the 'supply side' may be more conveniently discussed in terms of that decomposition. Note in this context that the state is also a fuzzy concept with the usual distinction—not operationally valid in some developing countries—between the legislative, the executive and the judiciary. In economic discussion, it is common to emphasise mostly the executive functions of the state, because it has a direct bearing on the formulation and execution of economic policies. We shall generally narrow down the problem by thinking of the role of the government, i.e. mostly the executive functions of the state in economic development. Nevertheless, its legislative functions, especially in relation to property rights in land in predominantly agrarian economies would also receive some attention in the course of our discussion.

Employment and the Participation Ratio

Particularly at times like the present, when the failure of central planning in earlier command economies has been only too apparent, it is worth reminding ourselves that the early years of central planning in most of these countries saw an almost dramatic increase in the participation ratio. By drawing in under-employed labour from traditional agricultural into land-improving activities through various agricultural cooperative organisations, especially countries like China and Vietnam enjoyed a pattern of high extensive growth in the immediate post-revolution period, roughly for a decade or so.[2]

As far as can be judged from various historical experiences of capitalistic development, there is no obvious counterpart to tapping one of the main sources of economic growth through a state-sponsored rapid increase in employment and the participation ratio.[3]

The reason for the absence of any dominant pattern of extensive growth in the market economies is not far to seek. The rule of the market dictates labour to be used only up to the point where its use is profitable to the private employer at market prices, in other words, the marginal-value product of labour has at least to equal the wage rate. The short-term advantage of extensive growth arises from deliberately pushing the utilisation of labour beyond this point. So long as the marginal product of labour remains positive, something is gained by employing the hitherto unemployed labour, especially in rural construction works like irrigation, drainage, road-building, etc., which can be carried out in a labour-intensive manner. Nevertheless, it was a mistake of central planning to believe that such employment creation can sustain itself for long.

The pattern of extensive growth is beset with two different sets of difficulties. The first relates to the decline in labour productivity and the second relates to the problem of financing during the process of extensive growth. Since the logic of this strategy lies in more than recouping in terms of the volume of employment what may be lost in terms of labour productivity, there is a strong tendency for labour productivity to decline, at least in the early phases. The problem seems more manageable in the case of agriculture, because many of the simplest forms of capital formation in agriculture have a large component of construction work which can be carried out by almost bare-handed labour drawn from the large pool of open or disguised unemployment in the early stages of extensive growth. The consequent shift in the *composition* of output and employment in favour of immediate non-consumable (investment) goods with also a higher absolute level of employment implies that the quantity of consumption goods produced per *employed* person is lower, i.e. labour productivity measured in terms of immediate consumable goods must fall, although in the longer run this may be more than recouped through the higher capital formation in agriculture. The pattern of extensive growth in agriculture therefore implies a reduction in per capita consumption of the already employed population in the short period and a sacrifice of *their* present consumption for the future. For the society as a whole, it may mean no sacrifice as it implies redistribution from the already employed to the unemployed plus additional output by employing the so far unemployed.

The 'financing' of the pattern of extensive growth hinges essentially on the question of how to effect the redistribution of consumption from the already employed to the formerly unemployed. Three broad options seem available: (1) direct transfer by the state through consumption rationing, (2) inflationary redistribution through the market mechanism, and (3) some forms of property tax.

Given a minimum socially acceptable real wage rate, any attempt to utilise labour beyond the point where the marginal product of labour falls below that wage would involve deliberate employment creation through redistribution of income by the state. If income from property is unimportant, this involves redistribution of income from the already employed to the unemployed, perhaps through some elaborate rationing system of consumption goods. However, this invariably creates a serious problem of incentives to work on the one hand, and an elaborate bureaucracy on the other to handle the problems of rationing. Moreover, as the problem of incentives appear increasingly severe under this pattern of extensive growth, the government has an almost natural tendency to resolve them bureaucratically, e.g. by setting plan targets, trying to monitor work-in-progress, etc. Bureaucratisation of the planning process weakens the incentive structure even more. It is a vicious circle that we have observed as the common experience in so many centrally planned economies.

In the mixed, developing economy, attempts to raise the participation rate through extensive growth are likely to encounter a somewhat different type of problem. The real wage may still need to be reduced, but instead of direct rationing, it may come about through the mechanism of 'forced savings' associated with inflation. Essentially, the prices of consumer goods would have to rise faster in percentage terms than money wages to redistribute income in favour of property income. Since, by and large, the property owners would have a higher propensity to save than the wage (and normal salary) earners, the reduction in the real wage rate entails higher savings to 'finance' the process of extensive growth.[4] However, two political implications of this process deserve special emphasis. First, inflation can be a very unjust and inefficient way of financing extensive growth in a mixed economy. Because it requires reducing the real wage to an extent where it not only finances the higher wage bill resulting from drawing in the unemployed workers into the extensive growth pattern, but also has to finance the higher consumption by the property owners, resulting from the redistribution of income in their favour. To put it dramatically, even an extremely regressive tax falling exclusively on wages could be less burdensome from this point of view than forced savings by the workers under inflation.[5]

Second, the financing of a higher level of investment through forced saving generated by inflation is not only grossly iniquitous, it can also become an ineffective instrument of policy. For instance, successful real wage resistance by the workers could lead to an unending process of inflation without generating the higher saving necessary to finance a higher level of investment. In that case, the economy would be exposed to all the social costs of unending inflation, without necessarily achieving a higher rate of (extensive) growth. Therefore, on grounds both of equity and of the danger of unending inflation, the price mechanism appears to be ill-suited to 'finance' the strategy of a high rate of extensive growth in a mixed economy.

The alternative to forced saving by the workers is to devise a scheme of taxation whose incidence falls mostly on property income. A particularly attractive solution that has been suggested from time to time in that context is the imposition of a sort of 'capital gains' tax on the various improvements in the value of private land which would be expected to accompany typically the process of extensive growth in a predominantly agrarian, mixed economy. However, such a scheme of taxation is likely to encounter severe problems posed by private ownership rights in land. It is not easy to design land improvement schemes on a large scale (e.g. major irrigation, road, drainage, etc.) by respecting strictly private property rights in land; nor is it administratively or legally easy to ascertain and attribute the increases in land value to private holders of land, especially if such improvements are brought about without the prior consent of all the individual property holders in land who are likely to be affected by the scheme.[6] It seems without considerable decentralisation of the taxation scheme at the level of local government, this method would have little chance of success in large countries.

The justification for this tax can be viewed as a classic case of 'external economies' generated by public investment while the benefits are internalised by private property owners in land. However, the market does not seem to offer any easily implementable solution as to how to finance the cost of creating these external economies in the first place. And yet, to create such external economies is precisely one of the central problems facing the development of backward agriculture.[7] It may be emphasised in that context that unless the state is empowered with legislative and executive rights to generate external economies through public investment whose cost it would recoup subsequently from taxing the private beneficiaries, the problem of recurring deficit in public finance (e.g. government budget) would arise. The sensible solution is not to preach the virtues of a balanced budget or financial austerity, but to devise ways to tax private beneficiaries of public investment.

Industrialisation and the Occupational Structure

The strategy for industrialisation of an underdeveloped, predominantly agrarian economy formed the core of traditional development economics in the post-war years. The question of industrialisation was closely linked with changing the structure of occupation. The empirically justified assumption underlying that discussion was the relatively high labour productivity in industry compared to agriculture which carries surplus labour. Consequently, industrialisation was seen as the route that allows overall productivity and per capita income to rise through intersectoral labour transfer from agriculture to industry. In discussing the role that the market might play in that context the main question was whether the price mechanism could be relied upon to induce industrialisation at a more or less acceptable pace.[8] Economic intervention by the state could be justified in terms of various forms of 'market failures', i.e. the failure of the temporal as well as intertemporal price mechanism to give correct signals towards the required direction of economic change. A remark in passing is that this paradigm assigns to the state primarily an executive role in economic development which is defined by the scope of conventional welfare economics, but overlooks largely the legislative role that it might also have to play regarding property rights, as mentioned earlier.[9] In more recent years, the 'market-failure' argument has been counterpoised against the 'government failure' argument in various forms. Its gist is to point out that, if the market mechanism cannot be expected to function in a perfectly competitive manner, nor can the government be expected to act always more wisely than the market to satisfy the dictums of welfare theory.

The argument about government failure has two extreme versions. In the radical view, the government would seldom act in a wise, neutral manner, because it must attend particularly to the interests of the 'ruling class' that it represents. At the other end of the spectrum, we have the 'public choice' theory of the government, where the government acts more or less like a glorified, selfish individual to serve its own interest. For instance, it may regulate production to generate quasi-rents from the artificial restrictions on production in order to have a share in it. If, in the eyes of the radicals, the economic policies of the government are driven mostly by the interests of the ruling class, in those of the neo-liberal conservatives they are driven by a hopelessly self-seeking government which has only its own interest in mind. In either case 'government failure' looks no less (or more!) plausible than 'market failure' in guiding resource allocation for industrial development, because fundamentally the neutrality of the government as a social institution is questioned. And, even if neutrality could be assumed, one could argue that, while market prices may not contain adequate information, there is little reason to believe that the government would have better information. To put it in a nutshell, lack of neutrality and lack of better information seem to be the two basic reasons for neo-liberal scepticism about government intervention in economic development.

Posed as a general problem of 'market failure' versus 'government failure' , the issues must look indecisive. They can only be settled on the basis of political prejudices with little room for reason. However, this is subject to an important proviso. While political prejudices are extremely important we have also learnt from historical experiences. Government control in an extreme form resembling a command economic structure without any regard to the market forces has been known to encounter insurmountable difficulties in the longer run. This observation holds despite the fact that it may raise the participation ratio in the short run, and also provide essential public goods like higher literacy and better public health care. Experiences of many socialist countries point both to these short-term gains, as well as insurmountable long-term problems.

As a stylised fact, state-led industrialisation typically meant removing what are identified usually as the major macro-economic constraints on development. Under central planning production of capital goods was rapidly increased by directing most of the public investment towards heavy industries, according to the orthodox Marxist postulate of 'the leading role of department 1'.[10] In so far as industrial investments are concerned, this analytically meant putting the 'acceleration principle' in reverse. Thus, the positive feedback from increased demand (capacity utilisation) for consumer goods to inducement for higher investment for raising the capacity for consumer goods production ceased to operate. In its place, the volume of pattern of investments were guided by non-market bureaucratic decisions, which in turn through the multiplier and income elasticities of demand created a corresponding level and pattern of demand. Put more simply, under central planning, the increase in capital-goods production governed the production of consumption goods through time (acceleration principle in reverse), rather than the other way round. It meant that no strong feedback from the level and pattern of demand for consumption goods to the level and pattern of investments was accommodated in such an industrialisation strategy. Ignoring market forces in this way boiled down to getting the time sequence in the development of industries almost systematically wrong. It deserves emphasis here that, despite its ruthless bias against the poor, the market mechanism has been capable of fostering growth with interruptions of business fluctuations, by allowing the demand-generating multiplier effect of investment to interact with the acceleration effect, influencing the level and composition of investment.[11] In a fundamental sense, both the level and the pattern of investment in a market economy tend to be *demand-led*, i.e. the process of income generation reflected in the level and pattern of market demand determines what and how much should be produced. No doubt, it contains a strong bias against the poor, because their low purchasing power does not allow their needs to be reflected in the market. And yet, the alternative of a *supply-led* process of growth, where the level and composition of investment and output are largely state-governed and bureaucratically determined, encounters even more serious problems through time as the experiences of the centrally planned economies have shown. In this specific sense, the arguments about the failure of the government to govern the process of industrialisation have some validity in the light of the experiences gathered. It may often be true that the government is neither 'neutral' nor sufficiently 'informed' to sponsor a viable pattern of supply-led growth—as various critics of the role of the state in development have so frequently pointed out.

Nevertheless, the lesson to be learnt from this experience is not the ruling conventional wisdom that the state should have a 'minimalist' role, hardly going beyond investments in social infrastructure, like education and health. Experience and our theoretical understanding of it point to something quite different, namely that the economic role of the state must change according to the stage of economic development and the particular situation. Thus, with a lot of surplus labour in agriculture, the case is still overwhelmingly strong for the state in its executive as well as legislative capacity to be involved in a pattern of extensive growth. But at the same time, the fact must be recognised that extensive growth is a transitory, initial phase of capital formation in agriculture and the state has to withdraw subsequently rather than scuttling private incentives in agriculture over a long period.

On the other hand, the decision which industries to develop and in what sequence need not be a supply-led process even when the state has an active 'industrial policy' to pursue. The pattern of industrialisation, as already pointed out, must incorporate adequately the influence of the market. In essence, it must be a demand-led process. The state would still have an important economic role to play, but that must be directed more towards influencing the pattern of demand through time, than towards bureaucratic control of a process of supply-led growth.

In a developed market economy, demand management is identified almost exclusively with Keynesian expansionary fiscal and monetary policies. While these short-period policies are still important to overcome the short-run deficiencies of effective demand, economic development also involves longer-term structural problems of demand management. And, even in a predominantly demand-led process of industrialisation, the role of the state in this respect deserves special emphasis. For instance, land reform, agricultural price support or an employment guarantee scheme are not only important on distributional or incentive considerations; they may be useful also for their influence on the structural aspects of demand management. The essential problem is easy to see. In a predominantly agrarian economy, demand management in the longer run would be highly problematic (and probably iniquitous), unless labour productivity rises rapidly in agriculture, because the volume of agricultural surplus plays a dual role. It provides essential wage goods and raw materials for industry on the supply side and it generates demand for industrial goods by agriculture on the demand side, at least in so far as the internal market is concerned. In that context, it is perhaps not altogether an accident that countries like Japan, Republic of Korea or Taiwan, which otherwise followed successfully a market-oriented, demand-led industrialisation strategy in the post-war period, had as their initial condition significant land reform aimed at productivity improvements in agriculture through various measures such as land redistribution, revision of tenurial conditions, agricultural credit, marketing reforms, etc. The improved agricultural productivity provided them with an expanded home market for industrial goods which in some cases could be a testing ground for export promotion and in others, it complemented the export market to yield greater scale advantages.

To avoid misunderstanding of the nature of demand-led industrialisation it should also be pointed out that the time sequencing of investment is not determined in this context simply by the backward and forward demand linkages of inter-industrial transactions, which featured prominently in the 'balanced versus unbalanced growth' debate in the 1960s. The time sequence of investment is determined instead by the level and pattern of *final* demand. In other words, it is the demand generated in the sphere of final rather than inter-industrial demand which has a critical role to play. Let two examples suffice to illustrate the point. First, if a developing country succeeds in promoting its exports rapidly, the external market plays a leading role. In that case, the investment sequence, operating through the 'acceleration principle', goes from developing those directly exported goods to the investment goods and services needed for exports. (Perhaps a small country like Singapore or Hong Kong concentrates more on services than on the manufacture of investment goods.)

On the other hand, if a country does not succeed in promoting its exports at a sufficiently rapid pace, the expansion of its internal market for consumption goods has to take the leading role. In that case, the 'acceleration principle' underlying demand-led growth, works largely by propagating the impulse of growth from the internal or home market for consumption goods to the 'derived' demand in the markets for services and investment goods. The role of the state could be market-friendly because it is demand-led, in both the former outward and the latter inward-oriented case. However, in the latter case, it has an even greater role in terms of demand management in the home market not only through monetary and fiscal policies, but also through structurally sustaining demand through measures such as agricultural productivity growth, and initiating programmes of rural employment creation in a decentralised manner.

While demand-led industrialisation can proceed by relying primarily either on the internal or the external market, a special advantage of relying on export promotion is the international discipline it enforces in terms of quality and cost efficiency on domestic production. However, this needs also to be weighed against the greater difficulties encountered in transmitting the impulse of growth from higher exports to the domestic production structure of an underdeveloped economy. For instance, the capital goods and services needed to maintain the quality of export cannot usually be produced at home. When imported, they tend to weaken the demand impulse of the accelerator-type mechanism.[12] Thus, in contrast to the successful cases of export-led growth which integrate export promotion with domestic production structure, we also have frequent instances of 'export enclaves' that are mostly de-linked from the domestic production structure of the developing economy. The lesson seems to be that, even if the external rather than the internal market can play the leading role in a demand-led process of industrialisation, the external market cannot be relied on, for transmitting automatically the impulses of growth to the domestic production structure. The state would have a role to play in integrating the external demand impulse in the domestic production structure so that export promotion does not degenerate into islands of disjointed 'export enclaves'.[13]

Sectorial Labour Productivity and The Role of Agriculture

An implicit assumption underlying the traditional strategy of industrialisation has been that a changing composition of GDP would also lead to a corresponding change in the occupational distribution. However, the assumption that industrialisation measured by a changing composition of GDP in favour of the manufacturing sector would also mean intersectoral labour transfer in favour of manufacturing has not been borne out by several recent experiences. For instance, almost all countries of South Asia in the post-World-War-II period have experienced a significant change in the composition of GDP in favour of industrial output, but with only a relatively small decline in the proportion of workforce in agriculture. This means arithmetically that labour productivity in agriculture has declined relative to the overall productivity level in the economy.[14] This declining agricultural productivity relative to other sectors needs to be viewed against the fact that the sectorial labour-productivity differentials between the developed and the developing countries tend to be highest in agriculture (about 15 times) compared to industry and organised services (3 to 5 times).[15]

However, the relatively low labour productivity in agriculture is not purely, or even primarily, a technological phenomenon. It is not primarily a technological gap created by lack of technical knowledge; instead, very often its origin is in the socioeconomic structure of a developing country and in the nature of economic management. In other words, it is the consequence of economic policies and of production relations in agriculture. Better techniques improving productivity cannot be adopted on a large enough scale in agriculture because of the barriers created by the agrarian economic structure. Conventional market-oriented economics tends to be simplistic and to put the entire blame on wrong government price policies which do not encourage the peasants to produce more. There is some truth in this, especially in the case of sub-Saharan Africa until the mid 1980s. However, like most half-truths, this can be a highly misleading over-simplification.

On the supply side, price response by the farmers requires a minimum of economic infrastructure such as control of water to grow alternative crops, credit and marketing reform to avoid distress sales, local storage facilities and road links to the market. It is difficult to visualise how the price mechanism alone can create these pre-conditions for price response, especially by the small farmers, without involving the state. In a parallel vein, even long-term private investments in land improvement in the form of minor irrigation, feeder channels, etc. are unlikely to occur on an adequate scale unless the state plays an active role in assuring ownership rights or long-term secured use-right of land to the tenants and consolidation of fragmented land-holding. These are pre-conditions which not the market, but the state can fulfil in its legislative and executive capacity, especially in a large, predominantly agrarian economy.

It also needs to be emphasised in this context that the international gap in land productivity is considerably lower than in labour productivity. For instance, most of the poorest developing countries in Asia harvest between one to two metric tonnes of rice per hectare, while the new varieties of rice have raised average yields to over six tonnes per hectare in America, Australia, Japan and South Korea.[16] Thus, while land productivity differences are only about three to four times, the labour productivity difference is as high as 15 times between the developed and the developing countries. This points to the compulsion of intensive use of land with sharply diminishing return to labour in an overcrowded agriculture in many developing countries. In other words, the problem of agricultural productivity cannot be solved without creating greater opportunities for alternative gainful employment, especially of family labour in small-sized farms on the one hand and raising land productivity in agriculture on the other. The traditional answer of development economies to this question has been to rely on industrialisation to transfer labour out of agriculture. But all arithmetical projections in populous agrarian economies (e.g. in South Asia) suggest that the required pace of industrialisation would be almost certainly unfeasibly high to make any significant dent into the problem within a reasonable period of time.[17] In general, market forces cannot do the job of raising agricultural productivity without the pre-conditions being present and, for some of the reasons mentioned earlier, state-sponsored industrialisation has also failed to transfer labour from agriculture to industry in a gainful manner. The way out of this development impasse in large, populous and predominantly agrarian economies is far from clear. But two elements which reinforce each other in the process of development seem essential. First, the state needs to be actively involved in raising agricultural productivity, primarily through public investment in agriculture. Both the nature of private property rights in land as well as the 'free rider' problem, make public action essential for large-scale land development, irrigations, drainage and rural communication network. Fortunately, in the early stages extensive growth can provide some help in this respect. This has to be supplemented by adequate price incentives to the direct producers. But 'getting prices right' alone cannot be expected to do the job unless the state creates the pre-conditions, preferably through extensive growth. Second, higher labour productivity in agriculture would normally create also non-agricultural income earning opportunities in rural areas. And by raising the level of agricultural surplus available to be exchanged for manufacturing, it would also boost the demand for domestic industrial products and create the basis for demand-led, market-friendly industrialisation so long as the intersectoral terms of trade do not move drastically in favour of either sector.[18] The government needs to play a critical role, both in raising the level of agricultural productivity through public investment and in maintaining a steady expansion of the home market for manufactured goods through an intelligent intersectoral terms-of-trade policy as well as other demand management policies. Without such an active involvement of the government, which must be able to decentralise decisions and financing of local projects there market no escape route from poverty, with or without market liberalisation, in large, agrarian economies.

Summing Up

1. Any attempt at raising the 'participation ratio' through extensive growth must be viewed as a transitory phase. While extensive growth requires large-scale government involvement, the danger of bureaucratisation of economic decisions is also exceptionally high in this phase. And unless this danger can be avoided, the extensive growth strategy may later turn out to be counter-productive (Section II).
2. The sterile controversy over 'market failure' versus 'government failure' needs to be avoided as far as possible. Instead, a fruitful focus of the enquiry could be the time sequence of investment decisions, in the process of industrialisation. The main thrust of our argument has been that the sequence should be determined primarily by considerations of final demand in a process of demand-led growth but not by supply linkages. In that respect, the analysis is Keynesian/post-Keynesian and differs from more conventional thinking in terms of only the supply side. However, demand management must also be

'structural', focusing on such factors as improvement of productivity in agriculture suited to local requirements through decentralisation (Section III).

3. There seems no escape route from poverty in large, populous, agrarian economies without a rapid rise in labour productivity in agriculture. This would have the double potential of creating non-farm income opportunities in rural areas and expanding the internal market for manufactured goods. Public investment and involvement by the state to reorient property rights in land are essential for raising labour productivity in agriculture. Neither economic liberalisation nor the price mechanism can achieve this on its own.

Notes

1. Let X = income (GDP), N = population and L = labour force. Per capita income, y, is derived in the text as:

$$y = \frac{X}{N} = \frac{L}{N} * \frac{X}{L}$$

$$= \left(\frac{L}{N}\right)\left(\frac{X_a}{L_a} * \frac{L_a}{L} + \frac{X_j}{L_i} * \frac{L_1}{L} + \frac{X_s}{L_s} * \frac{L_s}{L} = k\sum_j x_j w_j, \sum_j w_j = 1\right)$$

where $k = \frac{L}{N}; x_j = \frac{X_j}{L_j}; and\ x_j = \frac{L_j}{L}$

2. In analogy with the Ricardian idea of extending the margin of cultivation from the more to the less fertile soil, one could visualise the growth process as extending the margin of employment, rather than raising sectoral labour productivities through mechanism. The latter would correspond to intensive growth.
3. Perhaps the closest analogy is the public works programme, especially followed by Hitler. However, in so far as public works programmes are undertaken in a market economy, their main purpose is to affect aggregate demand which may raise labour productivity also in the manufacturing sector through higher capacity utilisation.
4. This is also the essence of the so-called Cambridge (or post-Keynesian) theory of distribution, formulated by Kaldor (1955–6). See also Kahn (1972).

5. See Bhaduri (1986, pp. 189–190).
6. One needs to distinguish between the ownership and the use (tenurial) right of land, especially in the context of backward agriculture with extensive renting in and renting out of land on various terms.
7. Water management, consolidation of spatially fragmented land holdings, rural roads, etc. belong to this category of creating 'external economics' in backward agriculture.
8. The 'dual-economy' literature initiated by Arthur Lewis' influential article (1954) has many variations on this theme. See especially Fei and Ranis (1961) and Lewis (1979).
9. See Chakravarty (1973) for an excellent analytical survey.
10. Formalised by the Feldman-Mahalanobis model. See Domar (1957) and Mahalanobis (1953).
11. Recalled that even the simplest multiplier accelerator interactions can produce either growth or fluctuations (but not both), depending on the structure of time-lags.
12. It may not even be feasible in terms of available foreign exchange.
13. However, this may be a more viable strategy in small economies, where the 'enclave' is the economy! The case of Hong Kong and Singapore come readily to mind. But even in such cases, the export activities have to transmit the impulse to the domestic service sector for sustained growth.
14. For a survey of Indian experience, see Dandekar (1992).
15. Based upon computations made by the author, using 1980–81 data from the United Nations and World Bank sources.
16. For a scientist's view of some of these problems, see Perutz (1991).
17. Capitalist development in Western Europe was greatly helped by migration to America. Such 'easy option' seems no longer available to today's developing economies. They have to rely on internal devices for bringing about changes in the occupational structure to reduce pressures on an overcrowded agriculture.
18. Both on the basis of analytical reasoning and an econometrically computable model (see Storm 1993) it has been pointed out in the case of India that 'too high' a price of agricultural (food) products reduces the real income of urban consumers and via Engel's law reduces the demand for manufacturing. On the other hand, 'too low' a price of agricultural products reduces the income of the agriculturists to depress the demand for manufacturing.

References

1. Bhaduri, A. (1986), *Macroeconomics: The Dynamics of Commodity Production*, London, Macmillan.

2. Chakravarty, S. (1973), Theory of Development Planning: An Appraisal in H.C. Bos, H. Linnemann and P. de Wolff (eds.), *Economic Structure and Development*, Amsterdam, North-Holland.
3. Dandekar, V.M. (1992), 'Forty Years After Independence' in B. Jalan (ed.), *The Indian Economy*, New Delhi, Viking, pp. 33–84.
4. Domar, E. (1957), 'A Soviet Model of Growth' in *Essays in the Theory of Economic Growth*, New York, Oxford University Press, pp. 223–261.
5. Fei, J.C.H. and G. Ranis (1961), 'A Theory of Economic Development', *American Economic Review*, 533–565.
6. Kaldor, N. (1955–6), 'Alternative Theories of Distribution', *Review of Economic Studies*, 23, No. 2, 212–226.
7. Kahn, R.F. (1972), 'The Pace of Development' in *Selected Essays in Employment and Growth*, Cambridge, Cambridge University Press.
8. Lewis, W.A. (1954), 'Economic Development with Unlimited Supplies of Labour', *The Manchester School*, May, pp. 131–191.
9. Lewis, W.A. (1979), 'The Dual Economy Revisited', *The Manchester School*.
10. Mahalanobis, P.C. (1953), 'Some Observations on the Process of Growth of National Income', *Sankhya*, 12 September, pp. 307–312.
11. Perutz, M. (1991), *'Is Science Necessary'*, Oxford, Oxford University Press, especially pp. 7–35.
12. Storm, S. (1993), *Macroeconomic Considerations in the Choice of an Agricultural Policy*, London, Avebury.

12

An Analysis of Semi-Feudalism in East Indian Agriculture *

I

This paper attempts to concretise the notion of 'semi-feudalism', as applied to the context of east Indian agriculture and also, examine some of the economic consequences that follow from it. In the course of the argument, it will also be possible to indicate the development of certain internal economic tendencies, which will ultimately contribute to the gradual transformation of this mode of production over time. To analyse the basis of historical change in the semi-feudal organisation of production, I shall study the interaction between the 'productive forces' and 'production relations' which leads to historical development. Undoubtedly, this historical process may be hastened by conscious political action on the part of individuals. But I am unable to comment meaningfully on this political aspect of the historical process. For, I do not believe, it is possible to make any relevant political analysis, without actively participating in bringing about the historical change. Indeed, there is always this very definite limit to a pure 'intellectual understanding' of a social system—we can never understand a system fully without being involved in changing it. This is the explanation for the obvious shortcoming of this paper—it lacks the

---

* Published in *Frontier*, Autumn, 29 September 1973 V6 (25–27)

accompanying political analysis. Nevertheless, in spite of its obvious weaknesses, I hope this paper may still have some usefulness in explaining why the economic system of semi-feudalism behaves, as it does.

II

Broadly speaking, there are *four prominent features* of agriculture in eastern India (and particularly in West Bengal, with which I am somewhat familiar) which justify the term 'semi-feudal'. These features are:

1. An extensive *non-legalised* sharecropping system.
2. Perpetual indebtedness of the small tenants.
3. The characteristic feature of the 'ruling class' in rural areas—they operate *both* as landowners and lenders to small tenants.
4. The specific historical character of rural 'markets' where small tenants have incomplete access to the market and are forcibly involved in *involuntary exchange* through the peculiar organisation of this sort of 'markets'.

In order to understand how the combined operation of these four features of east Indian agriculture has led to the semi-feudal mode of production, we must study these characteristics in greater detail now.

1. Sharecropping

The system of sharecropping is extensively prevalent in east India and particularly in West Bengal, under various names like 'Adihari', 'Bargadari', 'Bataidari' or 'Kishani' system. In West Bengal, as a rough estimate it has been suggested[1] that the sharecroppers constitute more than 30 per cent of the agricultural labour force and cultivate about 40 per cent of the total arable land in the State. There are approximately 24–25 lakh of Bargadars in this State, of whom only 8.9 lakh are legally registered as tenants in the record of rights. The rest are mostly tenants-at-will, who can be evicted more or less any time the landowner pleases.

At least on paper, registered tenants enjoy considerable rights. The West Bengal Land Reforms Act of 1955 stated that the tenants sharing no cost of cultivation should receive 50 per cent of the produce, while in other cases the tenant should get 60 per cent. The West Bengal Land Reform (Amendment) Act of 1970 raised the minimum share of the tenant to 60 per cent and the maximum share to 75 per cent, depending on whether he shares the cost of cultivation or not. It also gave special hereditary rights to tenants.

These laws are of little value in practice, because we must recognise that on an average 2 out of every 3 tenants are not registered and hence cannot enjoy these legal rights. As late as 1970–71, in the districts of Birbhum, Nadia and Murshidabad in West Bengal, I found that the 'agreed' (indeed, many tenants were under the impression that this is the 'legal') share of unregistered tenants varies typically between 33 to 40 per cent—around one-third share, and is almost the 'law' in practice set by conventions for unregistered tenants. We have reason to believe that the phenomenon of unregistered tenancy is probably even worse in many areas of Bihar. For example, as late as April 1973 in the Pandaual Block of Madhubani District in Bihar, "the CPI-led Kishan Sabha pointed out (to the Working Group on Land Reforms of the National Commission of Agriculture) that not a single Bataidar was recorded during the survey and settlement field operation which was concluded in that area only recently. *According to them all the staff of the Settlement Department were 'bought over' by the land-owners, as a result of which they stubbornly refused to record any sharecropper.*"[1] I shall identify this system of sharecropping, largely based on unregistered tenancy, as the first prominent feature of semi-feudalism. Unregistered tenancy with constant threat of eviction, gives the landowner a highly *personalised* form of economic power over his tenants, which is a distinguishing feature of feudal relations of production.

2. Perpetual Indebtedness

The small tenant is almost always indebted. He borrows grains during the agricultural lean season, mostly to pay back in grain just after the harvest from his "legally stipulated or agreed" share. On an average, for each kilogramme of paddy that he borrows in the lean season, he has to pay back 1½ to 2 kg of paddy after the harvest—implying something like 50–100 per cent paddy rate of interest over 4–5 months! This extremely unfavourable condition of borrowing does not usually leave the small tenants with enough food to survive from this harvest to the next, and the serious problem of survival from harvest to harvest can only be overcome by borrowing again for consumption until the next harvest comes. Thus, the perpetual indebtedness of the small tenants based on their regular requirement of consumption-loan continues. The reader may consider the following stylised example to visualise the state of perpetual indebtedness: Suppose the produce of land operated by a Bargadar is 100 maunds and his minimum consumption requirement is 28 maunds. If he gets 40 per cent of the produce, then his legal share is 40 maunds. But, because of the outstanding past debt of 12 maunds, he has to pay back 12 maunds as principal after the harvest *plus* say, another 12 maunds as interest charges at 100 per cent interest rate. Thus, after paying back 12 + 12 = 24 maunds, as 'adjustments' from past debts, out of his legal share of 40 maunds, he is left with only (40–24) = 16 maunds. Since, his minimal consumption need is already assumed to be 28 maunds, he must borrow again (28–16) = 12 maunds, thereby perpetuating a constant cycle of indebtedness, even when he is paying back full principal and interest every year. However, many share-croppers are not even so fortunate and get more and more into debt which they can never pay back—one bad harvest, some extra borrowing due to family emergencies like illness or social obligations like wedding expenses and religious rites, and the Bargadar is in the grip of hopelessly accumulating debt which he can never pay back. Anybody who has ever cared to talk to Bargadars in West Bengal or Bihar will immediately realise how serious this problem of perpetual indebtedness is, which is the second prominent feature of semi-feudalism in agriculture.

3. Landowners as lenders of consumption-loan

The definite economic character of semi-feudalism in east Indian agriculture however follows from the fact that the lender of consumption-loan is typically also the tenant's landowner. The tenant leases in land from the same man to whom he is perpetually indebted, which virtually reduces him to the state of a traditional serf. This is where the semi-feudal system gets its full grip on the tenants—*the tenant is more or less tied to his particular landowner so long as the latter wants, partly because he cannot move out in search of a new land-owner without settling his debt and also, partly because as a 'loyal' tenant he can get some credit from his land-owner in difficult times,* a security which he may not enjoy with a new landowner. *The feudal element of tying the tenant to a particular landowner operates indirectly though legally the tenant is free to move.* And unlike under capitalistic relations of production, the labour market takes a personalised, fragmented form and the "highest stage of commodity production,"—when labour is also sold as a commodity,—is never reached under such semi-feudal relations.

The semi-feudal landowner uses *two modes of exploitation* for extracting from the tenant—he exploits the tenant through his traditional property right on land as well as through usury and *the economic basis of semi-feudalism is the combined operation of these two models of exploitation.*

Several direct observers of Bihar and West Bengal agriculture have noticed this phenomenon. From Burdwan District in West Bengal, we have F.R. Frankel's reports "Throughout the year, the Bargadar is dependent on advances from the landlord for payment to agricultural labourers—which are not met by landowners—and for consumption loans for food, clothes, medicine or other family emergencies. At the end of the crop season, these advances are deducted from the sharecropper's one-third of the produce as first charge on the crop. After allowing for such deductions, it is not unusual for sharecroppers to be left with 12 per cent to 15 per cent of the total output, about 4 to 5 maunds per acre. One sharecropper interviewed reported that he had received no paddy at all during the previous year after 'adjustments' for all loans had been made against his crop share. Such cultivators survive mainly by taking even largest loans, thus falling into a state of perpetual indebtedness . . ."[2] My data for 26 West Bengal villages in the districts of Birbhum, Nadia and Murshidabad show that while the legally agreed share of the sharecropper was around 40 per cent, in effect after loan 'adjustments' with his landowner, the tenant typically got 10–16 per cent of the output. This impression is also strengthened by Dr. Pradhan. H. Prasad's recent survey of the Koshi Command Area in three districts of Bihar: "There were reports of widespread indebtedness in the area . . . in Monghyr district households normally taking consumption loans were found to be about 59% of the total households . . . The widespread poverty compels the rural poor consisting of mainly sharecropper and agricultural labour households to take consumption loans at a very exorbitant rate of interest whereby indebtedness becomes a permanent feature of these households and they are, thus, compelled to accept semi-slave condition of living . . . These creditors are mostly big landowning class."[3] In short, two modes of exploitation—usury and property rights in land—coupled with the landowner's basis of economic power through insecure tenancy and tenants' indebtedness to him, lend the present economic system of east Indian agriculture the definite character of semi-feudalism.

4. Organisation of Rural 'Markets'

Organised market is essential in an 'exchange economy' (where 'exchange value' rather than 'use value' has come to dominate) and in this sense, development of the market is an accompanying feature of commodity production. It is evident that unlike even the smallest industrial enterprises, a peasant household may directly produce most of its consumption requirements and could thus be involved in market transactions only in a rather marginal way. This will be the result of 'subsistence farming' guided by 'use value'. Nevertheless, even subsistence farming of small tenants and poor peasants is forcibly integrated into the market by the credit nexus of semi-feudal production relations. *This is not commodity production where they produce for the market in search of profit, rather they produce for individual landowners and moneylenders to settle past debt. The market for products thus also becomes personalised and fragmented* where the poorest cultivators are further exploited through their *involuntary* involvement. This is the sort of 'market relations' which correspond to semi-feudal production conditions.

Lack of access to the organised money market (because they have no asset to borrow against) places the tenants completely at the mercy of the semi-feudal landowners and moneylenders, who dictate as absolute monopolists the *terms and timing of* 'borrowing'. This, in turn, reduces their flexibility as sellers in the market for products. They are forced to borrow during agricultural lean periods when prices are very high in the local market and pay back right after the harvest when the prices are very low. Consider this actual example: a kisan in Birbhum borrowed when the price of paddy was Rs. 60 per maund and paid back when the price came down to Rs. 20 per maund. Thus, for each kg of paddy borrowed, he had to pay back *in kind* 3 kg of paddy implying a 200 per cent paddy rate of interest over a few months! The landowner managed this simply by *fixing the timing* of lending and repayment as well as the mode of repayment. Thus, the lack of access of the small tenant to the organised money market (banks, cooperatives, etc.) ensures that he is open to exploration through usury, while the existing credit nexus involuntarily involves him as a 'seller' in the market when prices are low and as a 'buyer' when prices are high. *This is the phenomenon of 'distress sale' where actual small cultivators are victims of price fluctuations, while profit from trading in the market is the privilege of the class manipulating the credit nexus in rural areas.*

In received economic doctrine, one is taught to imagine the market as an economic organisation facilitating division of labour and specialisation in production through exchange. Academic economists get busy demonstrating how the market widens the choice of available commodities to the producer in spite of his specialised production.[4] But, what is the sense in all this in a situation where exchange is mostly involuntary on the part of small peasants? *Underlying semi-feudal market relations is the rural power relations based on credit nexus and insecure tenancy rights:* the organisation of the market comes to reflect the existing power relations in rural areas which in turn gives such 'markets' a specific historical character corresponding to semi-feudal production relations. *This has little in common with more 'impersonal' market formations under capitalistic production relations. Thus, the surface phenomenon of market change and transaction or monetisation does not necessarily indicate symptoms of capitalistic development in agriculture—it may very well be an accompanying feature of semi-feudal production conditions.*

To sum up then, the main feudal element of *personalised economic power* has continued to persist and grow in east Indian agriculture, Tenants are tied to *particular* landowners through constant threat of eviction and perpetual indebtedness to landowners. This makes the 'labour market' fragmented and personalised. On the other hand, the markets for credit and products are so organised as to reflect the existing power relations in rural areas, which in turn, makes the market for products also fragmented and personalized, with involuntary exchange as the rule rather than the exception in such markets.

III

The existence of semi-feudalism in east Indian agriculture has important economic consequences. They have not yet been studied in detail and we know very little about the historical development of semi-feudalism in former Zamindari areas of British India. Without a fuller view of history, it is not possible to analyse meaningfully the major consequences following from the semi-feudal mode of production and all I can do here is to venture a few suggestions. They relate only to the *contemporary* agricultural scene in eastern India.

First, the economic power of the *semi-feudal class is not entirely based on their legal property right to land.* **Unregistered tenancy** is one important aspect of the problem and the other aspect is their operation as **lenders of consumption-loan** to tenants (and other forms of 'fixed' and 'working' capital). It follows that political movements like 'land grab' within this system are unlikely to succeed even for a strict economic reason. Without a complete re-structuring of the entire system of rural credit, one cannot get at the heart of the problem. It has been a common experience during the

Second United Front Government in West Bengal that much of the surplus land redistributed to the landless (under the 10B clause) soon came back to the 'jotedars' and semi-feudal landowners simply because *the land could not be cultivated by the poor peasants due to lack of 'working capital'*. It needs to be stressed here that working capital includes here, nor only seeds, etc. needed for cultivation but also the minimum consumption needs of small cultivators, which was traditionally given as consumption-loans by the semi-feudal landowners. This experience should teach us how entrenched the semi-feudal system is in West Bengal and, if we are willing to learn from experience, then at the next round of political movement, *land redistribution must proceed simultaneously with the provision of fixed and, particularly, working capital.*

I do not intend to imply that lack of provision of working capital was the main cause of the failure of the land redistribution movement. A politically biased legal system did its best to prevent even the distribution of surplus land above ceiling. In West Bengal, already injunctions over 60,000 cases pending in courts have prevented even the government from obtaining the ownership of 1.45 million acres of land under the Land Acquisition Act of 1955.[5] *A class-biased administrative and legal system, political opportunism of all the partners in the United Front everything contributed to the failure of the land redistribution programme.* Nevertheless, these should not blind us to the strict economic aspect of the problem where failure to make provision for 'working capital' was also a major contributory factor. Whether land-redistribution on such a marginal scale as carried out by the United Front could ever have (or was even intended to have) a significant political impact is another matter.

The second important *economic consequence of the existing semi-feudal relations is that it tends to perpetuate agricultural backwardness.*[6] Since the semi-feudal land-owning class derives income both from land-ownership (i.e. the owner's share of the produce) and from usury (interest on consumption-loan primarily), they have an economic interest in perpetuating the economic misery of the tenants. If this, in turn, requires maintaining low productivity of land to prevent the sharecroppers from becoming economically better off, the semi-feudal landowners may well do it. *For economically better-off tenants will require less consumption loan and in some situations, it is possible that the loss in income from usury will more than outweigh the gain from higher productivity to the semi-feudal landowners.* In such cases, even on pure economic grounds, the semi-feudal landowners may restrain the use of improved agricultural technology like sinking a tubewell. Though most landowners seldom will go into such clever economic calculations, I tend to believe that they broadly understand this feature of the system and this partly explains the absence of 'progressive farming' in these areas.[7]

But still more important is the question of class-power under semi-feudalism. Since their power is substantially based on the tenants being constantly indebted to them (and I even suspect that widespread unregistered tenancy is closely linked with the weak economic position of tenants arising partly from indebtedness), it seems plausible to argue that the semi-feudal landowners will try to maintain their political power by keeping undisturbed this phenomenon of perpetual indebtedness through consciously perpetuating stagnation and low productivity in agriculture by restraining technological improvements.

This is a clear case where semi-feudal production relations act as fetters on the release of productive forces—technology is constrained by property relations. Or, to put it somewhat differently, the mode of surplus extraction through usury gets linked with the way in which this surplus may be utilised. Under semi-feudal conditions, surplus extraction and utilisation have got entangled in such a way that perpetuation of agricultural backwardness serves the interest of the ruling class in rural areas.

This leads me to believe that in eastern India, we are now in a situation where improvement in agriculture cannot easily be accommodated by the existing social relations of production. Contradictions are growing between productive forces and production relations and according to any materialistic interpretation of history, such a situation is ripe for historical change.

IV

Nevertheless, it will be mere wishful thinking on my part to claim that *without* conscious political action, such historical change will also result in a more just social order. For, the *release of improved technology can be accommodated in very many ways by changes in the semi-feudal production relations and many of these changes will go still further, against the rural poor.* Without organised political power of the rural poor, the indications of historical change already taking place do not hold out much hope and I only want to venture a guess regarding how the semi-feudal system has already begun to change in West Bengal in areas where productivity has increased mostly through public irrigation work.

Continuation of semi-feudalism requires that the landowner must not let the tenants get economically stronger and get out of his economic grip. Consequently, *the logic of the situation demands that the entire extra output from improvements in technology (e.g. better irrigation, seed, etc.) must be expropriated by him so as not to allow any strengthening of the economic position of the tenant.* For, this will perpetuate the same nexus of rural credit, unregistered tenancy, etc. and keep the economic power of the semi-feudal landowning class undiminished. This they may try to do by bringing down the agreed share of the sharecropper from its existing 33 to 40 per cent or by charging a rent for the use of tube-well water, etc.). Or, they may simply evict tenants and go in for cultivation with wage-labour (which will be a movement in the direction of capitalistic development). All these are possibilities and various observers of the process of 'green revolution' have mentioned them in their field-studies.

It appears to me however that in West Bengal, cultivation with a *special form of attached wage labour* at places known as the 'Munishi system'—is gaining ground. The special characteristic of this system is that it combines the rural credit nexus of semi-feudalism with some capitalistic elements of wage-labour cultivation. In this system, during the agricultural lean seasons wage labourers and former tenants are given consumption loans on condition that they work at much-lower-than-the-market-wage-rate during the agricultural peak seasons (this is how the interest rate is charged also). By this method, the former tenants are being convented into attached farm labour—the so-called 'Munishi system'—and 'free' wage-labour is being tied to particular owners during the agricultural peak seasons, at a very low wage rate. Thus the hold on the wage rate as well as availability of labour during peak seasons are being maintained through more or less the same old semi-feudal credit nexus, while landowners are carrying on cultivation at a low wage cost even under improved technology without having to share its benefits. This appears to be the tendency in areas where agricultural productivity has recently gone up through public irrigation facilities and this may well turn out to be the next step in the historical evolution of the semi-feudal system, unless determined political action by the landless and poor peasants shape history differently.

Notes

1. N. Banerji, *Bargadars and Institutional Finance,* Directorate of Land Records and Surveys, West Bengal, January 1973, p. 2.

2. D. Bandyopadhyay, *Impressions on the Prevailing Agrarian Relations in the Districts of Madhubani and Muzaffarpur in Bihar,* April 1973.
3. Francine R. Frankel, *India's Green Revolution: Economic Gains and Political Costs,* Princeton University Press, 1971, pp. 167–68.
4. Pradhan, H. Prasad, 'Employment Structure in Rural India', paper presented to the Seminar on the Political Economy of Indian Agriculture, Calcutta, March 1973.
5. This sort of reasoning underlies 'gains from trade' type of argument in orthodox international trade theory.
6. *Economic and Political Weekly,* 17 March 1973.
7. A technical elaboration of this sort of reasoning is to be found in Amit Bhaduri's 'A Study in Agricultural Backwardness under Semi-Feudalism.' *Economic Journal,* March 1973.

13

Productivity, Production Relations and Class Efficiency: Illustrations from Indian Agriculture*

It is almost tautological to say that poor countries remain poor because they have low labour productivity. Nevertheless, this self-evident statement hides more than it reveals. Even at the crudest level of disaggregation it is striking that the gaps in labour productivity vary enormously across sectors. Not only is labour productivity the lowest in agriculture compared to that in industry and the service sector in almost every country, but even more importantly the gap in labour productivity between rich and poor countries tends to be the largest in the agricultural sector. On a rough estimate relating to the early 1980s, labour productivity in agriculture is about twenty times higher in the developed compared to the developing countries. In contrast, in industry and the service sector the gap is only about five times (Bhaduri, 1993). Coupled with the fact that the occupational structure is biased heavily in favour of agriculture in the developing countries, this provides an immediate arithmetical explanation of the marked international disparity in income. The strong compulsions towards industrialisation aimed at changing the

* From: *Economic Development and Agricultural Productivity*, edited by Amit Bhaduri and Rune Skarstein, Cheltenham, U.K., 1977, pp. 121–130.

occupational structure rapidly as well as the pressing need to raise productivity in most developing countries can be understood easily in this context.

However this gap in agricultural productivity is considerably lower when output per unit of land is considered. Again, at the superficial level of arithmetic it indicates the over-crowded nature of agriculture in many developing countries. Models of economic dualism with unlimited supply of labour from agriculture (Lewis, 1954; 1972) tried to capture the implication of this situation for industrialisation. While dual economy models concerned themselves mostly with the process of intersectoral labour transfer through industrialisation, the consequence of over-crowding within traditional agriculture opened up yet another important problem. Overcrowding of agriculture usually means landlessness as well as the preponderance of small and marginal peasant households with tiny plots of land in relation to their available family labour, especially when land ownership is very unevenly distributed. The question naturally arises whether such a structure of land-holdings depresses agricultural production significantly. Any attempt to answer this question satisfactorily cannot ignore the complex interrelation between labour productivity and production relations in agriculture. In this sense, the level of labour productivity also becomes a social phenomenon which cannot be explained entirely in terms of technology.

It is common sense to postulate that the tiny land-holders would try to use their land as intensively as possible as a strategy for survival, particularly if they have no other opportunities to earn income by using their family labour, especially women and children. In terms of standard economic analysis, family labour would tend to be used more and more intensively on tiny land-holdings until the diminishing marginal product of labour on those small and marginal holdings becomes virtually zero; on larger holdings hired labour would be used less intensively, only to the point where the marginal product of labour equals the given real wage rate in the market to maximise commercial profit. Thus, on the basis of relative scarcity of land in relation to family labour having zero opportunity cost, standard economic theory predicts that the smaller farms would have higher yield per unit of land compared to the larger farms. Obviously, this implies that labour productivity would be lower in the smaller-sized than in the larger-sized farms.

A large empirically oriented literature developed in India around this point. Known as the 'size-yield' controversy, it soon recognised that even in traditional agriculture with similar technologies for large as well as small farms, an unambiguous inverse relation between the yield of a single crop and the size of holding could not usually be established (Bharadwaj, 1974). It was realised that the higher labour input per acre in smaller farms would express itself in many different ways, depending on the nature of production relations under which the nearly landless peasant family operates. For instance, higher labour input may alter the crop-composition, allowing for more labour-intensive and higher-valued crops. However, which crops would be grown may not be dictated simply by the income-maximisation motive of the small peasant. He may be forced to grow a highly labour-intensive cash crop like jute (in parts of eastern India) because he took in advance a cash loan for working capital against a future contract to produce and sell back jute at a pre-determined price—which is lower than the market price—to his moneylender. The observed statistical predominance of small farmers in a labour-intensive crop like jute could thus be the result of surplus family labour coupled with arrangements for a working capital loan into which small peasants are forced to enter. It would be somewhat misleading to treat this decision to produce, say jute, simply as a voluntary decision, guided only by the motive to maximise income by pushing marginal product of family labour to zero, as it ignores the interlink between the product market and the credit market.

One could observe even more complex patterns of interlinkage in reality. A nearly landless family, which is able to lease in some land, may use family labour intensively to improve that leased-in land through drainage, irrigation and so on, provided it has sufficient security of tenancy. Thus one might expect small holdings that are either owner-operated or have secured tenancy to have more land-improving durable investments carried out through the small owners' or tenants' family labour than similar sized holdings under unsecured tenancy. The interlinkage here works through the labour and the land market through the degree of security of tenancy, or the extent of inter-temporal use-right of land in general.

The main thrust of the argument so far can be summarised briefly. The relative scarcity of land in relation to (family) labour in smaller holdings would normally lead to higher labour input per unit of land in accordance with standard economic theory. However the particular form in which this more intensive labour utilisation takes place tends to be mediated by the specific relations of production, generating different patterns of interlinkage in each case. Such interlinkage means that the particular form of family labour utilisation is often governed not entirely by the self-interest of the small peasant, but also by the interest of his moneylender or landlord or someone else in a similar dominant position to exploit him through these interlinkages in transactions. Both the theory of 'forced commerce' with its sharper focus (Bhaduri, 1983; 1986), and its more general formulation as the theory of 'interlocked transactions' (Bharadwaj, 1974) were intended to provide a framework for understanding this type of phenomenon. Since such interlocked transactions appear in various guises in backward agriculture, it is important to examine their implications for productivity growth.

Orthodox economic theory predictably examines the implications of such interlocked transactions in terms of their static resource allocative efficiency and Pareto optimality (Bardhan, 1980; Braverman and Srinivasan, 1981; Braverman and Stiglitz, 1982). This approach is misleading in so far as it asks the wrong questions about backward agriculture for two related reasons. First, the main problem of agricultural backwardness with surplus labour lies in insufficient accumulation, which slows down land-saving innovation as well as creation of new income-earning opportunities in agriculture. It is far from evident that the solution to these problems lies in trying to improve the static allocation of given resources. Indeed the central problem is to augment the resource base of backward agriculture through productive investment. Hence it is more fruitful to focus on the problem of the 'incentive to invest' in this context, that is, both the barriers to productive investment as well as the ways to stimulate it in the context of backward agriculture.

Second, Pareto optimality provides no helpful guidance even for analysing the 'welfare implications' of the situation, in so far as the distribution of income and wealth is governed by relations of economic power. The theory of interlocked transactions was designed to help us in analysing how power is exercised, especially through the various exchange relations in land, labour, credit and product 'markets' in backward agriculture. Whether such exchange relations have Pareto optimal properties is largely irrelevant in this context. The more powerful party can usually better his position by manipulating the distribution of income through such interlocked transactions in his favour in a non-Pareto optimal situation, rather than by trying to attain Pareto optimality. As a result the real problem of analysing economic power is obfuscated rather than illuminated by concepts such as

Pareto optimality. Instead, the concept of 'class efficiency' (Bhaduri, 1991) is more relevant for analysing phenomena such as interlocked transactions. An institutional arrangement is class efficient if the more powerful class can maintain a higher income in its favour, despite the lower productive efficiency of the system. Productive efficiency (including rules of Pareto efficiency) may be violated deliberately if it helps in manipulating sufficiently the distribution of income in favour of the more powerful class.

Analysis from this angle of class efficiency of institutional arrangements, like various forms of interlocked transactions that are widely prevalent in backward agriculture, opens up a new perspective. These institutional arrangements may be maintained, when necessary through the deliberate sacrifice of productive efficiency, on the grounds of class efficiency. As a result, agricultural backwardness characterised by low productive efficiency may continue, with highly uneven distribution of both income and power within such agriculture. The possibility of this trade-off between productive efficiency and class efficiency mediated through the existing production relations should become the focus of our enquiry, in explaining how production relations exert their influence on the level and growth of productivity.

The model of semi-feudalism was constructed (Bhaduri, 1973) to show why the incentive to invest in land improvement may be weak in situations where the semi-feudal landlord is also the moneylender to his tenants. Low productivity of land in traditional agriculture resulting in low income-share for the tenant keeps him perpetually dependent on his landlord for regular consumption loans.[1] So long as the landlord earns a higher interest income from advancing consumption loans than from raising land yield, he might have little economic incentive in undertaking land-improving investments. In contrast, sufficiently 'large' improvements in land yield may be economically attractive to him. While it might reduce the tenant's dependence on consumption loans and therefore also reduce the landlord's interest income, that loss would be out-weighed by the landlord's share from sufficiently 'large' gain in the yield from land. The argument could be further elaborated by introducing complications due to supervision cost, in so far as the debt-dependence of the tenant on the landlord might also reduce the supervision cost of the landlord. However even without such embellishment, the basic thrust of the argument should be clear. A landlord with considerable personal power over his tenants, largely due to their debt-dependence on him, chooses between the role of a 'rentier' in a patron-client relationship and that of an 'entrepreneur', by deciding on whether to invest in land improvement or not.

Although this model of semi-feudalism provided a precise illustration of how production relations might exert a crippling influence on the productivity growth in land if landlords choose their 'rentier' role, it overplays misleadingly an orthodox idea. Almost mechanically, it placed too rigid an emphasis on the idea that debt-dependence as a part of the production relations belongs to the 'super-structure' and that this super-structure would change if the 'base' of productivity growth changed significantly. Some recent empirical investigation from areas near to the original study (Bhaduri, 1973) shows how almost exactly the opposite might happen (Sarkar, 1988, 1991). New technology involving high-yielding varieties was introduced through larger advances of working capital loans from the landlord. The tenant now became indebted to his landlord for both consumption and production loans. Old production relations involving debt-dependence at an even higher level and crop-sharing continued, while land productivity increased due to the application of new technology.[2] The moral of the story is important: in traditional agriculture, the relation between production relations on the one hand and labour productivity, yield levels and their growth on the other, is not hierarchical in any causal sense. This is because the distribution of gains from increases in productivity can be manipulated by manipulating institutional arrangements to suit class efficiency. It is essential to understand more precisely in this context the pressures that operate on the class distribution of income, as considerations of capturing productivity gains through class efficiency mediate between changes in productivity and in production relations.

The general argument may be illustrated by a well-documented example. Based on considerable empirical evidence from several countries, it has been claimed that, despite being largely neutral with respect to the size of the holding, the high-yielding variety seeds and the Green Revolution technology lead to disproportionately large gains for the landlord compared to the tenants (Ruttan and Binswanger, 1978). On the basis of this evidence it is plausible to argue that, at least in some cases, new technologies could be introduced, precisely because the disproportionate distribution of gains acted as the shock-absorber, not to upset the existing production relations despite large changes in land yields.

However this pressure on income distribution need not operate only when new technology considerably increases the productivity of land. For instance, empirical evidence suggests that even 'customary' share often varies inversely in relation to land quality in crop-sharing arrangements (Cooper, 1983).[3] Although detailed empirical studies over time are lacking, it is plausible to argue in line with this cross-sectional evidence that higher yield achieved through durable land improvement in an area would tend to change the customary share in favour of landlords for capturing disproportionately the productivity gains (Griffin, 1974).

One could perhaps get an interesting insight by generalising this argument: the extent of manipulability of institutions and production relations to alter the sharing of productivity gains is a barometer of the unevenness in the underlying distribution of economic power; the more even that balance of power, the less manipulable are the production relations and the economic institutions within which the growth in productivity takes place. It would then follow that the restrictive role of production relations on productivity growth in backward agriculture might, almost paradoxically, be stronger, precisely when economic power is more evenly balanced between the contesting classes to make the production relations less easily manipulable. In other words, greater equality in terms of political power would not necessarily generate greater agrarian dynamism, particularly so long as investment decisions rest mostly with the landlords in backward agriculture.

The link between certain types of economic arrangements and institutions on the one hand and class efficiency on the other is established through the economic interest of the dominant class. Nevertheless, it is often a misleading oversimplification to postulate the interest of a class as completely homogeneous. Tensions exist almost invariably between the broad collective interest of the class and the individual interest of its members. Such tensions may typically increase with possibilities for rapid change in agricultural yield or productivity in backward agriculture. To illustrate the point more precisely, we return to the model of 'semi-feudalism' mentioned earlier. The rigidity in the relations of production in terms of dependence on consumption loans taken regularly by the tenants may tend to act as a barrier to the introduction, not only of 'small' but also of 'large' technical changes; whereas 'small' changes may be economically unattractive, the 'large' changes may be politically or socially unattractive in so far as the latter is 'large' enough to upset these production relations. However such large changes would also hold out the prospect of correspondingly large profits.[4] This might attract individual landlords to go against their collective class interest for realising individual economic gains. Thus there would be a limit to class efficiency; the mechanism manipulating institutions differently would come into operation when individual interests begin to become less homogeneous within a class.

A schism between the private profitability of individual landlords and their collective economic interest as a class may come into play in this case because potential productivity gains are sufficiently large to lure individual landlords and undermine in the longer run the existing production relations in backward agriculture (Bhaduri, 1991).[5] Indeed, it may be argued that large-scale public investment in agricultural infrastructure in such a situation is not only a technological improvement but it also has a political dimension, in so far as it also puts pressure on changing the existing relations of production by fragmenting the interest of the ruling class. To sum up, when economic power is very unevenly distributed, production relations can be manipulated rather easily by the more powerful to accommodate productivity change. This pattern of agrarian change is driven primarily by considerations of class efficiency. However when economic power between the classes is more evenly balanced, the production relations become less easily manipulable. Such rigidity in the relations of production may still be undermined though by a significant divergence between individual and class interest that may arise from the possibility of capturing 'large' productivity gains by individual landlords through private investment.

Interlocked transactions, mentioned earlier, are significant because they are often 'informal' and constitute an important part of the more easily manipulable production relations in the backward segment of Indian agriculture. However the role of such interlocking seems to have been largely misunderstood in conventional analysis. It is often argued that such interlocking of transactions is simply an extended form of contract between two parties such as the landlord and his tenants or the moneylender and his debtors. This view is misleadingly incomplete. It presumes that a 'contract' means more or less the same thing in backward agriculture as in the organised market economies. The crucial difference lies in the fact that the terms of a contract in backward agriculture are often not defined independently of the way in which they are meant to be enforced. For instance, it is not a well-defined and impersonal 'bankruptcy law' which applies uniformly to all loan contracts. In contrast, the implicit enforcement device contains the 'hidden script' of the contract and, unlike an organised market economy, the enforcement device is not uniform for all contracts. This can be illustrated by analysing how usurious interest rates are formed in backward agriculture (Bhaduri, 1977; 1983; Basu, 1984).

The essential difference between 'usury' and high interest rates is that in the former case it is the borrower but not the lender who has to bear the risk of capital loss in case of default of the loan. This arrangement operates mainly through the undervaluation of collateral which a relatively helpless borrower has to accept because his collateral is not easily marketable elsewhere (for example, encumbered land, future harvest or labour service).[6] Thus the commonplace idea that a higher interest rate is charged to cover the higher margin of risk of default faced by the lender has to be reversed altogether under usurious practices where the risk of default gets transferred from the lender to the borrower through the undervaluation of collaterals. This transfer of the risk of default mostly to the borrower can be interpreted as an enforcement device of the loan contract in so far as the borrower, threatened by his potential capital loss, has little incentive to default under any such arrangement. However, viewed from the lender's angle, the lender may have a strong incentive to induce default through charging higher interest or by enticing the borrower to take a larger amount of credit at a lower interest rate. These are the typical ways for the lender to realise net capital gains by seizing undervalued collaterals in so far as the value of the collateral to the lender outweighs the value of the defaulted loan (Bhaduri, 1977; Basu, 1984).[7] In these circumstances, the implementation of the loan contracts may also be altered because the device for the enforcement of the contract through the undervaluation of collateral affects the very implementation of the contract by encouraging default.

For such a system to operate extensively in backward agriculture, collateral undervaluation has to be carried out with respect to arrangements between particular lenders and borrowers. The personal valuations of collaterals of the borrower can be undervalued by a lender because they are not easily 'marketable' elsewhere. However for a particular lender advancing loans against some specific collaterals, these otherwise less marketable collaterals may have especially high personal value. For instance, an agricultural moneylender may lend against the collateral of encumbered land of a poor peasant with the intention of acquiring, at least temporarily, the use-right of that land. Nevertheless for another type of lender, say a professional moneylender who has no direct connection with cultivation, such use-right of land may have little personal value. Similarly, a trader-moneylender would also not be interested in the use-right of land but may prefer to lend against the collateral of undervalued future harvest of the poor peasant. In contrast, a landowner may prefer to lend against the undervalued collateral of the future labour service of his tenant. In each of these cases a particular collateral is seen to have a higher personal value for a specific type of lender, but not uniformly for all of them. Empirically there is some evidence to suggest that this leads to 'sorting behaviour' by different lenders on the basis of the particular collaterals they prefer to lend against, for example the trader-lender may generally prefer to lend against future harvest whereas the agriculturist-lender may prefer land as collateral (Yotopulos and Floro, 1992).

The impact of such sorting behaviour by the lenders on productivity change would tend to be complex because of the coexistence of many types of lenders. For instance, in the case of an agriculturalist-lender who seizes the use-right of the land of a poor peasant who has defaulted, the impact on land productivity is likely to be positive as the agriculturalist might use it efficiently with more modern technology. On the other hand, a trader-lender can hope to seize the collateral of future harvests regularly at low price through loan contracts, provided the peasant remains sufficiently impoverished to enter regularly into such unfavourable loan arrangements.[8] In these circumstances, the trader-lender is unlikely to have a strong incentive to lend for improving the productivity of the land.[9] Thus, the coexistence of a variety of moneylenders with different motives to lend by sorting out collaterals offered by various borrowers may generate a complex pattern. This, in turn, might affect both the availability of credit and its distribution. In particular there may be significant mismatch between the private lenders' personal motives for advancing credit and the borrowers' requirements. Its adverse consequences would be felt in terms of land yield and labour productivity, especially on the smaller farms with limited access to alternative sources of borrowing. This again illustrates how class efficiency may govern the private credit system to hinder productivity growth, even if the underlying class interests of the lenders are not entirely homogeneous.

Notes

1. Although, as already mentioned, small holdings may have higher land yield in traditional agriculture, the tenant's dependence on consumption loans arises due to the very small absolute size of the holdings in relation to his survival needs. Moreover, given the size of the holding per tenant, higher land yield also means labour productivity.
2. Sarkar's data suggest that net yield per acre reported a relatively modest increase. It is plausible that the interest on working capital loan increased disproportionately compared to the productivity gain per acre to keep debt dependence largely unaffected, with landlords continuing as the main source of credit.
3. The data relates mostly to the pre-World War II period in Bengal. Similar data from pre-revolution China were reported by Chen Po Ta.
4. In particular, public investment in irrigation, drainage and so on as well as better communications such as roads linking to a major centre may create pre-conditions for such 'large' increase in yield and labour productivity through supplementary private investment.
5. See Bhaduri (1981) for a model formulating divergence between the different rates of return on investment through 'externalities' in backward agriculture.
6. In principle, this is similar to the way the 'pawn-shops' work frequently. The pawn-shop principle of transferring the risk of default to the lender by undervaluing his collateral is also the basis of usury.
7. Again, the analogy with the pawn-shop should be obvious; see preceding note.
8. Floro (1987, p. 245) suggests that the trader-money-lender emerged in many cases in the Philippines because of the introduction in the 1960s of the new technology which increased the importance of purchased inputs and input traders.
9. Again, this is subject to the qualification discussed earlier that the improvement in land productivity would not be so large as to lead to a gain from 'normal' commerce which would outweigh his gain from 'forced' commerce.

14

Structural Change and Economic Development: On the Relative Roles of Effective Demand and the Price Mechanism in a 'Dual' Economy*

1. Structural Change and Development: Some Stylised Facts

One of the most robust facts in development economics, exhibited by cross-section data across countries as well as time series data of individual countries, is an inverse relationship between per capita GDP and the percentage of labour force engaged in agriculture. Richer countries have a smaller percentage of their labour force in agriculture, and in the primary sector.[1] This is reinforced by time series data; as countries become richer over time, the relative importance of the primary sector declines in terms of both its percentage contribution to GDP and the proportion of labour force employed. The numbers are indeed strikingly systematic in this respect: towards the end of the last century, in 1995, older industrialised countries like the UK and the USA had less than 3 per cent of their total labour force engaged in agriculture, producing less than 2 per cent of the GDP, Japan, which industrialised more recently, had less than 6 per cent

---

* From: *Rethinking Development Economics*, edited by Ha-Joon Chong. London, Anthem Press, 2003, pp. 220–235.

of the labour force, while (South) Korea still had 12.5 per cent employed in agriculture, contributing 2 per cent and 6 per cent respectively to GDP. Brazil had nearly 20 per cent of its workforce in agriculture, contributing 9 per cent of the GDP, while Mexico had 24 per cent in agricultural employment, contributing only 5 per cent of the GDP. At the other end of the spectrum, poorer countries like China, India or Bangladesh, all had more than half of their labour force engaged in agriculture (China 54 per cent, India 67 per cent and Bangladesh 63 per cent), while agriculture's contribution to GDP was 20 per cent in China, 28 per cent in India and 25 per cent in Bangladesh.[2] Although these numbers are merely illustrative (and there are a few statistical 'outliers'), they reveal the pattern of structural changes that typically accompany economic development. Three propositions roughly sum up that pattern:

1. The relative importance of the agricultural (and the primary) sector declines in terms of both the percentage of labour force employed there, and its percentage contribution to GDP, as per capita GDP increases in the course of economic development.[3]
2. However, the percentage of labour engaged in agriculture is usually considerably higher than the percentage contribution made by the agricultural sector to the GDP, implying that labour productivity is lower in agriculture compared to the national average. This holds for both the developed and the developing countries. Thus, from the above figures, we may calculate that, in relation to their respective national averages, the labour productivity in agriculture was about 67 per cent in the UK and in the USA, 33 per cent in Japan, 48 per cent in South Korea, 45 per cent in Brazil, 21 per cent in Mexico, 35 per cent in China, 42 per cent in India and 40 per cent in Bangladesh.[4]

3. Available data (not presented here) also tend to show that intersectoral differences in labour productivity are in the ratio of 1 to 2.5 for the developed economies, i.e. labour productivity in industry or in the service sector is about 2.5 times higher than that in agriculture. However, in developing countries, the same ratio tends to be much greater, perhaps as high as 8 to 10 times.[5]

The main thrust of these propositions, based on stylized facts, is to emphasise the pressure typically put on developing countries to industrialize at a rapid pace. Not only is agriculture marked by a considerably lower labour productivity than the national average, but the intersectoral productivity gap also tends to be especially large in developing countries. Therefore, transferring labour from the agricultural to the non-agricultural sectors entails large gains in overall labour productivity and in per capita income, propelling the process of economic development through structural change.[6] Nevertheless, this is merely an arithmetical truism. The real economic issues are to identify the nature of constraints and the processes that operate on the demand and on the supply side of a developing economy to regulate the process by which these structural changes occur. To this central problem we now turn.

2. Agriculture-Industry Interaction: Price and Quantity Adjustment in a Dual Economy

It has been an old idea in the history of economic thought to link the '*social division* of labour', that is to say the extent of diversification of the economy into different branches of activity with agriculture generating the *surplus* needed to support the consumption by workers in the non-agricultural activities. This link was seen as early as in the seventeenth century by Sir William Petty,[7] and became a central tenet in later Physiocratic writings. Francois Quesnay's *Tableau*

Economique exhibited how agricultural surplus supports through intersectoral exchanges other non-agricultural activities.[8] From the point of view of later theoretical developments in this area, at least two contributions of the Physiocrats seem to be of lasting value. First, they defined agricultural surplus as the 'gross produce' of agriculture *minus* 'productive consumption' by the farmers. 'Productive consumption' consists of agricultural raw materials required in its own production, and the subsistence, self-consumption by the farmers. The really fruitful Physiocratic idea was not the identification of agricultural surplus with rent and land revenue, which might have been valid in their particular socio-economic context, but their view that, rather than the total agricultural product, only the surplus—a predetermined quantity, or an exogenous variable obtained by deducting the self-consumption of the peasants from agricultural value added—enters the process of intersectoral exchange to support the consumption by workers and artisans engaged in the non-agricultural sectors for diversifying the economy.

Second, the Physiocratic notion of agricultural surplus as exogenous was justified in so far as both agricultural output and the self-consumption by the farmers are considered as given, the latter coinciding with subsistence consumption. In principle, however, this notion could be used for a more flexible formulation. Not only might higher agricultural price provide stronger incentive to increase agricultural output in the manner taught usually by textbooks (although empirical evidence on this point is ambiguous in developing countries) but more interestingly the availability of industrial goods, as well as their relative price in terms of agricultural goods, might also influence the amount the peasants decide to retain for self-consumption. And when these considerations are deemed to be important, the level of agricultural surplus becomes an endogenous variable, influenced by other factors within the system, for example the level of availability of industrially-produced consumer goods and their relative price in terms of agricultural goods.[9]

As reconstruction and decolonisation became part of the international agenda after the Second World War, many of the Physiocratic and classical economists' concerns with economic development through structural change began receiving greater attention. Lewis' seminal paper on the dual economy[10]—a concept used earlier by Boeke[11]—was meant to capture the economic process through which the traditional, largely subsistence sector of a developing economy gets modernised. Lewis distinguished the 'modern' from the 'traditional' sector on the basis of the different methods by which production is organised in them. This corresponds only roughly to the division between agriculture as the traditional, and industry as the modern, sector of a 'dual' economy; but it echoes an old Physiocratic idea in so far as the Physiocrats were the first to recognise that production in agriculture is organised differently from that in industry, requiring an analytical division between the two sectors.[12]

Both in Lewis' own model, and in a whole series of models of the 'dual' economy that it subsequently inspired,[13] a pivotal role is played by the assumption that the *supply* of agricultural surplus is exogenously given, while the real wage rate in terms of agricultural goods (e.g. 'food') for which labour supply is unlimited remains constant. The consequence of this assumption is to determine the level of industrial employment sustainable from the supply side simply as the ratio of agricultural surplus divided by the real wage rate. Any attempt to raise the level of industrial employment beyond that point would be thwarted, according to Lewis and his followers, by the price mechanism, namely the intersectoral terms of trade, or the price of industrial goods in terms of agricultural goods, because a faster pace of industrialisation would raise further the demand for 'food' and therefore the price of agricultural goods. Real wages in terms of foods, which is assumed to be constant, can remain constant only if the money wage rate also rises in the same proportion as the price of food. With industrial prices unaffected, this increase in money wages would squeeze profit in industry, while the terms of trade would move against industry. Using a version of 'Say's Law', in the form of the pre-Keynesian assumption that industrial profit as saving determines industrial investment, Lewis argued that the squeeze on industrial profit would slow down industrial investment and growth, until industrial employment returns to the level sustainable by the exogenously given agricultural surplus and the real wage rate.[14]

Using this Lewis-type dual economy framework as the benchmark, one can see how the argument could be developed further in two almost diametrically opposite directions. On the one hand, all the special structuralist assumptions of the dual economy model could be removed to make it look like the textbook competitive market economy. In that case, higher industrial growth, creating greater demand for 'food', would raise the relative price of agricultural goods, only to create stronger incentives to supply more agricultural surplus. With agricultural surplus no longer exogenously given, higher industrial growth through the working of the price incentives could become feasible. Moreover, the higher price of agricultural goods at any given rate of money wage would imply lower real wage. Thus, if labour supply is unlimited at a given money, rather than real wage, rate, a higher level of industrial employment could be sustained through agricultural price rise for any given amount of agricultural surplus. Thus, both through the price incentive to agricultural suppliers, and through a reduction in the real wage rate, the structural constraints on industrial growth in the economy may be relaxed considerably. It would not be too much of an exaggeration to claim that this sort of reasoning often underlies the emphasis that the 'Washington Consensus' of the IMF and the World Bank placed on 'getting prices right', particularly for the agricultural sector, and making the labour market 'flexible'.

The main problem with this view is that it makes the developing economy look almost like the perfectly competitive market economy of the textbooks. However, this is achieved only by assumptions, ignoring the peculiar structural characteristics that the dual economy model was meant to highlight. As a matter of fact, one could enrich the model by proceeding in the opposite direction, through incorporating additional, structural features. Perhaps the most important feature, originally due to Kelecki,[15] is to recognise that in agriculture, isolated peasants and farmers carry out production. Their supplies arrive in the market after harvest, prior to price formation. Given the level of supply, prices are formed subsequently in relation to the state of demand. In this sense, agricultural prices tend to be flexible in response to variations in demand, and can be claimed to be largely *demand-determined*. This flexibility of agricultural prices has been a well-documented fact in both developing and developed countries. For instance, 'with the exception of 1958, US wholesale prices of domestically produced food crops fell (absolutely) in every recession year since the World War II'.[16]

In contrast to agricultural prices, industrial prices tend to be markedly less flexible in response to variations in demand. This is because, unlike in the case of agriculture, industrial prices are usually set prior to sales, while variations in demand are absorbed mostly through inventory changes. Since industrial prices are set prior to sales, i.e.

without prior accurate knowledge of the state of demand, the standard procedure is to cover unit variable cost with some (usually fixed percentage) mark-up on that cost to allow for profit net of depreciation, interest payment on loans, etc. In this sense, industrial prices tend to be largely *cost-determined,* on the assumption that the state of demand would be 'normal', while deviations from this normal state are usually met through inventory rather than price change in the short run.

This distinction between relatively flexible, demand-determined agricultural price, and relatively inflexible, cost-determined industrial price, when incorporated as a further structural feature of the dual economy model, has important economic consequences. Perhaps the most important consequence is the possibility of 'stagflation' in a dual economic structure.[17] With agricultural surplus assumed to be exogenously given, and a constant (subsistence) real wage rate in terms of 'food' as postulated in Lewis' original model, industrial growth at a pace faster than that sustainable by the available supply of agricultural surplus would lead to higher demand for 'food', and therefore higher demand-determined agricultural price, as had been argued by Lewis. The higher price of 'food' would raise the *money* wage rate proportionately in industry to keep the subsistence real wage rate constant. However, unlike the 'profit squeeze' in industry postulated in the Lewis model, the higher money wage will be transmitted to higher cost-determined industrial price. If mark-up is a fixed percentage on unit variable cost, assumed to be equal to wage cost per unit of output in a closed economy, the percentage rise in industrial price (as well as in agricultural price) will be equal to the percentage rise in the money wage rate. Thus, the consequence would *not* be a squeeze on industrial profit, at Lewis had argued in the context of rising food prices, because industrial profits would be maintained by rising industrial price at that fixed mark-up, making the terms of trade between industrial and agricultural price inflexible in contrast to the Lewis model. The consequence would be stagflationary price rise in both sectors at a rate equal to the rise in the money wage rate.

A further interesting variation on this theme of stagflation in a dual economy occurs by combining it with another important fact of economic life, namely Engel's Law. This postulates that the demand for food tends to be inelastic with respect of variation in income. It can be argued plausibly that a rise in the price of food would typically result in a higher proportion of the money wage of the industrial worker being spent on food if the increase in money wage is proportionally less than that in food price. This would reduce the proportion of money wage left for spending on industrial goods. Consequently, higher food price could reduce overall effective demand for industrial goods, unless it is compensated by a correspondingly higher level of expenditure by the farmers from the higher income they earn from the higher price of food.[18]

The empirically robust assumption that industrial prices tend to be highly sensitive to cost but not to demand also casts doubt on the efficacy of the terms of trade mechanism in maintaining balance between expansion in both the agricultural and industrial sectors. As we already saw, it can result in almost completely inflexible terms of trade and stagflation in a dual economy. Even more significantly, this opens the way for output rather than price adjustment in the industrial sector in response to excess demand, when that sector is operating under excess capacity. Note, however, that the existence of excess capacity in industry is usually assumed, and this tends to reinforce the rationale for the rule of mark-up pricing widely observed in industry.[19] In this context it becomes especially important to examine how the dual economy operates, when demand-determined price adjusts in the agricultural sector, but quantity adjusts in the industrial sector with excess capacity and cost-determined mark-up pricing. This indeed was the route pursued particularly by Kaldor to bring to the forefront Keynesian considerations for revising our understanding of the role of demand in a dual economy framework.[20]

Kaldor suggested that agricultural surplus plays a critical role in the process of industrialisation, not so much by providing the supply of essential wage goods emphasised by Lewis and Kalecki, but by creating demand for industrial goods.[21] A larger volume of agricultural surplus entails a larger market for industry, bringing into operation the (trade) multiplier mechanism for the industrial sector. Thus, by treating agricultural surplus as largely autonomous, its role can be compared analytically to that of exogenous investment or export in the standard Keynesian model of income determination.

However, while this argument is suggestive, it has a serious lacuna.[22] Agricultural surplus creates demand for industrial goods by first being converted into monetary purchasing power. Thus, there is the problem of realising monetary income from agricultural surplus. In a closed economy without government, it is industry which provides this market for the conversion through the industrial wage bill spent on 'food'. As a result, a greater degree of interdependence from the demand side exists between agriculture and industry in a closed economy than Kaldor's argument suggests. Note that this interdependence arises because all transactions have to be made in terms of money, and not through barter, i.e. as a result of money's being used as a universal medium of exchange.

The importance of this argument relating to monetary exchange becomes all the more apparent if we consider the role of the government in maintaining a minimum 'support price' for agricultural products. Since any amount of agricultural surplus can be sold at that price, there is no problem of realisation of that surplus into monetary purchasing power. However, this resolves the problem of realisation of surplus only in so far as the agricultural sector is concerned. Viewed from the perspective of industry, the problem of demand still remains unresolved. Unless this monetary purchasing power of agriculture is spent on industrial goods, industry would suffer from insufficient demand, although there is no problem of the realisation of agricultural surplus into monetary revenue. That this problem can be serious has become clear, for instance, by recent experiences in post-Green Revolution India. In 2001, India had a stock of some 60 million tonnes of foodgrains in government godowns, while 325 million people lived below the 'poverty line', and some 50 million people were on the brink of starvation.

The Indian experience in recent years has yielded a shameful paradox, in that 'too much' food is procured through the support price system, while too many people remain on the brink of starvation.[23] While this simply means that the poor have too little purchasing power, it assumes further significance in the context of a closed, dual economy model of agriculture-industry interaction. It shows why the realisation of agricultural surplus into monetary purchasing power through government intervention is merely one facet of the more complex problem of managing effective demand in a sectorally-interdependent monetary economy. Because, unless this purchasing power is spent on domestic industrial goods, industry might suffer from insufficient demand and excess capacity, while the excess purchasing power is held by the agricultural sector in monetary assets. This may raise (agricultural) households' savings, without matching investment demand. In short, it is an illustration of the Keynesian 'paradox of thrift' in a dual economy: the use of money as a 'store of value' by the farmers leads to the failure of Say's law in a monetary economy.

Viewed from the opposite perspective, in the dual economy it is the slow pace of expansion of the industrial sector which can be said to result in insufficient demand for agricultural goods or for 'food', through insufficient expansion of the industrial wage bill. While this provides the rationale of a support price system for agricultural goods, it could obversely be argued that a faster pace of expansion of the industrial sector (e.g. through public investment in infrastructure, etc.) would have tended to alleviate the same problem. Thus, assuming the 'fiscal discipline' of a given government budget, the problem of the *composition* of public expenditure between the support price system for agricultural goods on the one hand, and the need for increased public investment for stimulating the demand for agricultural goods on the other, remains an important issue for the management of demand.

Outside the simplest dual economy model, at least two additional complications must be reckoned with in this context of managing demand. First, the incidence of (direct and indirect) tax tends to vary between the incomes of the two sectors; typically, the tax rate turns out to be higher for industry than for agriculture. Consequently, the support price system for agriculture tends to place a greater strain on the public finance position in so far as, through this policy, less money usually returns to the government as tax revenue, compared to an equivalent amount spent on industry to raise its capacity utilisation. Second, in an open economy, with trade in goods and services largely liberalised, serious administrative and political problems might arise concerning the maintenance of the agricultural support price at a level different from the international price.[24] Moreover, there is a further problem, in that the monetised purchasing power of agricultural surplus through the support price policy may largely leak out into imported goods without creating the necessary demand for domestic goods. Expansion through public investment might also involve a similar problem, especially because demand may leak out through the import of capital goods. It is worth noting that the less developed the industrial sector of a country is, the more generally pressing is the problem of managing demand due to import leakage. An oft-presented counter-argument is that agricultural surplus may be exported to alleviate simultaneously the problem of effective demand through the 'foreign trade multiplier' and the foreign exchange constraint. The plausibility of this argument depends on whether agricultural goods can be sold at all in the international market, and in particular without affecting too adversely the export price (i.e. the 'small country' assumption). Indeed, the very rationale for managing demand at home arises from the fact that most developing countries capable of exporting mostly primary agriculture-based products have grounds for 'export pessimism'. [25]

3. The Terms of Trade as Policy Instrument

So far, we have shown that the dual economy framework emphasises how excess demand, arising from an imbalance between the different rates of expansion of 'traditional' agriculture and 'modern' industry, might typically lead to price adjustment in agriculture, but to quantity adjustment in industry. Although simple, this is a particularly useful framework of analysis in so far as several controversial policy issues in development economics hinge largely on whether excess demand affects mostly quantity, as is postulated in Keynesian economics, or price, as presumed in neoclassical economics. Consequently, the importance assigned to the 'terms of trade', i.e. the relative price of industrial goods in terms of agricultural goods, could be very different depending on how price and quantity adjustment are woven into the analysis. As we already saw, the Lewis-type analysis relies on price adjustment through *flexible* terms of trade to calibrate intersectoral imbalances in demand or supply. By contrast, the 'stagflation' phenomenon emphasised first by Kalecki, or the role of agricultural surplus in generating effective demand for industrial goods emphasised by Kaldor, have in common the idea of a 'structurally' determined terms of trade, which is relatively *inflexible* to the pressures of excess demand or supply. In so far as the terms of trade shows any secular tendency to move, in this framework it is influenced mostly by structural factors like different rates of labour productivity growth in industry and agriculture, segmentation of the labour market along the sectors, and other factors that are not directly related to excess demand.

However, one could consider the same problem from the opposite angle in so far as the terms of trade might be considered not as an endogenous but as an exogenous variable. It could be treated as an instrument of policy, i.e. an exogenous policy parameter (especially in the context of planning), rather than an endogenous variable determined within the model.[26] This approach to the terms of trade has played a significantly important role in the past, for example, in the Soviet Industrialization Debate of the 1920s.

Following the introduction of the New Economic Policy in the spring of 1921, Preobrazhensky[27] criticised it on the ground that it opened the Soviet economy to the risk of a relapse into a dominant private economy. The new state sector, he felt, would not be able to generate sufficient investible surplus to finance its growth at a decisively faster pace than the private sector. When 'taxing' a private sector consisting mostly of agriculture, Preobrazhensky suggested that the terms of trade should be made so unfavourable to agriculture that farmers would be forced to exchange an 'unequally' large amount of agricultural goods for a few essential industrial consumption items like salt, fuel or cloth. Thus, the amount of agricultural surplus made available for industrialisation could be increased by changing the terms of trade *against* agriculture. This strategy of extracting agricultural surplus forcibly through the price mechanism would have the additional advantage that relatively few resources would need to be devoted to the production of only those few essential consumption goods, while the growth of heavy, capital goods industries could proceed faster with more resources devoted to them.

This strategy of forcibly extracting agricultural surplus by turning the terms of trade against agriculture runs contrary to the normal role of the price mechanism, because it adversely affects the price incentive to the agricultural suppliers. At the same time, however, it might also increase the demand for essential industrial goods through the operation of Engel's Law on those particular industries.

The strategy of extracting agricultural surplus by deliberately turning the terms of trade against agriculture did not go unopposed in the Soviet Debate on industrialisation of that period. Bukharin, in particular, opposed it on the ground that the peasants might simply withdraw from such unfavourable exchange, if this policy were followed too rigorously. Instead, he advocated a more moderate policy of expanding light consumer goods industries, which would provide sufficient consumer goods as well as reasonable terms of trade in order that peasants could engage voluntarily in intersectoral exchange. Bukharin's strategy was also meant to strengthen the political alliance between the industrial workers and the peasants, while Preobrazhensky's policy would have put it under considerable strain.

It is now a matter for history that Soviet industrialisation continued at a rapid pace while agriculture got collectivised, at least partly to overcome the problem of extracting agricultural surplus. In the process, an almost laboratory experiment of how the interaction between industry and agriculture may ago wrong due to forced industrialisation, took place. It is best summed up in the words of an experienced journalist-traveller to the Soviet Union in the 1950s:

"Hundreds of thousands of peasants partake steadily in what is a kind of passive revolt against the collective system. They concentrate on their private plots, at the expense of the work of the collective as a whole, sabotage procedures, and are careless of procedures and state property. They resent the rigidity of the system, taxes, and the prices they get for obligatory delivery quotas, and hence produce just enough to support themselves. Some say that they are worse off then their grandfathers who were serfs. Above all, they lack incentive. The peasant does not produce more, because even if he gets a substantial cash income as many do, he has no 'spending power'. Nothing worth buying is in the shops. This brings up one of the dramatic paradoxes of the Soviet economy. The government must, in order to improve the standard of living of the country as a whole get more out of the farmer, but at the same time is unwilling or unable to release more consumer goods to the farmer in order to stimulate him to more production."[28]

If the Soviet experience with forced industrialisation highlighted the damaging consequences of treating agriculture merely as a passive sector that would adjust easily to the needs of an unwarrantedly high rate of industrial growth, the post-Green Revolution experience in some developing countries like India warns, albeit less dramatically, against committing an error of the opposite type. This results in an overemphasis on generating surplus in agriculture without creating adequate conditions for the expansion of domestic industries at a sufficiently rapid pace to absorb that surplus. The Soviet example highlights the mistake of trying to extract agricultural surplus, without engaging the peasants voluntarily in intersectoral exchange through reasonable terms of trade, and availability of industrial consumers' goods. By not providing adequate incentives, it failed to generate a sufficiently high volume of agricultural surplus to cope with the rising demand from industry. In this sense it highlights the basic concern of the Lewis-type model, in which the supply of an adequate level of agricultural surplus plays the central role. Consequently forcible extraction, rather than voluntary generation of agricultural surplus, became an unfortunate feature of Soviet planning and collectivised agriculture.

By contrast, rapid growth in agricultural production was promoted by the technology of the Green Revolution, while the minimum support price system provided the necessary price incentive to agricultural producers. In some cases, agricultural surplus grew more rapidly than agricultural production, because the new technology was concentrated mostly in selected regions (in particular those with good access to water), and in the hands of relatively well-off, surplus farmers. In a situation of balanced intersectoral 'trade', the rapidly growing volume of agricultural surplus would have translated into correspondingly rapid growth in the demand for industrial goods. In turn, this would have also led to a rapid expansion in industrial production by relaxing the demand-constraint. In contrast to Lewis, this was the type of scenario that was emphasised by Kaldor. It rightly underscores the equally important aspect of agricultural surplus as a generator of *demand* for industrial goods, in addition to its role as a supplier of 'food' to the 'industrial' workers. Nevertheless, when industry does not expand at a sufficient pace to absorb the growing agricultural surplus, the support price system has to be relied on to provide price incentive for farmers, and to convert their surplus into monetary income. And yet, as observed in the Indian case, this incentive system for agriculture alone may not be sufficient, in so far as it lacks a complimentary policy instrument to ensure that the monetary purchasing power created through the support price system is actually spent on domestic industrial goods. If the farmers tend to hold too high a proportion of their money income either as a 'store of value', or spend it on imported goods—unlike the scenario painted by Kaldor, and in stark contrast to the Soviet case, the economy would run into a persistent problem of apparent 'over-production' of surplus foodgrains. This would be particularly true if industrial employment does not expand sufficiently to create demand for surplus agricultural food production. In a dual economy, the Keynesian 'paradox of thrift' might manifest itself as the 'paradox of poverty amidst plenty'. This is a scene of widespread under-nutrition, even starvation, coexisting with rising inventories of foodgrains in government storage, while industry languishes due to insufficient demand. Unfortunately, this is a paradox not altogether unknown in some developing countries.

Notes

1. 'Primary' sector includes agriculture, mining, fishing and animal husbandry. We use the term 'primary' sector and 'agriculture' interchangeably, implicitly referring to countries where agriculture is the predominant form of activity in the primary sector.
2. International Labour Office (ILO, 1999) is the source of the employment data, while the World Bank (WB, 2000) is the source of the value-added data.
3. Strictly speaking, this statement applies to the time series data of individual countries, rather than to the international cross section data. However, this proposition is consistent with both cross section and time series data. Limitation of space forces us only to mention this in passing, without going into the details of the historical time series of individual countries.
4. Let, $Y = GDP$, L = Labour force, $Y/L = X$ = national average labour productivity and, X_a = labour productivity in the agricultural sector. Then, for example, in the case of Brazil, we have $X_a = (0.09Y / 0.2L) =$ 0.45 X etc., as the basis of the calculations given in the text.
5. Bhaduri 1993, p. 173, table 6 A.2; based on 1980 data.
6. See Johnston 1970 for a survey.
7. Petty 1963.
8. See Meek 1962.

9. As we shall discuss later, this point is particularly relevant in understanding certain aspects of the Soviet experience with the agricultural sector.
10. Lewis 1954.
11. Boeke 1942.
12. Bharadwaj 1987.
13. E.g. Fei and Ranis 1964: Jorgenson 1961; Zarembka 1970; Dixit 1973.
14. A slight variation on this argument is to use the assumption of profit maximisation in industry. With given real wage in terms of agricultural goods, we have in self-evident notations, by assumption (W/P_a) = constant. As the terms of trade (P_i / P_a) moves in favour of agriculture, i.e. (P_i / P_a) falls, the product wage in terms of industrial goods (W/P_i) has to rise to keep real wage (W/P_a) constant, because $(W/P_i) = (W/P_a) \times (P_a/P_i)$, a relation which is satisfied if (W/P_i) and (P_a/P_i) rise proportionately. The higher product wage in industry which equals under profit maximisation the marginal product of labour in industry is attained by reducing the level of industrial employment and output.
15. Kelecki 1971.
16. Okun 1981, p. 136.
17. Kaleeki 1976; Kaldor 1976.
18. Taylor 1983; Krishnaji 1992; Storm 1993. See in particular Krishnaji (1993 p. 105), who argued empirically that, 'other things remaining the same, rising cereal prices depress the demand for manufactures' in the context of the widespread poverty in India.
19. Ef. Bhaduri and Falkinger 1990.
20. Kaldor 1967, 1978, 1989; also Taylor 1983.
21. So long as the terms of trade are relatively inflexible (under conditions discussed earlier), the demand for industrial goods in real terms is provided for any given level of agricultural surplus.
22. Bhaduri and Skarstein 2001.
23. That this is not merely a problem of 'food security', or maintaining a buffer stock of essential food, is clear for two reasons. First, with so many people near starvation, it is not apparent what 'food security" is supposed to mean, unless it is defined exclusively in terms of protecting the interest of only that section of the urban population which is covered by the public distribution system. Second, reported estimates suggest that around 20 per cent of the stock of procured foodgrains is lost every year through poor storage (a substantial quantity of which is said to be eaten by rats.)
24. In a global system, developing countries face considerable international pressure to liberalise their agricultural markets. At the same time, however, the lower income and purchasing power of the average consumer in developing countries create political, even

humanitarian, pressure at home to maintain lower food prices more in line with that lower, average income, while paying the farmers a 'politically acceptable' price. The support price system with subsidy on food emerges as a compromise.

25. Despite lower wages, lower land and labour productivity in many developing countries result in their unit cost of production in agriculture being higher than that in many developed countries.
26. Important price-like, macro-economic variables — e.g. the interest rate, the exchange rate or the wage rate — are often treated as instruments for policy formulation. The terms of trade between agriculture and industry could also be thought of as one such macro-economic policy instrument.
27. Preobrazhensky 1965.
28. Gunther 1958, p. 394.

References

1. Bhaduri, A. and Falkinger, J., 1990, 'Optimal Price Adjustment under Imperfect Information', *European Economic Review,* 34 (4), pp. 941–52.
2. Bhaduri, A., 1993, 'Alternative Development Strategies and the Rural Sector' in A. Singh and H. Tabatabai (eds.), *Economic Crisis and the Third World Agriculture,* Cambridge, Cambridge University Press, pp. 149–78.
3. Bhaduri, A. and Skarstein, R., 2001, 'Effective Demand and the Terms of Trade in a Dual Economy: A Kaldorian Perspective', *Cambridge Journal of Economics* (forthcoming).
4. Bharadwaj, K., 1987, 'Analytics of Agriculture-Industry Relation', *Economic and Political Weekly,* 17, pp. 19–21, AN 15–AN 20.
5. Boeke, J.H., 1942, *Economies and Economic Policy in Dual Societies,* Haarlem, Tjeenk Willnik.
6. Dixit, A., 1973, 'Models of Dual Economies' in J.A. Mirrlees and N.H. Stern, (eds.), *Models of Economic Growth,* London, Macmillan, pp. 325–52.
7. Fei, J.C.H. and Ranis, G., 1964, *Development of the Labour Surplus Economy,* Homewood Illinois, Richard D. Irwin.
8. Gunther, J., 1958, *Inside Russia Today,* London, Hamish Hamilton.
9. International Labour Office (ILO), 1999, '1999 Key Indicators and the Labour Market CD-Rom', Geneva, ILO.
10. Johnston, D.F., 1970, 'Agriculture and Structural Transformation in Developing Countries: A Survey of Research', *Journal of Economic Literature,* 8 (2): 369–404.
11. Jorgenson, D.W., 1961, 'The Development of a Dual Economy', *Economic Journal,* 71 (2): 309–34.

12. Kaldor, N., 1967, *Strategic Factors in Economic Development,* Ithaca, Cornell University Press.

——, 1976, 'Inflation and Recession in the World Economy,' *Economic Journal,* 86 (4): 703–14.

——, 1978,' What is Wrong with Economic Theory' in his *further Essays on Economic Theory,* London, Duckworth, pp. 202–13.

——, 1989, 'Equilibrium Theory and Growth Theory' in F. Targetti and A.P. Thirlwall, (eds.), *The Essential Kaldor,* London, Duckworth, pp. 411–33.

13. Kalecki, M., 1971, 'Costs and Prices' in his *Selected Essays on the Dynamics of the Capitalist Economy,* Cambridge, Cambridge University Press, pp. 43–61.

——, 1976, 'The Problem of Financing Economic Development in a Mixed Economy', in his *Essays on Developing Economies,* Hassocks, Harvestor Press.

14. Krishnaji, N., 1992, 'The Demand Constraint: A Note on the Role of Foodgrain Prices and Income Inequality' in his *Pauperising Agriculture: Studies in Agrarian Change and Demographic structure,* Bombay, Sameeska Trust.

15. Lewis, W.A., 1954, 'Economic Development with Unlimited Supplies of Labour', *The Manchester School,* 22 (2): 139–91.

16. Meek, R.L., 1962, *The Economics of Physiocracy* (Essays and translations by Ronald Meek), London, George Allen and Unwin.

17. Okun, A.M., 1981, *Prices and Quantities: A Macroeconomic Analysis,* Washington DC, Brookings Institution.

18. Petty, W., 1662, *A Treatise on Taxes and Contributions* in C. H. Hull, (ed.), *The Economic Writings of Sir William Petty,* Cambridge, Cambridge University Press, 1899; New York, revised Augustins M. Kelly edition, 1963.

19. Preobrazhensky. E., 1965, *The New Economics,* London, Oxford University Press, (first published in Russian in 1926).

20. Storm, S., 1993, *Macroeconomic Considerations in the Choice of an Agricultural Policy: A Study into Sectoral Interdependence with Reference to India,* Hants, Avebury.

21. Taylor, L., 1983, *Structuralist Macroeconomics,* New York, Basic Books.

22. World Bank, 2000, 'World Development Indicators, 2000 CD-Rom', Washington DC, World Bank.

23. Zarembka, P., 1970, 'Marketable Surplus and Growth in a Dual Economy', *Journal of Economic Theory,* 2 (2): 107–21.

15

Increasing Returns and the Division of Labour in the Theory of Economic Development*

Invited lecture given originally in the plenary session of the annual conference of the European Society for the History of Economic Thought, Rethymno, Crete, 14–17 March 2002. It intends exploring the connection between some aspects of economic history and theory.

Classical concern with economic growth and development was rekindled towards the end of the Second World War, as reconstruction and decolonisation became part of an international agenda. Thinking about development and underdevelopment, some economists pursued a suggestive line of enquiry to argue that countries develop through processes that reinforce themselves over time. Thus, Rosenstein-Rodan (1943) argued in favour of a 'big push', consisting of several complementary investment projects, needed to set in motion such a self-reinforcing process. Myrdal found that disparities between ethnic groups (1944) and countries (1957) tend to widen due to the operation of a similar "principle of circular and cumulative causation". Kaldor (1989) explained regional and

---

* Published subsequently in a revised version in G.Vaggi and George Stathakis (eds), *Economic Development and Social Change*: Historical Roots and Modern Perspective, Routledge, London and New York, 2007.

international imbalances through the self-reinforcing process of increasing returns, and argued that standard "equilibrium economics" is incompatible with this framework of analysis.

Self-reinforcing mechanisms appear in different fields of enquiry, e.g. as auto-catalysis in bio-chemical reactions or, as positive feedback in engineering systems. Examples also abound in economics. Current price rise may lead to expectations of even greater price rise to generate "bubbles", a self-reinforcing "herd instinct" of agents may produce patterns of collective behaviour to produce "mania, panics and crashes" in the financial markets (Kindleberger, 1978). Even some fundamental norms of the market culture like trust, and respect for commercial contracts may be reinforced through an increasing number of market participants accepting them.

Almost since the birth of political economy as a distinct branch of enquiry, the presence of such self-reinforcing positive feedback, especially in manufacturing has been known. Petty (1623–87) recognised not only the importance of agricultural surplus in sustaining the **social** division of labour between agriculture and manufacturing, he also pointed out the possibility of cheaper production through the **technical** division of labour and **spacial** agglomeration of manufacturing activities: ". . . for in so vast a city (like London), Manufactures will beget one another and each Manufacture will divide into as many parts as possible, whereby the work of each Artisan will be simple and easy. As for Example. In the making of a watch, if one Man shall make the Wheels, another the Spring, another shall engrave the Dial-Plate, and another shall make the Cases, then the Watch will be better and cheaper, than if the whole work be put upon any one man" (Petty, 1963: 471–2; quoted in Groenwegen, 1998: 219).

Social as well as technical division of labour in a competitive economy was assigned a central role in Adam

Smith's 'Inquiry into the Nature and the Causes of the Wealth of Nations' (1776). In the vision he presented, greater division of labour leads to higher labour productivity which, under the classical assumption of a constant real wage rate, generates larger surplus per worker.[1] Competition plays a critical role in the continuous reinvestment of that surplus. As the cost of production gets reduced through a greater division of labour, the long-run normal prices are lowered in a competitive economy which, in turn, put pressure on the capitalists to reduce costs further by taking recourse to even greater division of labour through the reinvestment of the surplus (cf. Kurz and Salvadori, 1998). Young revived this vision by pointing out that the division of labour operates on an economy-wide scale through continuous product differentiation, the emergence of new products, industries production methods and organisation which result in a self-reinforcing process of cumulative progress. He summed it up in ". . . the theorem that the division of labour depends in large part upon the division of labour" (Young, 1928: 233).

This grand Smithian vision of capitalistic development as a continuously self-reinforcing process, driven by the twin forces of competition and division of labour, raises many issues, some of which were more closely analysed by subsequent developments in economic theory. Ricardo (1817) brought into sharp focus the consequences of the obvious neglect of non-reproducible resources like land. It led him to the dismal view that economic development ends ultimately in a "stationary state" with zero profit; because profit tends to dwindle while the differential rent on land increases at its expense, as the economy expands bringing under cultivation less and less productive land at the margin yielding diminishing returns (cf. Pasinetti, 1959–60). Although 'capital' is a produced means of production, on the questionable assumption (Pasinetti, 2000) that it can be treated in a manner analogous to land, diminishing return to capital is postulated to occur in modern neo-classical theory as the capital-labour ratio rises, if capital accumulates through the reinvestment of saving at a pace faster than that of the exogenously growing labour force.[2] The Ricardian "stationary state" is then reinvented as an exogenously given "steady state" rate of growth, determined by the steady, exogenous growth rate of the labour force, which can be measured either in natural units without technical progress, or on efficiency units of labour if technical progress takes the specific form of augmenting only labour productivity (Solow, 1956; Swan, 1956). Diminishing returns is thus counterposed against increasing returns for analysing economic growth.

For a return to the Smithian view that the growth process is driven endogenously by the interacting forces of competition and division of labour without any exogenously binding constraint like labour, attention has recently been focused in the neo-classical tradition to interpret the division of labour in a manner that counteracts the marginal product of capital from diminishing. Currently available endogenous models of growth explore the general idea that the growing stock of capital that the reinvestment of savings would generate by itself leads to increasing division of labour through **social** 'learning by doing' (Arrow, 1962), embodied in a larger stock of 'human capital' (also Romer, 1986; Lucas, 1988). In effect, it by-passes the role of labour as an exogenous constraint, by postulating that the increasing division of labour, brought about by the production of further human capital can be achieved through a larger stock of physical capital (e.g. Arrow, 1962; Romer, 1986) or, through the stock of human capital and the proportion of labour time allocated to acquiring human capital through training (Usawa, 1965; Lucas, 1988). In either case, human capital is so defined as to augment the total stock of labour in efficiency units. When this efficiency effect is assumed to be sufficiently strong to neutralise the tendency of the marginal product of physical capital from falling, economic growth may be sustained endogenously, despite the exogenously given growth of the natural labour force.

The possibility of social learning creates a wedge between the private and the public view of economic optimality. For instance, if gross investment provides the route to social learning, private investors would fail to take this externality into account, and private optimisation would result in under-investment from a social point of view. It has long been known that the so-called fundamental theorem of static welfare economics, namely that every competitive equilibrium is Pareto optimal and vice versa, runs into difficulties because of various externalities in production and consumption (cf. Chakravarty, 1973). Social learning through capital accumulation extends this argument to the dynamic context of economic growth. It also warns against the Smithian reliance on competition to do necessarily a satisfactory job of maintaining dynamic efficiency in the presence of social learning, or other forms of externalities driving the division of labour.

However, the argument goes deeper than non-optimal temporal or intertemporal resource allocation in the presence of increasing returns, because it might render the very market form of competition **structurally** unstable. Marshall (1920) hinted at it in his famous Appendix H (see also Bharadwaj, 1989), and the incompatibility between his partial equilibrium analysis and the assumption of increasing returns was made explicit by Sraffa (1926). To restate the problem of structural instability of the market form with a simple example, consider only two competitive firms identical in every respect, and both subject to exactly the same extent of decrease in average cost with expansion in output. A small, accidental perturbation in favour of the market share of one firm, by reducing its average cost gives it only a slight initial competitive advantage. However, this almost negligible initial advantage might magnify cumulatively over time in a self-reinforcing manner, as lower average cost leads to higher market share to even lower average cost and so on, perhaps until one firm emerges as the monopolist, and the competitive market structure is irrevocably changed. Similar reinforcing mechanisms might also operate in the spatial competition between two industrial locations (Arthur, 1994). As a more dramatic example from sociobiology, consider the social organisation of insects. Ants or termites are known to practise so extensive a division of labour that the survival of the individual is practically impossible outside the group. In the construction of termites' nest, initially random deposits of building materials may occur in several places. When, by chance, one of these deposits become sufficiently large, a similar self-reinforcing process takes over, as termites begin to deposit preferentially materials on the larger heap, while the smaller deposits are abandoned altogether or joined by arch in particular cases (Nicolis and Prigogine, 1977: 452–6). Thus, the emergence of structures of orders in the formation of termites' nest, industrial districts, cities or monopolies share in common the same basic mechanism of self-reinforcement.

As these examples suggest, many self-reinforcing processes over time, including dynamic increasing returns and division of labour, have consequences that are not easily dealt with in standard economic analysis. **First**, temporary, even small disturbances, may have large and cumulative permanent consequences, at times incorporated in a new order as our previous example of the emergence of monopoly from competition suggests. Similarly, short-term macro-economic stabilisation policies that depress output and investment temporarily, may affect adversely the long-run growth prospect of the economy, if, for example, they retard social 'learning by doing' and human capital formation which reduces long-run productivity growth (Blackburn, 1999).

Second, the cumulative processes through which initial small disturbances magnify, usually take time. In a probabilistic framework, if the initial disturbances are random, fluctuations would occur initially, before any cumulative process is able to gather sufficient momentum to dominate the long-run dynamics. In the previous monopoly example, the fortunes of the two competing firms would fluctuate initially, if both are subjected to random shocks. Again, in the termites' nest-building example, the prospect of the location fluctuates initially among alternative sites of deposits. Fluctuations give way to order, when the self-reinforcing process becomes sufficiently strong through successive positive feedbacks in favour of one particular firm or building location. "Order through fluctuations" (Haken, 1978; Nicolis and Prigogine, 1977) is therefore a common phenomenon in many self-organizing systems, including economic systems which self-organize through self-reinforcing mechanisms like increasing returns and division of labour.

Third, each successive, positive feedback tends to 'lock in' the system more firmly, through its cumulative effect along a particular path or trajectory. In the monopoly example, as one particular firm cumulate the advantages of successive rounds of cost reduction through higher market share, a path-dependent outcome towards the industrial structure of monopoly becomes more probable. One could also think of two competiting technologies in the same manner. By chance, or even due to its initial superiority, as a particular technology gets adopted, the firm producing that technology might enjoy initially increasing returns to scale internal to the firm, due to the spreading out of some fixed overhead cost over a larger volume of sales. However, over time it might also have the advantages of the distributional network getting increasingly geared to spreading that particular technology, while social learning and training about it also become easier. Thus, under increasing returns technological trajectories have a tendency to get trapped in a particular path. However, had the initially left-out technology been adopted, it might even have become more efficient over time than the one actually adopted. Paradoxically therefore, dynamic increasing returns and division of labour which have long been recognised as a main source of achieving efficiency in production might also turn out to be a source of inefficiency in terms of the comparative costs of foregone opportunities over time (Arthur, 1994; David, 1985).

Although path dependence and locking-in seem fairly generic properties of many economic, social and political processes, the formalism required to capture them is only at an early stage of development. At each stage of such a process, usually several possibilities or choices exist. Its formalisation calls for a non-linear probability schema, and in some interesting cases it may be captured by a "generalized Polya process" (due to Arthur, Ermolieu and Karniouski, 1983, 1987; reprinted in Arthur, 1994). To illustrate intuitively this process, consider the economic example of locating a new industry among alternative industrial districts. If the probability of its being located in a particular district is postulated to depend on the proportion of total industries located already in that district, then the self-reinforcing mechanism appears only probabilistically, because the location actually chosen for the next industry may still be any one of the districts. The generalised Polya process demonstrates that, as industrial development continues, the proportion of industries located in a district ultimately settles down to an equilibrium (of 'fixed point' of the probability function), where the (ex ante) probability of locating a new industry in a particular district equals exactly the (ex post) proportion of total industries located already in the district. The chance element in deciding on industrial location ultimately has little influence. In general, however, several such (stable) equilibria or fixed points are possible, so that deterministic prediction of the equilibrium position may not be possible.

Contrary to Kaldor's view (1989) that the cumulative causation of dynamic increasing returns is incompatible in general with economic equilibrium, Polya-like processes exhibit the possibility of equilibrium or multiple equilibria, so long as the strength of positive feedbacks tend to decrease in each successive round. Thus, if the proportion of industries in a district initially is one-fifth or 20 per cent, as the next industry is located there, it becomes [(1+1)/(5+1)] = 33%; with the next one [(2+1)/(6+1)] = 43% and so on; i.e. while the feedbacks remain positive and self-reinforcing, in percentage terms they decrease non-linearly in strength at each round.[3] Without this additional assumption of positive feedbacks of decreasing strength at each round, self-reinforcing processes of increasing returns may indeed rule out the existence of equilibrium.

From the macro-economic point of view, however, a far more compelling reason limits the extent of the division of labour than the positive feedbacks of decreasing strength in a self-reinforcing process. Adam Smith had rightly observed that, "the extent of the division of labour is limited by the size of the market"; but he failed to analyse clearly what determines the size of the market. The interaction between the size of the market which is determined by aggregate demand, as the Keynes (1936)–Kalecki (1971) theory taught us, and the division of labour lies at the core of the macrodynamics of economic growth. And yet, post-war neo-classical growth models, exogenous or endogenous, share with the Ricardian model the unfortunate common characteristic of ignoring effective demand altogether. It is simply assumed instead, in a pre-Keynesian manner, that all savings are automatically reinvested in a world ruled by Say's law.[4] And yet, the matching between demand and supply is particularly problematic in the presence of increasing returns, as pointed out by Weitzman (1982). Because, suppliers inevitably become large under increasing returns, and they may fail to create adequate demand necessary to make continuous expansion of supply profitable.

Restated from a Keynesian perspective, the independence of investment from saving decisions forces us to recognise that the higher labour productivity and surplus per worker made possible by a greater division of labour need not be invested automatically by the firms. Because increasing returns exacerbate the tendency towards monopoly and market concentration, the share of profit in income may increase. How this impacts on the incentive to invest remains an open question. While Schumpeter (1942) emphasised "creative destruction" through rapid technical progress in an oligopolistic market structure, Steindl (1952) suggested that a higher profit share under greater market concentration might push the economy towards stagnation by depressing aggregate demand. However, in so far as a higher profit share lowers consumption demand but raises the profit margin per unit of sale to stimulate investment demand, the effect on aggregate demand remains ambiguous. Depending on which effect dominates, it might result in a lower-consumption induced stagnationist regime, or a higher-investment-led expansionist regime (Bhaduri and Marglin, 1990). Thus, the division of labour impacts in a complex way on the level of aggregate demand, and the size of the market. In the case of investment-led expansion with higher profit share, it can perhaps help the process of further division of labour in a self-reinforcing manner (cf. Young, 1928); but it might also hinder the same process in the consumption-induced stagnationist case. Without analysing these alternative patterns of interaction between the market size and the division of labour, we could end up telling the story of Hamlet without mentioning the Prince of Denmark!

Notes

1. Higher surplus per worker need not imply higher total surplus, because that depends also on the level of employment. Smith's (pre-Keynesian) discussion fails to explain how the levels of employment and output are determined.
2. Again, as in Ricardo's or Smith's discussion, the level of employment or output is not determined; instead, it is simply assumed that full-employment is maintained somehow, and that full-employment level of saving is automatically reinvested under the (pre-Keynesian) Say's law to drive the process of rising capital-labour ratio.
3. Obversely, if in successive rounds, the next industry is not located in that district, probability decreases from 20% to [1/ (5+1)] = 17% to [1/(6+1)] = 14% etc. Intuitively speaking, the intersection(s) between the increasing and the decreasing probability defines one or more Polya fixed points, at probability less than or equal to unity.
4. See previous en-notes 1 and 2, on this point.

References

1. Arthur, W.B., 1994, *Increasing Returns and Path Dependence in the Economy,* Ann Arbor, Michigan University Press.
2. Bhaduri, A. and Marglin, S., 1990, 'Unemployment and Real Wage: The Economic Basis for Contesting Political Ideologies,' *Cambridge Journal of Economics,* (14): 375–93.
3. Bharadwaj, K., 1989, 'Marshall on Pigou's Wealth and Welfare ' in her *Themes in Value and Distribution,* 159–75, Delhi, Oxford University Press.
4. Blackburn, K., 1999, 'Can Stabilization Policy Reduce Long-Run Growth?', *Economic Journal* (109): 67–77.
5. Chakravarthy, S., 1973, 'Theory of Development Planning: An Appraisal' in H.C. Bos, H. Linneman and P. de Wolff (eds.), *Economic Structure and Development,* Amsterdam, North Holland.
6. David, P.A., 1985, 'Clio and Economics of QWERTY', *American Economic Review,* Papers and Proceedings, 75: 332–7.
7. Groenweagen, P., 1998, 'Division of Labour' in H.D. Kurz and N. Salvadori (eds.), *The Elgar Companion to Classical Economics* (A to K), 217–22, Chelttenham, U.K., Edward Elgar.
8. Haken, H., 1978, *Synergetics,* New York, Springer–Verlag.
9. Kaldor, N., 1989, 'The Case for Regional Policies' in F. Targetti and A.P. Thirlwall (eds.). *The Essential Kaldor*: 311–26, London, Duckworth.
10. Kaldor, N., 1989, 'The Irrelevance of Equilibrium Economics, *op. cit: 373–98.*

11. Kaldor, N., 1989, 'The Role of Increasing Returns, Technical Progress and Cumulative Causation in the Theory of International Trade and Economic Growth', *op.cit,* 327–51.
12. Kaldor, N., 1989, 'What is Wrong with Economic Theory', *op.cit,* 399–410.
13. Kalecki, M., 1971, 'Determinants of Profits' in his *Selected Essays on the Dynamics of the Capitalist Economy,* 78–92, Cambridge, Cambridge University Press.
14. Keynes, J.M., 1936, *The General Theory of Employment, Interest and Money,* London, Macmillan.
15. Kindleberger, C.P. 1978, *Mania, Panics and Crashes,* New York, Basic Books.
16. Kurz, H.D. and Salvadori, N., 1998, "Endogenous Growth Models and the "Classical" Tradition' in H.D. Kurz and N. Salvadori, *Understanding 'Classical' Economics,* 66–89, London, Routledge.
17. Lucas, R., 1988, 'On the Mechanics of Economic Development', *Journal of Monetary Economics,* 22: 3–42.
18. Marshall, A., 1920, *Principles of Economics,* (8th edition), appendix H, London, Macmillan.
19. Myrdal, G., 1944, *An American Dilemma: The Negro Problem and Modern Democracy,* (Carnegie Foundation Study), New York, Harper and Row.
20. Myrdal, G., 1957, *Economic Theory and Underdeveloped Regions,* London, Duckworth.
21. Nicolis, G. and Prigogrine, I., 1977, *Self-Organization in Nonequilibrium Systems,* New York, John Wiley and Sons.
22. Pasinetti, L.L., 1959–60, 'A Mathematical Formulation of the Ricardian System', *Review of Economic Studies,* (26): 78–98.
23. Pasinetti, L.L., 2000, 'Critique of Neoclassical Theory of Growth and Distribution', *Banca de Lavoro Quarterly Review,* (53): 383–432.
24. Petty, W., (original 1662), *A Treatise on Taxes and Contributions* in C. H. Hull (ed.) *The Economic Writings of Sir William Petty,* Cambridge, Cambridge University Press, 1899; revised Augustins M. Kelly edition, New York, 1963.
25. Ricardo, D., (original 1817), *Principles of Political Economy and Taxation* in P. Sraffaa (ed.) *Works and Correspondence of David Ricardo,* Cambridge, Cambridge University Press, 1951, Vol 1.
26. Romer, P., 1986, 'Increasing Returns and Long-Run Growth', *Journal of Political Economy* (94): 1002–37.
27. Rosenstein–Rodan, P.N., 1943, 'Problems of Industrialization of Eastern and South-Eastern Europe', *Economic Journal* (53): 202–11.
28. Schumpeter, J.A., 1942, *Capitalism, Socialism and Democracy,* (3rd edition). New York, Harper Brothers.

29. Smith, A., 1776, *An Inquiry into the Nature and Causes of the Wealth of Nations,* the Glasgow Edition of the Works and Correspondence of Adam Smith (Vol. 2), in R.H. Campbell, A.S. Skinner and W.B. Todd (eds.), Oxford, Oxford University Press.
30. Solow, R., 1956, 'A Contribution to the Theory of Economic Growth'. *Quarterly Journal of Economics,* 70: 65–94.
31. Sraffa, P., 1926, 'The Laws of Returns Under Competitive Conditions', *Economic Journal,* (36) : 535–50.
32. Steindl, J., 1952, *Maturity and Stagnation in American Capitalism* (2nd edition), New York, Monthly Review Press.
33. Swan, T., 1956, 'Economic Growth and Capital Accumulation', *Economic Record* 32: 343–61.
34. Usawa, H., 1965, 'Optimum Technical Change in an Aggregative Model of Economic Growth', *International Economic Review,* (6): 18–31.
35. Weitzman, M., 1982, 'Increasing Returns and the Foundations of Unemployment Theory', *Economic Journal* (92): 787–804.
36. Young, A., 1928, 'Increasing Returns and Economic Progress', *Economic Journal* (38): 527–42.